Ways of Knowing in Science Series

RICHARD DUSCHL, SERIES EDITOR

ADVISORY BOARD: Charles W. Anderson, Nancy Brickhouse, Rosalind Driver,
Eleanor Duckworth, Peter Fensham, William Kyle,
Roy Pea, Edward Silver, Russell Yeany

R E A D I N G

C O U N T S

Expanding the Role of Reading
in Mathematics Classrooms

Raffaella Borasi & Marjorie Siegel

FOREWORD BY DAVID PIMM

Teachers College
Columbia University
New York and London

The "Reading to Learn Mathematics for Critical Thinking" project was supported by a grant from the National Science Foundation (Award #MDR-8851582). The opinions and conclusions reported in this book, however, are solely the responsibility of the authors.

Figure 2.1 and a portion of Chapter 2 originally appeared in Siegel, M., Borasi, R., & Smith, C. (1989). A critical review of reading in mathematics instruction: The need for a new synthesis. In S. McCormick and J. Zutell (Eds.), *Cognitive and social perspectives for literacy research and instruction* (pp. 269–277). 38th Yearbook of the National Reading Conference. Chicago: National Reading Conference. Used by permission.

Some of the instructional vignettes and findings reported in Chapter 4 originally appeared in Borasi, R., Siegel, M., Fonzi, J., & Smith, C. (1998). Using transactional reading strategies to support sense-making and discussion in mathematics classrooms: An exploratory study. *Journal for Research in Mathematics Education, 29*, 275–305. Used by permission of the National Council of Teachers of Mathematics.

Sections of "Mathematics and War," quoted extensively in Chapter 4, originally appeared in Davis, P., & Hersh, R. (1981). *The Mathematical Experience* (pp. 89–92). Boston: Houghton Mifflin. Used by permission of Springer-Verlag.

Chapter 5 is adapted from the original article by Siegel, M., & Fonzi, J. M. (1995, Oct/Nov/Dec). The practice of reading in an inquiry-oriented mathematics class. *Reading Research Quarterly, 30*(4), 632–665. Copyright © 1995 by Marjorie Siegel and the International Reading Association. All rights reserved.

Chapter 6 is a revised and expanded version of Siegel, M., Borasi, R., & Fonzi, J. (1998). Supporting students' mathematical inquiries through reading. *Journal for Research in Mathematics Education, 29*, 378–413. Used by permission of the National Council of Teachers of Mathematics.

Published by Teachers College Press, 1234 Amsterdam Avenue, New York, NY 10027

Library of Congress Cataloging-in-Publication Data

Borasi, Raffaella.
    Reading counts : expanding the role of reading in mathematics classrooms / Raffaella Borasi and Marjorie Siegel.
       p. cm.—(Ways of knowing in science series)
    Includes bibliographical references and index.
    ISBN 0-8077-3921-9 (cloth)—ISBN 0-8077-3920-0 (pbk.)
       1. Mathematics—Study and teaching. 2. Literature in mathematics education.
  I. Siegel, Marjorie Gail, 1952–   II. Title. III. Series.
  QA11 B6384 2000
  510'.71—dc21   99-057206

ISBN 0-8077-3920-0 (paper)
ISBN 0-8077-3921-9 (cloth)

Printed on acid-free paper
Manufactured in the United States of America

07 06 05 04 03 02 01 00   8 7 6 5 4 3 2 1

To our fathers,

Vincenzo Borasi

and

Jack M. Siegel

Contents

Foreword

This is a book that deals with several significant and complex issues facing contemporary mathematics teachers, issues that arise from the nature of text materials offered to students as educational. It is important to be clear at the outset that there is no general mathematics teaching method that is being proposed here, and the book is the stronger for it. With this book, we have a broad and systematic exploration by Borasi and Siegel of a generative place for reading in the teaching and learning of mathematics.

We are offered an informed and engaging account of a significant, long-term, classroom-based project that started with Borasi and Siegel offering a range of ideas to explore on the notion of "reading to learn mathematics," in conjunction with a focused and thoughtful presence in the classroom. In turn, the classrooms and the teachers fed much back into the work and thinking of these university-based researchers. Both duos shaped and were shaped by their work toward commonly-shared goals: It was a reciprocally beneficial encounter.

Mathematics is fundamentally concerned with texts—not textbooks necessarily, but the written in general. And, as the authors point out, so much of most students' experience of reading involves interacting (and even that seems too mutual a term) with textbook pages, worksheets, and within them, the still ubiquitous "word problem." In large part, you are what you read, and what you are offered to read in class significantly influences what you believe mathematics to be.

The declared aim of this book is to integrate reading into school mathematics. A second aim is about reintegrating mathematics into society, into humanity. In an important sense, the authors are working with an educational notion of numeracy: not what this word has come to mean in so many contexts, namely a pale "practical arithmetic," but in its original meaning as a full and equally important sibling to literacy, worthy of study throughout the secondary school.

Borasi and Siegel introduce texts about mathematics that can profitably be read in mathematics class, and they work alongside teachers in offering and developing specific techniques and strategies from literacy education that might help students get better at the business of interpretation. They are engaged in identifying and refining possible functions for reading and chose as their collaborators teachers who strive to create inquiry-based mathematics classrooms.

By focusing on certain strategies that students can bring to bear on a text, Borasi and Siegel's message is: There is always something that can be done. One need never be rendered immobile or mute, nor have to retreat. The authors believe in the importance of giving students a worthwhile challenge in school mathematics, and challenge does not only come from an increase in technical demand. Too often when faced with (very real) evidence of student difficulty in mathematics, the response has been to simplify, to dilute, to remove challenges in search of an increasingly vacuous "success."

We hear from students in this book about their difficulties in working with and creating an understanding from what they have been asked to read. But we also hear them being prepared to accept this challenge, supported by their teachers in terms of technique as well as encouragement, productively struggling both individually and in various collective settings with something that is both genuinely difficult and worthy of their attention.

The techniques they are offered are the means for making sense. Too often, in the classroom, the question asked is: Does it make sense? Better, would be to ask: What sense have you made of this? The former tends to funnel into a "yes" or "no" response and act as an obstacle to further discussion and inquiry. There is always more that can be said.

There is more, much more, that can be said about this book. But this is a prefatory text, a pre-text, and one that should not be permitted to get in the way of the real thing. So my writing will stop here, but the thinking generated by my engagement with this text will go on for a long time.

David Pimm

Acknowledgments

This book is the culmination of a collaboration that began in 1987 when we met at the University of Rochester. Writing and thinking together has been one of the great pleasures of this project, and throughout the project we have approached writing as a collaborative, rather than as a cooperative, undertaking. We have therefore chosen to list our names in alphabetical order in recognition of the collaborative nature of our work and our contributions as equal partners to the writing of this book.

The project reported in this book would not have been possible without a grant from the National Science Foundation, and we wish to acknowledge this important source of support as well as the encouragement of Ray Hannapel, who was then the Program Director for Research in Teaching and Learning. Additional funding was also provided by Teachers College, Columbia University, through a Dean's Grant to Marjorie Siegel. This grant provided support for further analysis of data collected in the NSF-sponsored study, and we are grateful for this support as well.

This project was not only an interdisciplinary collaboration but also a collaboration of teachers and researchers. We are grateful to the members of the "Reading to Learn Mathematics" professional development seminar—Denise Anthony, David Baker, Richard Fasse, Judi Fonzi, George Isgrigg, Tracy Markham, Laurie Platt, Donna Rose, Lisa Grasso Sanvidge, John Sheedy, Anna Sotiriadou, and Ken Steffens—for their serious yet playful exploration of what it might mean to expand the role of reading in learning mathematics in middle and high school settings. Our weekly conversations about the educational significance and practical possibilities of reading in mathematics classrooms did much to shape the unfolding project. The centerpiece of this project occurred during the year of classroom research that followed the seminar, when we collaborated with four of these teachers on the design and teaching of instructional experiences in which reading had a major part. To these teachers and their students goes a special thanks for welcoming us to their classrooms and helping us understand more fully what reading might contribute to their mathematics education.

We owe a special debt of gratitude to Judi Fonzi and Lisa Grasso Sanvidge, whose teaching is at the core of this book. The expanded understanding of reading presented in this book would not have been possible without the collaboration of these two remarkable teachers. Each took up the spirit of the project fully and invested it with her intelligence, professional vision and experience, and ethic of responsibility to students. The friendships we forged in the course of this work were due not only to the shared commitment of all involved but also to Judi and Lisa's enthusiasm, energy, generosity, and sense of fun. We were especially thankful that Judi Fonzi became a partner in the data analysis phase of the project and a co-author on several reports of findings. Her unique perspective on the integral role reading played in her teaching added immeasurably to our understanding of classroom events and kept us grounded.

We also wish to acknowledge the many contributions Connie Smith made as the research associate for the RLM Project. From the beginning, Connie was an invaluable colleague, assisting us in everything from locating the literature on reading mathematics to collecting, transcribing, and analyzing the miles of audio- and videotaped data that were generated. Her thoughtful insights and gentle manner greatly enriched both the intellectual and social dimensions of the project.

Over the years, we have been fortunate to have colleagues who have read our work and offered helpful feedback and encouragement. Steve Brown and Sandy Segal were early enthusiasts as well as encouraging critics throughout the project; David Bleich, Judith Green, Patty Anders, Chris Pappas, Frank Lester, Judith Sowder, and David Pimm helped us clarify and extend our ideas; and Patty Anders's generous review of the entire book manuscript gave us the sense that such a book might be helpful to teachers and teacher educators.

As the book neared completion, we benefited from the editorial suggestions of Brian Ellerbeck at Teachers College Press. A special thanks also goes to Tama Robertson for her help with the preparation of several figures on very short notice!

Finally, we would like to thank our families for sustaining us throughout this project with love, laughter, and a sympathetic ear. They believed in us and that made it all possible.

CHAPTER 1

Introduction

At a time when mathematics educators have come to regard writing and talking as valuable ways for learners to recast technical content in their own words, express their feelings about mathematics, and reflect on the process of doing mathematics, the literature on reading mathematics is still focused primarily on instructional strategies designed to help students comprehend word problems and learn the technical vocabulary of mathematics textbooks (Siegel, Borasi, & Smith, 1989). However much we might agree that students may need this kind of instructional support, this interpretation of reading mathematics limits the contribution that reading can make to mathematics instruction, as it makes a number of assumptions about *what, how,* and, most important, *why* students may read in a mathematics class that are at odds with constructivist views of learning and teaching (e.g., Fosnot, 1996) and humanistic conceptions of mathematics as a discipline (e.g., White, 1993).

The first of these assumptions is that well-formed word problems and perhaps some technical definitions and explanations presented in textbooks are the texts most relevant to learning mathematics. Although there is new interest in using children's literature in elementary mathematics instruction (e.g., Griffiths & Clyne, 1991; Schiro, 1997; Whitin & Wilde, 1992, 1995), it is rare to find studies and classroom descriptions in which texts other than worksheets and textbooks are incorporated into secondary mathematics instruction. Assumptions about *how* students read mathematics are as deeply embedded in the literature on reading mathematics as assumptions about *what* is read. In this literature, it is taken for granted that reading is a matter of extracting meaning from text—what Pimm (1987) has called the "mining" metaphor for reading. The assumption that readers must "mine" the text for meaning directs attention to features of the text without giving equal consideration to the role readers may play in making sense of such texts. Given this interpretation of reading, it is not surprising that the bulk of the research literature on reading mathematics has focused on developing and studying instructional strategies that help students deal with those aspects of technical mathematics texts thought to be difficult (e.g., Earp & Tanner, 1980; Moyer, Moyer, Sowder, & Threadgill-Sowder, 1984; Shuard & Rothery, 1984; Skrykpa, 1979). Finally, we must consider the assumptions that have been made about *why* texts are read in mathematics classrooms. With few exceptions, the purposes for reading mathematics have been restricted to those that serve a "techniques curriculum" (Bishop, 1988), and stress learning procedures that will enable students to accurately solve word problems and aquire the technical vocabulary used in textbook definitions and explanations. There are few investigations in which students read to gain a sense of historical context or contemporary uses for such techniques, to learn how mathematicians might have approached a particular problem, or even to set the stage for their own mathematical inquiries. Reading for purposes such as these highlights the development of understanding and reasoning as well as beliefs and attitudes associated with successful mathematics learning (e.g., National Research Council [NRC], 1989; National Council of Teachers of Mathematics [NCTM], 1989, 1991), reflecting a set of goals for mathematics education quite different from those of a "techniques curriculum."

When we juxtapose the new goals for learning mathematics advocated by many constituencies today and the assumptions underlying most research on reading mathematics, it becomes evident that educators have tended to underestimate the contribution that reading can make to mathematics instruction. If, on the other hand, educators take advantage of the theoretical shift toward generative and collaborative meaning-making that has occurred within the field of reading along with discussions about what counts as reading and the functions it may serve in classrooms, new ways of using text and reading to support mathematical learning become possible. This may be especially true in those mathematics classrooms where language serves as a way for students to negotiate meanings and representations as they construct knowledge together, a key characteristic of what we are calling inquiry-oriented classrooms (Siegel, Borasi, & Fonzi, 1998). It was the awareness of these new instructional possibilities that led us—a mathematics educator and a reading educator—to initiate an interdisciplinary project that explored the integration of reading in mathematics classrooms. This project, "Reading to Learn Mathematics for Critical Thinking" (RLM hereafter), involved the development, documentation, and analysis of reading experiences in selected secondary mathematics classrooms.

This book presents the key findings of the RLM Project and two follow-up studies in order to help mathematics and reading educators alike expand their views of what may "count" as "reading mathematics" and better appreciate the contributions an expanded view of reading could make to inquiry-oriented mathematics instruction. Because our work challenges many common expectations about reading mathematics, we thought it would be helpful to begin by providing readers with an image of the integration of reading in mathematics instruction we propose. To achieve this we present a short vignette, drawn from our classroom data, that exemplifies some of the new goals for mathematics instruction as well as the multiple perspectives on reading that informed the research presented in this book. A brief discussion of this vignette will also enable us to introduce the three complementary perspectives we have found useful in studying the contributions reading could make to mathematics instruction. We hope that together, the vignette and our analysis of it will make the detailed overview of the content and organization of the book, provided at the end of this chapter, more meaningful and useful for readers.

Narrative 1: The "Analog & Analytic" Experience— An Illustration of the Proposed Integration of Reading in Mathematics Instruction

The following vignette reports an instructional experience 7 hours in length that was developed in the context of an unusual high school course, "Math Connections," taught by Judith Fonzi. The overall goal of this course (described in Chapter 3) can be briefly described as broadening the students' conceptions of mathematics by exploring connections between mathematics and disciplines such as art, music, literature, and science. During the course, the students identified, planned, carried out, and reflected on several inquiries related to the theme of math connections. The following narrative is an abbreviated report of one of these experiences, which developed quite spontaneously toward the end of the course, as students tried to understand the nature and significance of analog and analytic thinking in the context of mathematics—the topic of an essay two students, Tim and Char, had been assigned to read and present to the rest of the class using reading strategies introduced earlier in the course (see Fonzi & Smith, 1992, 1998, for a full report of this instructional episode). The decision to devote class time to this inquiry was part of the teacher's effort to expand students' conceptions of mathematics. By exploring these two approaches to mathematical thinking, she hoped students would rethink their implicit belief that the analytical approach was the only one that counted as "real mathematics" and begin to appreciate the place of an analog approach in mathematical practice.

The two-page essay entitled "Analog and Analytical Mathematics" from Davis and Hersh's (1981) popular book *The Mathematical Experience* introduced these two fundamental ways of thinking by means of the following explanation:

> Analog mathematizing is sometimes easy, can be accomplished rapidly, and may make use of none, or very few, of the abstract symbolic structures of "school" mathematics. It can be done by almost everyone who operates in a world of spatial relationships and everyday technology. . . . In analytic mathematics, the symbolic material predominates. It is almost always hard to do. It is time consuming. It is fatiguing. It requires special training. . . . Analytic mathematics is performed only by very few people. (pp. 302–303)

Each approach was further illustrated by a series of examples, such as the following:

> Problem: How much liquid is in this beaker? Analog solution: Pour the liquid into a graduated measure and read off the volume directly. Analytic solution: Apply the formula for the volume of a conical frustrum. Measure the relevant linear dimensions and then compute. (pp. 303–304)

To make sense of this text, Tim chose to record in writing the questions and ideas he generated while reading the essay (his adaptation of the Cloning an Author strategy [Harste & Short, 1988] that had been introduced in previous classes), whereas Char, inspired by her previous positive experiences with the Sketch-to-Stretch strategy (Siegel, 1984, 1995), found it helpful to draw a picture of a situation from her own life that she felt exemplified the distinction between analog and analytical thinking. Despite the support provided by these reading strategies, the two students found the concepts discussed in the essay quite difficult, as shown by the following exchange in which they tried to share their tentative understanding of the text with the rest of the class. Because Tim entered the class saying he did not understand the piece, the class decided Char should explain her interpretation of the article first:

> I think I [understand it]. I'm kind of having second doubts, but maybe . . . I did "Analog and Analytical Mathematics" . . . but I read half of it and all of a sudden a lightbulb went off. And so I drew this neat little picture [showing her sketch of a map representing two routes from her home to her friend's house: a

straight, direct path labeled "analog" and a winding path labeled "analytic"]. . . . It's a really weird drawing now, but it was really cool then. . . . For both of these [paths]—it doesn't matter what you are doing—you get to the same point. Okay. So you are starting at the same point and you are getting to the same point but it is different how you get there. So I draw this— I thought of, like when I walk over to Tanya's house. Do I walk the fastest way? . . . Or, do I kind of like, go around the block just because I like to walk down that street? But I still get there. . . . I finished reading the paper, kind of, and it fit. [When questioned by another student, Char defended her sketch.] Well, that's what I got out of it. That analog—it's kind of like 2 + 2 = 4, and analytic is 1 + 1 + 1 + 1.

The teacher then turned to Tim and asked if he had anything to add:

Tim: Wait a minute, let me see here. I don't know if I put it right. But I saw analytic as the simple way of having things done. Like her [Char's] simple way of getting to Tanya's house. And I put analog as in the part—computing. Maybe analytic is like—us—what we are doing [in the "Math Connections" course] instead of having books and stuff. It's *thought* that's doing it. And with analog—it is writing down on paper and computing and stuff like that.
Teacher: Char? . . . Respond to what Tim said.
Char: I don't know how.
Shellie: Didn't you have the opposite?
Char: Yeah, it's just opposite. I don't know how I could respond. Maybe it's the way—maybe—I don't know.
Teacher: Okay, in its most general sense you said your picture showed analog as the straightforward method [and] analytic as [the] "round-about" method or a complicated [method].
Char: Maybe, it's just the way I think of mathematics compared to Tim.
Tim: I see it [mathematics] as the same. I just see it as the same as hers. Which one is the easiest?

Over the next two class periods, the whole class, with the help of the teacher, tried to resolve the controversy raised in this dialogue and come to an understanding of what distinguished one approach from the other. After the teacher had reviewed the information provided by

Tim and Char, and noted the confusion and even controversy over their interpretations of analog and analytic approaches, Tim brought up one of the examples discussed in the essay—the problem of evaluating how much water is in a glass—in an attempt to clarify the difference between the two approaches. He explained that the analytic approach to this problem would be to measure the base, height, weight, and circumference of the glass and compute the volume of the glass on paper; the analog approach, on the other hand, would be to pour the water into a premarked measuring cup. As the class worked together to try to make sense of this explanation, they discussed the correct way to compute the volume of a cylinder of water and then actually carried out the analytic procedure described in the essay by doing the required computations. The teacher and the students also proposed and discussed other examples—some of which were not even among those discussed in the essay—to further understand what would be an analog and analytic approach in each of those cases. But despite all these efforts, the class was not able to come to a satisfactory resolution of what really distinguishes analog and analytic thinking in mathematics.

In an effort to help the students better understand the nature of these complementary approaches and their relevance to learning and doing mathematics, the teacher thought it would be worthwhile for the students themselves to use both of these approaches to create and prove their own theorem. To prepare them for this challenging activity, the class watched a video, "The Theorem of Pythagoras" (Project Mathematics! 1989), that implicitly illustrated the use of both analog and analytic approaches in proving this fundamental theorem; along with viewing the video, students were asked to undertake specific assignments such as creating a set of index cards recording examples of analytic or analogic approaches used to prove the Pythagorean theorem (because these approaches were never identified as such in the video) and writing a journal entry about what they learned about each approach. As students shared their cards and journal entries in a whole-class discussion, the teacher created a generalized list of students' ideas for and examples of each approach on the board. She then asked the students to identify themselves according to their preferred ways of approaching things (analog or analytic), on the basis of the criteria recorded in the list, so that they could form small groups that were heterogeneous with respect to approach. Each group was given the task of "creating a theorem about two figures that have the same area, and proving it using both an analytic and an analog approach."

In the small groups thus formed, the students spent two class periods generating specific conjectures about equivalent figures and proving/refining them. Throughout this process, the continuous creation and critical "reading" of diagrams played a crucial role, especially as students shared and discussed their tentative conjectures and proofs with the rest of the group. For example, the sketches presented in Figure 1.1 were the focal point of the conversation that developed in one group as the students tried to find a rectangle having the same area as a 4 x 4 square. In the course of creating and proving their theorem, the students also referred often to a sheet of area formulas provided by the teacher as well as to the list of analog and analytic approaches compiled earlier. Some groups also looked at a math textbook to see how theorems were written. And when the teacher noticed that many students were struggling to find ways of developing analog proofs for their theorems, she decided to assign the reading of an excerpt from an article on paper folding (Pappas, 1987), along with a written journal response to that text, so as to provide them with some inspiration and concrete models for their own work.

Finally, the students shared the theorems they had created with the rest of the class, often using some of the figures and/or texts that they had generated as support in their presentations. The students were also asked to write a fictional story that conveyed something about the social or historical context within which their group's theorem had developed. To help students become aware of these aspects of mathematics, "historical snippets" about the Pythagorean theorem, previously collected by the instructor from a variety of texts, were read and discussed, thus offering the students some models for this final writing assignment.

Multiple Perspectives on Reading in Inquiry-Oriented Mathematics Instruction

The previous vignette has shown that *what*, *how*, and *why* students read can indeed take more varied forms in mathematics instruction than suggested by existing research and practice on reading in mathematics classrooms. At the same time, the nature of the learning experiences reported in the previous pages makes clear that the kind of mathematics instruction we are hoping to support through such reading experiences is very different from what takes place in most mathematics classes today.

As the "Analog & Analytic" narrative suggests, our study sought to understand the contributions reading could make to the improvement of mathematics instruction in classrooms where teaching and

Figure 1.1. Sketches produced in the course of creating and proving a theorem about two figures that have the same area.

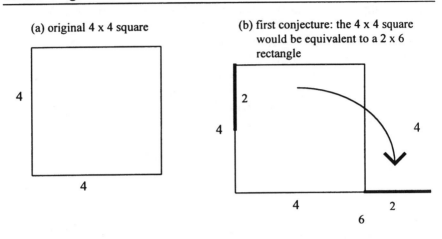

(a) original 4 x 4 square

(b) first conjecture: the 4 x 4 square would be equivalent to a 2 x 6 rectangle

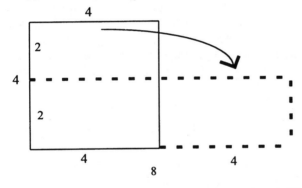

(c) second conjecture: the 4 x 4 square would be equivalent to a 2 x 8 rectangle

learning are defined in terms of inquiry (Borasi & Siegel, 1992, 1994; Siegel & Borasi, 1994)—a perspective illustrated by the experiences portrayed in the previous narrative and further articulated in Chapter 2. More specifically, our goal has been to explore how reading can offer mathematics students opportunities to:

- Construct and negotiate the meaning of important mathematical ideas, including issues related to the nature of mathematics.
- Support engagement in mathematical inquiry and problem solving.

- Encourage the development of conceptions and attitudes about mathematics associated with successful mathematics learning.
- Contribute to the negotiation of classroom norms and practices consonant with an attitude of inquiry.

As we began the RLM Project, the main hypothesis guiding our work was that learning opportunities such as those identified above could be offered by experiences that involved reading what we initially called "rich math texts" (such as the essay "Analog and Analytical Mathematics" [Davis & Hersh, 1981]) using reading strategies designed to help students make sense of such texts and serve as springboards for further reflection and/or learning activities. This hypothesis was grounded first of all in the belief that expanding the range of texts read in mathematics classrooms beyond textbooks and word problems would be important in order to expose mathematics students to issues that have thus far been neglected in traditional mathematics courses— such as how specific mathematical concepts or techniques are used in the real world, how professional mathematicians approach problems, how some of the results found in math textbooks came about, current debates about the "truth" of mathematics results, and even discussions about learning styles and problems. At the same time, findings from recent research on reading had shown that what students might actually "get" from any such text would depend in large part on *how* and *why* these texts were used in a mathematics classroom. Reading strategies rooted in a transactional theory of reading (Rosenblatt, 1938, 1978, 1994)—such as those employed by Tim and Char in the previous vignette—seemed particularly appropriate for our purposes. Rosenblatt made *exploration* the central metaphor of her theory, and these strategies were designed in such a way as to actively engage readers in explorations of meaning by writing, drawing, or talking during and/or after reading. From this perspective, reading becomes a process of meaning-making characterized by the negotiation of different perspectives and the production of new connections and questions. The learning experiences generated around the reading of the essay "Analog and Analytical Mathematics" (Davis & Hersh, 1981), described in the previous vignette, are thus examples of the kind of "reading to learn mathematics" episodes (RLM Episodes hereafter) we developed and studied collaboratively in different instructional settings during the initial phase of our research.

The RLM Episodes developed in these settings, especially those episodes designed by two teachers whose beliefs and practices could be characterized as inquiry-oriented, confirmed our hypothesis about the value of such experiences for mathematics students. Yet our analysis of these experiences suggested that there were additional ways reading could contribute to the inquiry-oriented mathematics classroom that we had not considered when we began the study. For example, even just looking at the reading that took place in the "Analog & Analytic" narrative, we could identify the use of several texts other than "rich math texts"—such as students' journals, lists of ideas recorded on newsprint, definitions and theorems reported in the textbook, and even multimedia texts like Char's sketch or "The Theorem of Pythagoras" (Project Mathematics! 1989) video. Furthermore, often these texts were not read in an exploratory or generative manner. For example, students' journals were read aloud to *make public* the students' thinking; some students looked at theorems in their textbook in order to *get a model* for writing their own theorem; and when each student perused the list of characteristics of analog and analytical thinking the class had generated, it was not to comprehend the meaning of specific items but, rather, to help him or her *make an informed decision* about which small group to join for the activity of creating their own theorem.

When considered in relation to recent research on reading as a *social practice* (e.g., Green & Meyer, 1991; Luke, 1991; Street, 1984), these observations suggested the value of a systematic study of *all* the reading experiences that occurred in a long-term instructional experience (such as the semester-long course on "Math Connections" from which the previous vignette was taken) and not just those experiences that involved reading "rich math texts" in an exploratory or generative way. The goal of such an analysis would be to make visible the many ways in which reading practices serve as vehicles through which mathematics instruction is enacted in classrooms. Identifying the reading practices that occurred in an *inquiry-oriented* mathematics class could not only help mathematics teachers become more aware of how these practices communicate particular beliefs about doing and learning mathematics, but also illustrate the specific reading practices one teacher used to create a classroom community of practice that valued collaboration, student participation in decision making, generative and reflective thinking, complex problems, and the struggle involved in creating, enacting, and transforming ideas. The results of this study indeed provided new insights on reading in mathematics classrooms that, without undermining the value of "reading rich math texts generatively" explored earlier, led us to reconsider what could "count" as reading in a mathematics classroom and thus further expand our vision of a new integration of reading and mathematics instruction. These insights may be helpful to mathematics teachers both conceptually and practically in that teachers may begin to see how different ways of reading become ways of "living and learning mathematics" (Whitin, Mills, & O'Keefe, 1991) in a particular classroom. They may also find the specific examples of reading practices useful as resources in the design of inquiry experiences for their own students.

Finally, in order to further articulate the role that reading could play in supporting students' mathematical inquiries, we decided to look at our classroom data from yet another perspective. In particular, we became interested in identifying the specific *functions* that reading played in "math inquiry cycles," such as the one illustrated by the students' inquiry on analog and analytic thinking—that is, learning experiences designed to engage students in inquiry as Dewey (1933) described it: a four-part cycle of problem sensing, problem formation, search, and resolution. Although we are not suggesting that all inquiry-oriented mathematics instruction consists of this kind of learning experience, we believe that "math inquiry cycles" are emblematic of inquiry-oriented instruction in that they invite students to experience firsthand the ambiguity and nonlinearity associated with the mathematical thinking of professional mathematicians as well as the power of generating mathematical knowledge. As such, participating in math inquiry cycles may result not only in meaningful learning of specific mathematical concepts and processes but in a new awareness and appreciation of the nature of mathematics along with increased confidence in mathematical ability.

The analysis we undertook helped us identify a variety of functions reading can serve in math inquiry cycles and show how these functions support students' mathematical inquiries. For example, in the "Analog & Analytic" Inquiry Cycle, reading and presenting the original essay provided a stimulus for the whole inquiry as the controversy that arose served to *make things problematic to raise questions worth exploring*; looking up definitions and theorems in the course of developing their own theorem instead enabled students to *gather tools and/or models necessary to carry out their inquiry*; reading the paper-folding article had yet a different function, as the teacher assigned it with the intention of *pushing the students' inquiry further* when she realized that most groups had difficulty identifying analog ways to prove their theorem. Our analysis also suggested that the reading functions thus identified were associated with specific components of math inquiry cycles and, furthermore, represented ways of reading that could be best described and discussed in light of multiple reading theories.

Although each perspective introduced in this section is grounded in a distinct theory of reading and thus emphasizes certain interpretations of reading over others, we have come to regard these interpretations as complementary ways of "seeing" reading in mathematics classrooms. Taken together, these perspectives offer an expanded view of the nature and role of reading in classrooms and suggest the rich possibilities for teaching and learning mathematics that may flow from this view.

Scope, Content, and Organization of the Book

Our goal in this book is to contribute to an understanding of how reading could enrich students' learning experiences in inquiry-oriented mathematics classes by building on perspectives from both the reading and the mathematics education literatures, and on the analysis of classroom experiences in secondary schools. The core of the book (Chapters 4, 5, and 6) reports the major findings of the three complementary analyses we conducted, each grounded in one of the three theoretical perspectives—reading as transaction, reading as a social practice, and reading as functional—outlined in the previous section. Each of these studies examined extensive classroom experiences developed by two inquiry-oriented mathematics teachers, Judith M. Fonzi and Lisa Grasso Sanvidge, first in the context of the RLM Project and later in some experiences these teachers initiated and carried out independently. The decision to focus on these two teachers grew out of our respect for them as teachers and our observation that their classrooms offered the richest sites for studying the potential of integrating reading into mathematics instruction. Indeed, it was the power and inventiveness of their teaching that inspired us to undertake the multiple analyses presented in this book, as our initial idea could not account for all the ways that reading had been incorporated into their mathematics instruction.

Narratives of selected instructional experiences serve as the centerpiece of each of these core chapters. The purpose of these narratives is not only to illustrate the multiple ways reading can support the learning and teaching of mathematics but also to introduce the major findings of each study in the context of practice by means of a parenthetical commentary embedded in each narrative. In an effort to make the book more readable, we have tried to limit a discussion of the research methodology used in each of the three studies we report. Readers wishing to learn more about the procedures used to analyze the data will find this information in the Appendix.

To provide a framework for the findings reported in the core chapters, the book begins with a discussion of the theoretical grounding for our study and a description of the research and instructional settings for the classroom experiences examined throughout. More specifically, in Chapter 2 we make explicit the overarching inquiry framework, goals for learning mathematics, and theories of reading that inform our work; then, from these views, we construct an emerging vision of integrating reading into mathematics instruction that can be compared to the existing research literature on this topic. In addition to positioning our work with respect to the discourse and research in various related fields, we believe this chapter is important in light of the interdisciplinary nature of our study and the dual audience for whom this book is intended. Our hope is that this chapter will acquaint mathematics educators with important developments in the field of reading education they may not be familiar with, and vice versa. Chapter 3, instead, describes the RLM Project and its follow-up studies, and provides background information about the teachers, schools, students, and courses featured throughout the book.

Finally, in Chapter 7 we attempt to draw together the results of the three studies presented in Chapters 4, 5, and 6 by revisiting our original question of *what*, *how*, and *why* students could read in inquiry-oriented mathematics classes. Implications for practice that emerge from the expanded view of reading mathematics developed in this book and directions for future research that follow from our work are also considered in this final chapter.

CHAPTER 2

Frameworks for Rethinking Reading in Mathematics Instruction

The image of reading and mathematics instruction presented in the "Analog & Analytic" vignette reported in Chapter 1 is not one that usually comes to mind when we think of school, especially secondary schools. Without a close look at the thinking behind such instructional experiences, it may be hard to understand why a teacher might make the choices she did or to see what students might gain from participating in activities and discussions like those described in that vignette. The purpose of this chapter, therefore, is to make explicit the beliefs that guided the teaching and research described in this book. This involves four elements: (a) a discussion of the beliefs that have led us to characterize knowing and learning as inquiry, and their implications for classroom practice; (b) an overview of the goals for school mathematics that we sought to support throughout the project; (c) a review of the reading theories that informed the studies presented in Chapters 4, 5, and 6; and (d) a conceptual map of the existing literature on reading mathematics that produced the new integration of reading in mathematics we set out to study.

Given the interdisciplinary nature of the project, some readers may find the ideas and arguments in particular sections familiar, whereas other sections may offer a new understanding of the field with which the reader is less well acquainted. The challenge of learning about and making connections between the fields of reading and mathematics education was a highlight of our own experience with this project and one that allowed us to imagine possibilities for integration that neither field, by itself, had considered. We hope this discussion will do the same for the reader.

Building a Framework for Inquiry-Oriented Instruction

Despite the attention that has been paid to "reforms" in the teaching of mathematics in the educational literature, inquiry-oriented instruction such as the "Analog & Analytic" experience is still quite rare in U.S. secondary schools (Goodlad, 1984; NCTM, 1991). As a report of the 1995 Third International Mathematics and Science Study (TIMSS) has shown, classroom practices in the United States (and other countries as well!) continue to emphasize the transmission and display of knowledge in preparation for standardized tests (U.S. Department of Education, 1996). In what follows, we attempt to clarify what we mean by "inquiry-oriented" classrooms by examining the theory and research that have led us to conceptualize knowing and learning as inquiry, followed by a discussion of the implications this work has for classroom practice and the role of language in such classrooms.

Conceptualizing Knowing and Learning as Inquiry

Questions about what it means to know and to learn are enduring and, therefore, our discussion will focus only on the philosophers, anthropologists, sociologists, psychologists, and educators whose ideas have shaped our understanding of inquiry.

First among these is the theory of inquiry set out by the American pragmatist Charles Sanders Peirce (1839–1914) over 100 years ago. The starting point for Peirce's theory was his critique of the Cartesian assumption that absolute knowledge is attainable. In contrast, Peirce argued that all knowledge is indirect because we know the world through signs, and, because signs must be interpreted by other signs, there can be no guarantee that the knowledge we have is absolute. Thus Peirce rejected the idea that knowledge is stable and certain and proposed, instead, that knowledge is a process of inquiry, ever open to doubt. This does not mean he was a skeptic; rather, he maintained that we could not live with doubt on a day-to-day basis and therefore should not continuously doubt that which we take to be stable. At the same time, we should recognize the contingency of that stability and be ready to revise or reject knowledge found to be false (Skagestad, 1981). In short, Peirce rejected the foundational metaphor and posited a radically different view of knowledge in its place:

> To Peirce, knowledge is no longer regarded statically as a body of propositions resembling a more or less finished building, but dynamically as a process of inquiry. (Skagestad, 1981, p. 18)

The metaphor he used to capture this belief was that knowing is walking on a bog.

We never have firm rock beneath our feet; we are walking on a bog, and we can be certain only that the bog is sufficiently firm to carry us *for the time being* [emphasis added]. Not only is this all the certainty that we can achieve, it is also all the certainty we can rationally wish for, since it is precisely the tenuousness of the ground that propels us forward. . . . Only doubt and uncertainty can provide a motive for seeking new knowledge. (Skagestad, 1981, p. 18)

This metaphor captures well the key role that doubt plays in Peirce's theory of inquiry. In his well-known essay, "The Fixation of Belief," Peirce clarifies this point when he writes: "The irritation of doubt causes a struggle to attain a state of belief. I shall term this struggle *inquiry*, though it must be admitted that this is not a very apt designation" (1877/1982, p. 67). For Peirce, it is doubt that sets the process in motion, and most often this feeling of doubt arises when the knower encounters an anomaly—something that doesn't make sense in light of existing beliefs.

The characterization of inquiry as a struggle to settle doubt and fix belief makes it appear as if Peirce were describing the activities of isolated individuals, but in fact the concept of community figured prominently in his theory. Peirce regarded inquiry as a "public process carried out by a community of investigators" (Skagestad, 1981, p. 24) and believed that it was the function of this community to distinguish purely private thoughts from those that could hold up under public scrutiny; knowledge that could pass the test of the community was taken as "true."

Findings from the history and philosophy of science and mathematics lend further support to the idea that anomalies and doubt are central to inquiry and the understanding that knowledge is deemed "true" by virtue of intersubjective agreement. Kuhn's (1970) thesis regarding the growth of scientific knowledge has been especially influential in reconceptualizing inquiry in this regard. Drawing on historical examples from astronomy, chemistry, and physics, Kuhn argued that the production of knowledge in science is less a cumulative process than a revolutionary one in which the reigning paradigm or worldview is overthrown, not by more and "truer" facts but by a more powerful theory, one which could account for anomalies previously left unexplained. Still, for this new paradigm to take hold and become the basis for doing what scientists regard as "normal science," it must be taken up by the community of inquirers. If not, it fails to influence ongoing inquiry and is viewed as a curiosity (at best). Kuhn thus demonstrated that the logical and objective quality of scientific inquiry is a social achievement, and hence the knowledge produced by a community of inquirers is an artifact of that community's agreement about how to see the world.

Whereas Kuhn drew chiefly on the history of the physical sciences to develop his thesis, Kline's (1980) and Lakatos's (1976) analyses of some key events in the history of mathematics show that even in the discipline thought to be the most certain and rational, this image of inquiry as social undertaking applies. Kline's account of the creation of non-Euclidean geometries provides a clear example of the role played by the community in establishing the truth of a mathematical result. He writes:

> That Euclidean geometry is the geometry of physical space, that it is the truth about space, was so ingrained in people's minds that for many years any contrary thought such as Gauss's were rejected. . . . For thirty years after the publication of Lobatchevsky's and Bolyai's works all but a few mathematicians ignored the non-Euclidean geometries. They were regarded as a curiosity. Some mathematicians did not deny their logical coherence. Others believed that they must contain contradictions and so were worthless. Almost all mathematicians maintained that the geometry of physical space, *the* geometry, must be Euclidean. (Kline, 1980, p. 88)

It was not until several key papers were published that mathematicians began to question the "truth" of Euclidean geometry and consider that a non-Euclidean geometry could also be used to describe properties of physical space.

Recently, anthropologists and sociologists working in a field known as the sociology of scientific knowledge (SSK) have further elaborated the role played by community in the creation of knowledge. Ethnographies of research laboratories such as the Salk Institute (Knorr-Cetina, 1981, 1983; Latour & Woolgar, 1979) have been undertaken in an attempt to better understand what scientists are doing when they study plant proteins or the brain's endocrine system. By focusing on social practices of laboratory life, these scholars have shown that language and representations have a central place in the activity we call science. From this perspective, scientific communities are in fact "discourse communities," and the "truth" of a knowledge claim is established through a rhetorical contest. In other words, the construction of the argument is key to convincing the community of practice that the knowledge claim is warranted by the data. Here we can begin to see the shaping role that language plays in producing "truth," despite the fact that scientists do not characterize inquiry in this way (and may resist it, as Jonas Salk did after reading Latour and Woolgar's ethnography). In the context of the research laboratory, scientists understand the constructed nature of their work, but when they prepare papers for publication, they proceed as if their work involved mere description. Scientists work hard to convince the reader that their findings are not representations at all but unmediated nature, and that the reader has been convinced only by the evidence presented and the elegant logic of the inquiry. However, it is the rhetorical practices scientists use that turn inscriptions into "truth." From this perspective, then, scientific knowledge is socially constructed and achieves its privileged status as "fact" from a process in which dialogue and debate among colleagues in the laboratory is transformed into a statement with quotation marks around it and, finally, into a flat factual statement in a textbook (Latour, 1987). Ultimately, SSK researchers have found that the production of scientific knowledge is not qualitatively different from the production of everyday knowledge, because science depends, as does all human thinking, on the process of representation or sign-functioning.

Whereas philosophers such as Peirce helped us conceptualize knowing as a process of inquiry, and sociologists and anthropologists like Latour and colleagues showed us how social practices involving language and representations were central to doing inquiry, we turned to psychological theories of learning to help us understand how mathematics learning occurs. Three perspectives on learning in particular—constructivism, social constructivism, and situated theories of learning—influenced the way we thought about learning. Within the education community, these theories have been the focus of much discussion and debate (Cobb, 1994; Lave & Wenger, 1991; Phillips, 1995; Rogoff, 1990; Sfard, 1998; Steffe & Gale, 1994). In what follows, we do not review those debates but instead focus only on those theoretical considerations and research findings that contributed most to our emerging framework for inquiry-oriented instruction.

First, several studies on learning mathematics (see, e.g., Baroody & Ginsburg, 1990; Fosnot, 1996; Ginsburg 1983, 1989; Steffe, von Glasersfeld, Richards, & Cobb, 1983) have challenged the common-sense assumption that knowledge can simply be transmitted to individuals. Rather, drawing on Piaget's model of cognitive development and, later, on research inspired by the field of cognitive science, these researchers have shown that the learner must actively construct a personal understanding of mathematical concepts and techniques if meaningful learning is to occur. The starting point for learning is often the learner's realization that something doesn't fit with prior knowledge or explanations and as such doesn't make sense. Piaget (1970) called this phenomenon "disequilibrium" and regarded it as a key mechanism for learning. Constructivist perspectives on learning mathematics thus highlight the active, sense-making nature of learners' interactions with the environment.

The resurgence of interest in Vygotsky's (1962, 1978) work has led some mathematics education researchers to place more emphasis on the social dimensions of learning. The key tenet of what some refer to as social constructivism is that learning is necessarily social in the sense that it first occurs between people on an interpsychological plane and only later appears within the learner on an intrapsychological plane. As Cobb, Wood, and Yackel (1990) have stated:

> Social interaction therefore constitutes a crucial source of opportunities to learn mathematics in that the process of constructing mathematical knowledge involves cognitive conflict, reflection, and active cognitive reorganization (Piaget, 1970). As such, mathematical learning is . . . an interactive as well as constructive activity. (p. 127)

The idea that social interaction "mediates" thinking and learning in the Zone of Proximal Development (ZPD) extends the constructivist perspective by highlighting the influence that social interactions and the social arrangement of the classroom may have on learning. Still, some Vygotskian scholars (e.g., John-Steiner, Panofsky, & Smith, 1994; Wertsch, 1985, 1991) suggest that the attention paid to social interaction in the ZPD has overshadowed the most important of Vygotsky's ideas—the concept of semiotic mediation. As John-Steiner, Panofsky, and Smith (1994) note, "mediation refers to the tools, signs, and practices that contribute to qualitative changes in development [and], through social interaction, become internalized and thus available for independent activity" (pp. 139–140). For Vygotsky, then, thinking and learning were regarded as social both because mediational means such as tools, signs, and practices are products of sociocultural evolution and because they are learned through social interaction (John-Steiner, Panofsky, & Smith, 1994). Although social constructivists tend to emphasize social interaction over semiotic mediation, we regard both concepts as critical to understanding thinking and learning.

Finally, it is worth considering what Sfard (1998) calls the "participation" metaphor for learning. Rather than focus on the acquisition of knowledge, situated theories of learning focus on learning how to participate or become a member of a particular community of practice (Lave, 1988; Lave & Wenger, 1991; Rogoff, 1990; Sfard, 1998). From this perspective, the goal of learning is not so much the construction of meaning, either individually or through social interaction; instead, learning is a matter of learning to talk and act like a member of a particular community, taking on the language, identities, and practices of that community. Moreover, learning to participate in a particular community is a social process of "apprenticeship" (Rogoff, 1990) involving legitimate peripheral participation (Lave & Wenger, 1991). Thus situated theories of learning go beyond social constructivist theories and propose that social interaction is both the means and the endpoint of learning.

Although it is tempting to try to integrate these three perspectives on learning, that is not something easily achieved, owing to the differing assumptions and genealogy of each theory. Yet we found these perspectives helpful because each emphasized an aspect of learning that we regarded as important (cf. Cobb, 1994; Sfard, 1998) and that seemed to resonate with our emerging sense of knowing as inquiry.

Implications for Classroom Practice

A classroom in which knowing and learning are conceptualized as inquiry would look quite different from those we are most familiar with—especially in secondary mathematics! In what follows, we point to some of the key features of inquiry-oriented classrooms, which we developed by drawing implications from the theory and research summarized in the previous section and by analyzing the classroom practices of teachers who approached teaching and learning from the perspective of inquiry. Selected references to the "Analog & Analytic" experience described in Chapter 1 are used to illustrate some of these points.

First of all, classrooms that are inquiry-oriented tend to emphasize the full complexity of knowledge production. Teachers expect students to see the doubt arising from ambiguity, anomalies, and contradiction as a motivating force leading to the formation of questions, hunches, and further exploration, as opposed to the source of confusion. Therefore, teachers in inquiry-oriented classrooms are more inclined to help students use this confusion as a starting point for problem posing and data analysis and less concerned with clearing things up *for* them. For example, in the "Analog & Analytic" narrative the teacher resisted the temptation to clarify the students' initial confusion about analog and analytic thinking and chose instead to support *their* struggle to understand the differences between these two approaches. As the result of experiences such as these, students are no longer outsiders who regard knowledge as something handed down and preserved as flat factual statements in textbooks. Rather, as members of a community of practice, they come to understand that what ends up in textbooks is often the endpoint of a long debate, which may have been decided on the basis of the argument made and not the correspondence between the phenomenon and the statement describing it. In this way, the authority of textbooks is challenged and they become simply artifacts of a particular conversation. It is likely, therefore, that patterns of classroom discourse will move from what Richards (1991) has characterized as "school math" to those associated with the logic of discovery—that is, conjectures and arguments—which is common to the discourse of both professional mathematicians and mathematically literate adults.

An appreciation for the social dimensions of learning and the role played by community in the production of knowledge also means that inquiry-oriented classrooms are highly collaborative. Value is placed on becoming a participant in a community of practice within which meanings are negotiated. This does not mean that students need not construct personal understandings, but rather that collaboration and social interaction provide critical support for that process—as illustrated throughout the "Analog & Analytic" narrative—as well as for the development of student identities as mathematical knowers and learners. At the same time, the moral imperative of such classrooms respects diversity and individual perspectives so that the production of collective meanings does not become a tool for silencing difference.

Most important, inquiry-oriented teachers listen to their students (Confrey, 1991; Harste, Woodward, & Burke, 1984). They listen so as to understand their beliefs about learning and the background experiences they bring to specific inquiries, to invite their involvement in the framing and organization of the inquiry, to gain insight into the meanings and connections students construct, and to hear their concerns and questions about the inquiry process itself and the changes in classroom norms and values it engenders.

Inquiry-oriented classrooms also require students to take an active role within the class as members of a community of practice. This role requires a much greater degree of risk-taking as well as responsibility on the part of the student. Risk is woven into all aspects of the inquiry process, from the initial formation of the problem through to the final presentation and evaluation of end results. Much of the risk involves the sharing of "rough draft" thinking (Barnes, 1976) and, in particular, the use of talking, writing, and reading to shape and reflect on their thoughts.

The characteristics discussed thus far call for different teacher roles in inquiry-oriented classrooms. Here teachers spend less time transmitting information through the channels of talking or reading and take up the challenge of supporting student inquiry. This may involve designing activities that can help students move further in their inquiry (like those designed by the teacher in the "Analog & Analytic" narrative around "The Theorem of Pythagoras" [Project Mathematics! 1989] video and the paper-folding article), facilitating classroom conversations, providing access to relevant tools and resources, and so on. An important aspect of a teacher's work in an inquiry-oriented classroom involves negotiating a set of social norms and values with students that helps them learn what it means to know and learn in a particular classroom or school setting, and how they can successfully participate in and take up the possibilities such settings offer.

Finally, if the production of knowledge, including mathematical knowledge, involves the negotiation of meanings within a community of practice (Lave, 1988), then communication becomes integral, if not central, to doing inquiry. Richards (1991) highlights this point in his examination of mathematical discourse and notes that the discourse of school math (classroom discourse following traditional recitation patterns, and the language of textbooks) truncates the practice of inquiry in mathematical communities to the point that students cannot see or experience the zigzag quality so characteristic of mathematical knowing. Therefore, although talking, writing, and reading may be relegated to the sideline in traditional mathematics classrooms and may even serve to obscure the nature of mathematical work, this is less likely in inquiry-oriented classrooms because these modes of commmunication are used to support learning and participation in classroom life. Hence reading, writing, and talking in such settings require much greater attention from teachers—the central theme of this book.

Reconceived Goals for School Mathematics

Reconceiving mathematics instruction within the inquiry framework we have outlined calls for not only different assumptions, instructional practices, discourse, and classroom norms but also a quite different set of goals for school mathematics. It may be difficult to appreciate the value of the experiences described in the "Analog & Analytic" narrative, for example, if we do not value the need to help students consider and perhaps reevaluate their conceptions of mathematics or to understand how theorems are constructed and written, as that experience was designed to do. Consistent with the recommendations of mathematics education researchers working from a constructivist perspective as well as those made by influential professional organizations in the United States (e.g., NCTM, 1989; NRC, 1989), we believe there is a need to rethink the mathematical content we would like students to learn, pay explicit attention to the processes involved in learning mathematics, and address students' conceptions about the nature of mathematics as a discipline. In the remainder of this section, we briefly consider each of these major categories of instructional goals and the support they have received in the mathematics education literature.

First, there seems to be a consensus about the need to rethink the *mathematical content* that students should "learn." This point is especially evident in the curriculum recommendations described in the *Curriculum and Evaluation Standards for School Mathematics* (NCTM, 1989) and the TIMSS report (U.S. Department of Education, 1996), but is also supported by the instructional implications of much of recent research in mathematics education (see, e.g., the reviews reported in Grouws, 1992). In contrast to the traditional focus on arithmetic, algebra, and eventually calculus, the importance of knowing about branches of mathematics such as probability and statistics, number sense and estimation, geometry and measurement, and patterns and functions is now stressed, owing to the increased importance of these branches of mathematics in everyday applications. Furthermore, teachers have been encouraged to pay more attention to students' understanding of the "big ideas" within these branches of mathematics as well as within more traditional school mathematics topics (Steen, 1990). In the context of teaching algebra, for example, this would mean focusing on an understanding of what an equation is and what equations can allow us to do rather than on techniques for solving different kinds of equations; in geometry, it would mean paying attention to ideas such as the relationship between properties and functions of shapes rather than memorizing a lot of vocabulary and facts about specific figures out of context. Finally, the importance of appreciating the connections among the mathematics topics noted above as well as connections to other fields that use mathematics has also been highlighted (NCTM, 1989).

As part of this rethinking of the school mathematics curriculum, we have also seen a new emphasis on instruction that focuses on the *process of learning and doing mathematics*. It is significant, for example, that the NCTM Standards articulate the key goals for school mathematics in terms of processes (solving mathematical problems, reasoning and communicating mathematically) and attitudes (valuing mathematics, gaining confidence in one's ability to do mathematics) *above* learning specific content or basic skills (NCTM, 1989, p. 5). Support for this emphasis on process can be found in the vast research literature on mathematical problem solving. This body of work has attempted to identify the kind of knowledge and strategies needed to be a successful problem solver and to develop instructional practices that help students learn to use such strategies (e.g., Charles & Silver, 1988; Schoenfeld, 1985, 1987). Some of this work has focused on the importance of metacognition—awareness of and reflection on the process of framing and solving problems—in successful problem solving (e.g., see review reported in Schoenfeld, 1992). This interest in metacognition, along with other theoretical influences, has contributed to a growing appreciation for the mediating role of language in problem solving as well as new interest in research on students' use of language and other modes of representation to reason and communicate mathematically (e.g., Connolly & Vilardi, 1989; Janvier, 1987; Richards, 1991). Although research on these topics has been fruitful, more instructional approaches grounded in such research are needed to help students develop learning strategies that will enable them to frame and solve the kind of problems they are likely to encounter in mathematics classes and everyday life.

One aspect of learning mathematics that has received far less attention in the research literature, and even in documents such as the NCTM Standards, focuses on learning about *the nature of mathematics as a discipline*. Yet this seems a critical dimension of a student's mathematical education, especially in light of Schoenfeld's (1992) contention that "a fundamental component of thinking mathematically is having a mathematical point of view, that is, seeing the world the way mathematicians do" (p. 340). Support for this argument comes from several sources. Social constructivist and situated theories of learning, for example, highlight the social as well as cognitive aspects of learning and suggest that becoming part of a community of practice is essential to becoming an expert in a discipline (e.g., Bishop, 1988; Lave & Wenger, 1991; Resnick, 1988; Schoenfeld, 1992). As Resnick (1988) has noted, "becoming a good mathematical problem solver—becoming a good thinker in any domain—may be as much a matter of acquiring habits and dispositions of interpretation and sense-making as of acquiring any particular set of skills, strategies or knowledge" (p. 58).

Research on students' beliefs about mathematics also suggests that developing an awareness of the nature of mathematics is a crucial part of learning mathematics. These studies (e.g., Borasi, 1990, 1992; Buerk, 1981, 1985; Schoenfeld, 1989) have revealed a number of widespread beliefs about mathematics that are unfounded and hence dysfunctional for learners. For example, many students believe that:

- There is only one correct way to solve any mathematical problem— usually the rule the teacher has most recently demonstrated to the class
- Mathematics is a solitary activity, done by individuals in isolation
- Students who have understood the mathematics they have studied will be able to solve any assigned problem in five minutes or less
- The mathematics learned in school has little or nothing to do with the real world (Schoenfeld, 1992, p. 359)

These beliefs are cause for concern not only because they misrepresent the nature of mathematical thinking but because they promote unproductive learning strategies and habits of mind. Faced with a problem that involves more than the application of a stated algorithm, students who hold the above-mentioned beliefs may think, "It is no good to try to reason things out on your own; . . . staying too much on a problem is a waste of time; . . . history and philosophy of mathematics are irrelevant to learning mathematics" (Borasi, 1992, p. 208). Such ways of thinking may interfere with students' learning and may even put students at risk for developing math anxiety (e.g., Borasi, 1990; Buerk, 1981).

In calling for instruction that helps students appreciate the nature of mathematics and develop beliefs and strategies associated with the mathematics community, we should not forget that mathematicians continue to disagree about how to define the "nature" of mathematics (Brown, 1984). Nor should we forget that previous reform movements also tried to help students understand the nature of mathematics. Recall that this was an explicit goal of several of the New Math projects in the 1960s, although in that context it meant familiarizing students with what were thought to be unique and characteristic aspects of mathematical thinking, such as notions of structure and abstraction. Those working from a "humanistic" perspective on mathematics, on the other hand, have suggested a different interpretation of the nature of mathematics, one that would help students see mathematical knowledge as socially, culturally, and politically constructed. Rather than highlight the absolute and authoritarian image of mathematics, humanistic mathematics educators contend that mathematics is a human endeavor as fallible and value-laden as any other (e.g., Borasi, 1992; Brown, 1982; White, 1993). This view of mathematics takes on new significance in relation to an inquiry perspective on knowledge, especially if educators want students to see mathematics as a way of knowing that has value and meaning for their lives.

Rethinking Reading Theory and Practice

Along with new goals for school mathematics, the "Analog & Analytic" narrative suggests that reading is much more than "mining" the text so as to reconstruct the author's message, the most common way reading is thought of in secondary mathematics classrooms. Hence it may be useful to understand how researchers and educators in the field of reading came to think of reading as a generative process of meaning-making. This brief review may help explain some of the teaching practices described in the "Analog & Analytic" narrative—for example, encouraging students to use drawing or writing to make their own sense of an assigned text and then sharing those interpretations with their peers.

Among reading educators, theories of reading are as controversial as questions about the nature of mathematics and goals for teaching mathematics are for mathematics educators. Though disagreements remain, the last 30 years have witnessed significant changes in reading theory and research as a result of conceptual shifts in the fields of linguistics, cognitive psychology, and literary criticism. The image of reading that has emerged from this work is one in which readers are neither passive in the face of the text nor blind to the social event of which reading is part. Instead, readers are regarded as active meaning-makers who use their knowledge of language and the world to construct interpretations of texts in light of the particular situations within which they are read. In what follows, we briefly outline the ideas that influenced the development of a generative view of reading and then summarize the central tenets of this perspective, drawing primarily on Rosenblatt's (1938, 1978) transactional theory of reading. We then introduce several perspectives on reading, drawn from the fields of sociolinguistics and anthropology, that became relevant to our research as our understanding of how to conceptualize reading mathematics expanded.

Early Theoretical Bases for a Generative View of Reading

As early as 1965, the shift within the field of linguistics from behaviorist to mentalist theories of language led Kenneth Goodman and others to challenge the belief that reading was verbal behavior and begin to study reading as a language process. Goodman thus suggested that oral reading errors were not random mistakes but evidence of language use by readers. Readers relied not only on printed symbols but also on their knowledge of linguistic cues (semantics, syntax, and graphophonics) as they worked to make sense of a text (Gollasch, 1982). If oral reading errors were reconceptualized as "miscues," Goodman reasoned, they could serve as a window on the reading process. This insight led Goodman and his associates to collect miscues generated by hundreds of readers and use them to develop a psycholinguistic model of the reading process, which proposed that readers engage in a cycle of sampling, predicting, confirming, and integrating language cues and background knowledge to construct an understanding of the text (Gollasch, 1982; Goodman, 1967, 1985, 1994). Frank Smith (1971) reached similar conclusions about the importance of readers' use of nonvisual (i.e., language and world knowledge) as well as visual information when reading and, like Goodman, argued that reading was a matter of comprehending text, not identifying words, thus assigning readers the leading role in the process.

At about the same time, researchers in the emerging field of cognitive science turned their attention to the reading process as a way to better understand cognitive processes. The cognitive theories of reading comprehension they developed characterized reading as an interaction between reader and text, with the reader playing an active part (e.g., Adams & Collins, 1979; Anderson & Pearson, 1984; Rumelhart, 1977). Researchers repeatedly showed that even in cases where readers could recognize all the words, comprehension was not achieved until they activated the relevant background knowledge (e.g., Anderson, Reynolds, Schallert, & Goetz, 1977; Bransford & Johnson, 1972). The classic example of this finding is the sentence, "The notes were sour because the seams split," which makes little sense until the schema for bagpipes is brought to bear on the text being read (Bransford & McCarrell, 1974). Studies such as these led cognitive psychologists to conclude that readers must do more that accurately decode the words on the page in order to understand a text, and, for this reason, inferencing was given a central place in their accounts of reading comprehension. A major implication of this finding was the realization that no reader would comprehend a text in exactly the same way as another owing to differences in background knowledge, represented in memory as schema, and, therefore, texts functioned as blueprints rather than containers of meaning.

Using the theories and research outlined above as a basis, reading educators developed and investigated a variety of instructional strategies to promote active, meaningful reading (e.g., Beach & Hynds, 1991;

Pearson & Fielding, 1991; Tierney & Pearson, 1981/1994; 1992/1994). This work, in turn, led to new directions in the teaching of reading in elementary as well as secondary classrooms. Many teachers have thus begun to move beyond text-based strategies (e.g., defining technical vocabulary, answering literal questions) to strategies that encourage readers to bring their background knowledge to the text, monitor their own comprehension, engage in a dialogue with the author, think about the relationships among ideas within a text as well as across texts, and separate out important from unimportant ideas. As Pearson and Fielding (1991) note in the conclusion to their review of research on comprehension instruction:

> Students understand and remember ideas better when they have to transform those ideas from one form to another. Apparently it is in this transforming process that *author's* ideas become *reader's* ideas, rendering them more memorable [emphasis in original]. (p. 847)

Spurred on by this new awareness of reading as a process of generating and transforming meanings, reading researchers and educators turned to the work of literary theorists.

A Transactional Perspective on Reading

Among literary theorists, a similar shift toward characterizing reading as a dynamic process of generating meanings and readers as central actors in this process was underway (e.g., Bleich, 1978; Eco, 1979; Rosenblatt, 1978) as the influence of New Criticism began to wane. New Criticism, an approach to reading and interpreting literature that dominated the teaching of literature in high schools and colleges for many years, was based on the assumption that texts contain objective meanings that can be revealed through close readings of the text. Like psycholinguistic and cognitive theories of reading, "reader-response" theories of literary reading challenged the assumption that the meaning was "in the text" and instead focused on the processes readers used to construct interpretations. What distinguished reader-response theories, however, was their insistence that readers' experiences and responses serve as the starting point for interpreting a text. Interpretation thus became an inquiry into meanings rather than a search for a single, text-based meaning.

Rosenblatt's transactional theory of reading (1938, 1978, 1994) has been especially influential in helping reading researchers and educators appreciate that reading is a generative activity that involves more than reconstructing the author's message. Rosenblatt is critical of the ways schools have privileged text-bound meanings above all else and have thus taught children to read poems (and, indeed, all literature) in search of "facts" (Rosenblatt, 1980). Her argument, instead, is that the focus of reading literature should be the "lived-through experience" of the reader. With the publication of *Literature as Exploration* in 1938, Rosenblatt rejected the idea that the text is a static container of meanings and proposed that meanings instead arise from the *transaction* of readers and texts in particular contexts. She chose the term *transaction* to call attention to the way in which the reader and the text shape and are shaped by one another during the reading event, and turned the spotlight on readers' experiences while reading—what they felt, thought, wondered, questioned—in order to understand their transactions with texts. She argued that these experiences, not the ready-made responses students offered up to teachers who treated the text as the true source of meaning, should be the starting point for inquiry into the meaning of a work of literature.

Indeed, exploration is the central metaphor in Rosenblatt's theory of reading. From Rosenblatt's perspective, this exploration is an ongoing cycle of generative and reflective meaning-making, which begins with a tentative purpose or expectation that guides the reader as she or he encounters the printed text. The text, consisting of printed signs with the capacity to act as symbols, calls up in the reader past experiences, feelings, and images that the reader organizes and synthesizes to create a tentative framework that may be revised, rethought, or rejected as the event proceeds. As a result, each reading event is a unique negotiation of reader, text, and context so that, for example, a student reading a newspaper article to find out the results of a recent sports event at home is likely to look for and generate meanings very different from those she or he would if asked to read the same article in a mathematics class in order to locate and explain the meaning of the probability statements reported in the article. Hence, from the perspective of transactional reading theory, texts are open, variation in interpretations within and across readers is expected, and meaning-making is a generative activity that is best characterized as duplicating the activities of an author rather than duplicating the text.

One feature of Rosenblatt's theory that is often cited yet remains problematic from our perspective is her suggestion that readers adopt either an "aesthetic" or an "efferent" stance toward a text. She defined an *aesthetic* stance as one in which the reader focuses on the "lived through" experience while reading and an *efferent* stance as one in which the reader focuses on what is taken away from the experience. Several scholars (e.g., Berthoff, 1990; Willinsky, 1990) have criticized this dichotomy, noting that the either/or quality seems too limiting to explain the twists and turns in focus readers may take in any particular reading event. It seems possible that these categories were developed by Rosenblatt in response to her frustration with instruction that emphasized authoritative meanings rather than the reader's experience and are thus less a theoretical than a pedagogical move on her part (cf. Willinsky, 1990). The problem is that this move led her to offer a rich description of aesthetic reading but a rather thin description of the transaction that occurs when reading efferently. By focusing on the aesthetic rather than the efferent stance, Rosenblatt may have thus unintentionally lent support to the belief that literary texts should be read aesthetically and nonliterary texts efferently. The assumption underlying our work is that reading is a transaction even when the reader adopts an efferent stance and reads to take something away from the text, as the classroom narrative presented in Chapter 4 shows.

Rosenblatt's ideas have captured the imagination of educators concerned with the teaching of reading in both elementary and secondary schools and have led to the development of instructional practices that invite the exploration of texts from multiple perspectives. Rather than narrow down students' interpretations to fit a teacher's a priori interpretation, the concern now is for practices that encourage students to read literature for aesthetic engagement and to participate in literature discussion groups where their experiences can become the starting point for further reading and inquiry into meaning (e.g., Gambrell & Almesi, 1996; McMahon & Raphael, 1997; Peterson & Eeds, 1992; Short & Pierce, 1990). These practices reposition learners and teachers so that teachers become facilitators who help learners take control of their reading and learning rather than experts with authoritative meanings to impose on students (Harste & Short, 1988; Pearson & Fielding, 1991). As we have noted, though, this approach to reading has had a limited influence on the kind of reading that occurs in secondary mathematics classrooms, due in part to the conception of learning mathematics that dominates such settings but also, as mentioned earlier, to Rosenblatt's concern with the teaching of literature, which led her to emphasize the aesthetic stance in her writings.

To support generative reading in classroom settings, reading educators have developed a number of instructional reading strategies grounded in a transactional view of reading—such as Say Something (Harste & Short, 1988), Cloning an Author (Harste & Short, 1988), and

Sketch-to-Stretch (Harste & Short, 1988; Siegel, 1984, 1995), described in Chapter 4. These strategies are not intended to serve as prescriptions for what and how to think but rather to offer some vehicles that can act as springboards for dialogues, reflection, and inquiry and thus enable students to experience the risk-taking and flexibility that are required when readers negotiate meanings and interpretations.

A Social-Practice Perspective on Reading

In contrast to the research described so far, reading and literacy researchers influenced by sociolinguistic and social interactionist theories of language (Bloome & Egan-Robertson, 1993; Bloome & Green, 1984; Green & Meyer, 1991; Kantor, Miller, & Fernie, 1992; Myers, 1992) have not focused on reading as an individualistic activity, however influenced by the context it might be. For these theorists, reading is a social practice inasmuch as it is bound up with the negotiation of everyday life in particular settings, including classrooms. Hence these researchers have argued that reading cannot be defined a priori as a transactional process; instead, they make what "counts" as reading in particular cultural settings the focus of investigation. Furthermore, because these researchers seek an emic (i.e., insider's) understanding of reading, they do not automatically assume that engagement with print, however it is conceptualized, defines a reading event. For example, teachers and students in a particular classroom may, over time, construct a local meaning for "reading" that includes certain ways of talking and interacting (Green & Meyer, 1991). From a social-practice perspective, then, reading is social, not just because it occurs in a social context but because what it means to read is negotiated through social interaction (Bloome & Egan-Robertson, 1993; Green & Meyer, 1991; Kantor, Miller, & Fernie, 1992).

Anthropologists (Heath, 1983; Scribner & Cole, 1981; Scribner, 1984/1988; Street, 1984; Szwed, 1981/1988) have also argued against individualistic definitions of reading. In particular, they have rejected what Street (1984) has called an "autonomous" model of literacy—literacy as a neutral, technical skill—proposing, instead, that literacy be understood as a culturally defined set of practices, that is, ways of reading and writing that are constituted by specific purposes, social relations, technologies, and knowledge (Scribner & Cole, 1981). Anthropologists thus speak of multiple literacies rather than a single literacy. Whereas sociolinguists have emphasized the social construction of these literacies, anthropologists have called attention to the ideological nature of these practices, and especially the way in which different literacies represent different "identity kits," historically and culturally produced associations among ways of using language and ways of thinking, feeling, valuing, and acting (Gee, 1990). From this perspective, treating literacy as an individual rather than an ideological achievement (Street, 1984) is a way to keep questions of power and politics separate from questions of educational practice and policy.

In sum, theorists who view reading as a social practice have been less interested in studying instructional strategies for teaching reading than in studying what "counts" as reading in a community or classroom and how learning to be a certain kind of "reader" affects students' access to and opportunities for learning. These researchers thus suggest that educators abandon a priori definitions of reading and try, instead, to understand the local meanings of reading at work in a particular classroom.

A Functional Perspective on Reading

Sociolinguists and anthropologists also have a long tradition of thinking of language as functional, serving a variety of purposes in people's lives. Two studies, in particular, have been influential in the field of language education, prompting a shift in focus from form (i.e., grammar) to function, meaning, and context in studies of language learning and teaching. In the first, Halliday (1975, 1978) looked at the functions language served in the daily life of his preschool-aged son and identified seven such functions: instrumental (to satisfy material needs—"I want"); regulatory (to control the behavior of others—"Do as I tell you"); interactional (to interact with others—"Me and you"); personal (to shape identity—"Here I come"); heuristic (to learn about reality—"Tell me why"); imaginative (to create one's own reality—"Let's pretend"); and informative (to communicate a message—"I've got something to tell you"). Halliday thus argued that learning language involved more than learning the grammar of a language; rather, it was a process of "learning how to mean," by which he meant learning how to do things with language in interaction with others. As a result, language educators became concerned with the limited, school-specific functions typically observed in classrooms (i.e., the informative function tends to dominate) and began to call for instructional environments that provided students with more opportunities to use reading, writing, and talking for purposes that reflected language use in nonschool settings.

In the second study, an ethnography of the meaning and use of language and literacy in two communities, Heath (1983) also identified a wide variety of functions that reading and writing served, including reading/writing to build and maintain friendships and family ties, to learn of news, for enjoyment and recreation, to check or confirm facts or beliefs, to reinforce or substitute for an oral message, as a memory aid, and to accomplish the myriad of tasks (e.g., filling in documents, reading signs and labels) that are often taken for granted in daily life. In addition to calling attention to the cultural nature of language and literacy learning, Heath's work encouraged language educators to examine the gap between the functions that language and literacy play in communities and classrooms, respectively, and to develop instructional experiences that could help students bridge this gap by expanding their understanding and use of language/literacy functions. This work, in turn, suggests that a functional perspective on reading could make visible many more uses of reading (and writing) in a classroom than have been considered thus far in the educational literature.

Toward New Ways of Thinking About the Integration of Reading in Mathematics Instruction

Our exploration of new ways to think about the nature and role of reading in mathematics instruction took shape as we began to talk together about our respective fields of expertise. As we learned more about the theories, research, instructional practices, and problems faced in each other's field, we began to identify some striking parallels and similarities between an inquiry-oriented view of mathematics knowing and learning and the view of reading as a transactional process of meaning-making. One early heuristic we developed for making sense of the existing literature on reading mathematics was to construct a "grid" in which the perspectives on mathematics instruction and reading described earlier were contrasted with more "traditional" views of these domains, yielding four alternative interpretations of reading mathematics (represented in the grid reproduced in Figure 2.1). Although we eventually came to realize some limitations of this framework, the grid provided us with a useful way to map out the existing research on reading in the context of mathematics instruction and helped us identify "missed opportunities" we might be able to address.

First of all, we noticed that most of the existing literature on reading mathematics fell into Box 1, as it focused primarily on two dimensions: (a) the language of mathematics, with particular emphasis on strategies for teaching and learning the technical vocabulary of math-

Figure 2.1. A grid for framing the problem of reading mathematics.

	Mathematics as a Body of Facts and Techniques	Mathematics as a Way of Knowing
Reading as a Set of Skills for Extracting Information	1. Extracting information from technically oriented mathematics texts	3. Rich mathematical texts are read to gain information on important aspects of mathematics typically excluded from the mathematics curriculum
Reading as a Mode of Learning	2. Reading to learn so as to achieve the goals of a technically oriented mathematics curriculum	4. Reading to learn so as to understand mathematics as a "way of knowing"

Source: Siegel, Borasi, & Smith (1989), p. 272.

ematics, and (b) comprehension of word problems, with attention to the way the syntactic and semantic organization of word problems affects students' ability to solve them (for a more detailed report of this critical review of the literature, see Siegel, Borasi, & Smith, 1989). This is consistent with a definition of the problem of reading mathematics as efficiently extracting information from technically oriented mathematics texts, usually with the goal of accurately solving a problem presented in the text or understanding a procedure explained in the text. Consequently, researchers working within this interpretation concentrated on identifying what they believed to be the major *obstacles* presented by technical mathematics texts, and studying the effects of various instructional strategies designed to overcome these obstacles. Although this approach to reading mathematics has produced some instructional strategies that have been shown to improve students' ability to solve well-defined problems and help them better understand the language used in their mathematics textbooks, it seemed to us that it failed to capitalize upon the potential of reading to support students' learning in mathematics classes. In fact, the implicit belief that the "reading" component creates an *obstacle* to learning mathematics may have contributed to the trend toward minimizing the use of reading in mathematics instruction.

The interpretation of reading mathematics identified in Box 2 instead rejects the "mining" metaphor for reading and reflects the idea that reading is an act of constructing meaning through the negotiation of reader, text, and context, a perspective that gives the reader an active part. However, studies informed by this interpretation (e.g.,

Cohen & Stover, 1981; McCabe, 1981) still seemed focused on developing instructional strategies that would help students correctly interpret and solve word problems. Interestingly, these studies were conducted by reading educators, who may have simply taken "as given" traditional views about school mathematics—instead of challenging them as the mathematics education community has done.

Box 3, on the other hand, suggests the possibility and value of reading a wider array of mathematical texts—such as historical and philosophical essays on specific aspects of mathematics, magazine and newspaper articles about the applications of certain mathematical concepts, or even mathematical stories and poems. Classic collections such as *The World of Mathematics* (Newman, 1961) as well as more recent ones (e.g., Campbell & Higgins, 1984) reveal the existence of many such texts that are accessible to mathematics students. The publication of these collections in itself reflects some appreciation of the pedagogical value of these texts within the mathematics community. And yet, the authors seem to have felt that their task was accomplished once these texts were made available to teachers and students—a choice that reveals their implicit belief that reading is a straightforward matter of extracting information conveyed in a text. This becomes problematic, because mathematics teachers are usually unaware of reading research and instructional strategies that could support their students' active engagement with these texts. As a result, the potential contribution of these texts to school mathematics seems to have remained largely untapped.

Although we readily acknowledge that this grid is somewhat simplistic, it made us aware of the variety of meanings for "reading mathematics" within the literature and, moreover, that when reading educators (Box 2) or mathematics educators (Box 3) have worked in isolation, the theoretical innovations proposed have been limited by an "outsider" view of the other discipline. In contrast, Box 4 suggested to us the possibility of exploring the potentials identified in Boxes 2 and 3 by developing reading experiences in which students would actively make sense of "rich" mathematical texts using strategies grounded in transactional reading theory in an effort to achieve the goals of school mathematics articulated earlier. Our collaboration in the RLM Project thus began with the desire to capitalize on the potential that this new synthesis suggested and led to the study reported in Chapter 4.

As our work took shape in classrooms and in conversations devoted to data analysis, however, we became aware of the limitations of assuming *any* a priori definition of "reading mathematics"—even one as potentially rich as the one identified in Box 4 of our grid. Instructional experiences such as those described in the "Analog & Analytic" narrative showed us that indeed many "kinds" of reading were taking place in the inquiry-oriented mathematics classrooms we had studied other than the generative readings of "rich" mathematics texts we had originally set out to explore. This led us to undertake a systematic study of what "counted" as reading in one of the inquiry-oriented classrooms we had worked in, as we report in Chapter 5.

Moreover, it seemed that if we looked closely at the reading events developed in our classroom research, we might learn what they contributed to students' mathematical inquiries and how they could be best used to support such inquiries. A functional perspective on reading informed a study in this direction, as we report in Chapter 6.

Together, the three studies reported in this book represent an interdisciplinary and collaborative effort to better understand how reading can contribute to mathematics instruction. Combining our respective "insider" perspectives on the fields of reading and mathematics education and bringing multiple perspectives to bear on the classroom events we documented allowed us to identify new ways that reading could be integrated into mathematics classrooms. At the same time, engaging in collaborative action research with two unique mathematics teachers and their students challenged us to think "outside the box" and expand the interpretation of "reading mathematics" in ways we could not have imagined before entering their classrooms.

CHAPTER 3

Research and Instructional Settings

Although our reading of the literature on reading mathematics had demonstrated the need for interdisciplinary work on this problem, it was only when we began to collaborate with teachers in classroom action research that we were able to see how our initial ideas would play out in practice and how they might be revised and expanded. The lively conversations that occurred in every phase of our research challenged us to remain open to perspectives other than our own and to acknowledge and appreciate the complexities teachers face, as well as the compromises they must make, on a daily basis. Our collaboration with the two teachers featured in this book was especially significant, as their inquiry-oriented teaching practices showed us that reading could contribute to learning mathematics in even more ways than our original scheme suggested. In this chapter, then, we describe the research and instructional contexts that frame the instructional experiences examined in the remainder of the book. We begin with an overview of the RLM Project and the experiences and studies that followed it, before introducing the two teachers who designed and carried out reading experiences in their mathematics classes and the instructional settings in which they taught, learned, and researched.

An Overview of the "Reading to Learn Mathematics" (RLM) Project

The "Reading to Learn Mathematics for Critical Thinking" project was designed jointly by the authors—a mathematics education researcher and a reading education researcher—as an exploratory study aimed at creating a new integration of reading and mathematics. The collaborative and interdisciplinary character of this project emerged from conversations begun in fall 1987, when Margie arrived at the University of Rochester. Even while a doctoral student in mathematics education, Raffaella had been interested in the role that texts such as novels, stories, dialogues, and essays on the history and application of mathematics could play in expanding students' conceptions of mathematics as a discipline; working with Stephen I. Brown at the State University of New York at Buffalo, she put together a collection of such texts and wrote about the potential of "novel" texts in mathematics teaching (Borasi & Brown, 1985). However, as Margie shared her research on reading as a transaction, Raffaella began to see that she had not considered how these texts might be read. Margie's research on reading thus introduced Raffaella to a new way of thinking about reading such texts, and especially the need for students to approach texts as active meaning-makers. The idea that reading could become more integral to mathematics education in the ways Raffaella imagined was new to Margie, but her background in semiotic theory and research on transmediation (moving across symbol systems) helped her see the theoretical and practical possibilities of taking on this problem. As our conversations continued, we also became aware of parallel developments in theory, research, and practice in our respective fields and how each field could inform the other.

These conversations would probably not have been so stimulating and enjoyable, however, had we not also shared a number of beliefs, most notably the belief that schools often limited students' thinking and learning and that teaching and curriculum grounded in broader conceptions of both mathematics and reading were needed. We also believed in doing research that challenged the status quo of schooling and wanted our research to be educative for all involved. This led us to conceptualize our emerging research plan as collaborative action research, in which we would join with teachers to design, enact, and reflect on instructional experiences that integrated reading and mathematics in ways that fit Box 4 of our grid for framing the problem of reading mathematics (see Chapter 2). In short, our research combined curriculum design, professional development, and collaborative action research in classroom settings and crossed both disciplinary and institutional boundaries. And because this work involved many hours of conversation—whether in university seminar rooms, hunched over student desks in classrooms, or around our dining room tables—and because the participants featured in this book became friends as well as colleagues, we have chosen to refer to all participants by their first names throughout the book.

The overall research question informing this project was articulated in the original proposal to the National Science Foundation (Borasi & Siegel, 1988) as: How can mathematics instruction take advantage of transactional models of reading so as to foster critical thinking, defined as an attitude of inquiry (Siegel & Carey, 1989), and a deeper understanding of mathematics? More specifically, the intent of the project was to develop, document, and analyze, in collaboration with secondary school mathematics teachers, a set of classroom experiences in which the students would use reading strategies grounded in a transactional theory of reading to make sense of "rich" mathematical texts in order to achieve a better understanding of mathematical content, processes, and/or characteristics of mathematics as a discipline.

To achieve these goals, we planned and organized two main activities to be carried out in phases over a 2-year period:

- A professional development seminar for secondary mathematics teachers interested in exploring uses of reading in their teaching.
- Collaborative action research with a subset of the teachers who had participated in the seminar and were committed to developing and incorporating some reading experiences in at least one of their classrooms.

In what follows, we briefly describe each of these phases, with special attention to the last one because it was the source of most of the classroom experiences examined throughout the book.

The Professional Development Seminar

In spring 1989, the professional development component of the RLM Project took place. This experience was designed as a seminar for secondary mathematics teachers with the expectation that all involved would explore the ideas developed in the initial proposal and elaborate on what they might mean in practice. We hoped that the participating teachers would see the seminar as a forum for considering the possibilities of integrating reading in mathematics instruction, and as an invitation to collaborate in the classroom research phase of the project planned for the following year. The semester-long seminar, entitled "Reading to Learn Mathematics," was offered tuition-free at the University of Rochester and co-taught by Raffaella Borasi and Marjorie Siegel, the principal investigators of the research project. Ten mathematics teachers from a variety of schools in the area and two doctoral students in mathematics education (in addition to Constance Smith) participated in the course.

The course had two components: (a) engaging the participants in activities that would allow them to experience *as learners* the potential of using reading to support mathematics learning and (b) building a collaborative research team in preparation for the collaborative classroom research phase of the project (i.e., the development, documentation, and analysis of "reading to learn mathematics" experience in secondary school settings).

We began the course with a comprehensive unit on "Alternative Geometries" (a topic we expected to be unfamiliar to most of the participants), which was designed so that participants could learn about non-Euclidean geometries with the support of a variety of reading activities. The topic was introduced through a reading experience involving a story about New York City (previously written by one member of the group) that contains an implicit description of *taxigeometry*, a simple non-Euclidean geometry. The technical aspects of this geometry were explored with the support of a technical text on taxigeometry, whereas the broader implications of alternative geometries were examined through an essay on the historical development of non-Euclidean geometries and the mathematical novel *Flatland* (Abbott, 1952). A number of transactional reading strategies were introduced to help participants make sense of these texts. The strategies—Say Something, Sketch-to-Stretch, and Cloning an Author (Short & Harste, 1988), which are described in more detail in Chapter 4—encouraged the participants to connect their own background knowledge and experiences to the text and to actively engage in making meanings through talking, drawing, and writing. Because the strategies promoted group discussion of the ideas encountered while reading, participants were challenged to expand their perspective on the texts and their understanding of alternative geometries.

A second unit on the idea of "Infinity" was then developed. This time, however, decisions about the learning experiences to be designed (including decisions regarding which rich mathematical texts would be read and which reading strategies would be used) became the responsibility of the participants rather than the instructors. The purpose of this unit was to hand control of decisions about what to study, how to do so, and for what purpose to the participants so they could experience as a group what it was like to learn mathematics in the spirit of an "authoring curriculum" (Harste & Short, 1988). In an authoring curriculum, students become authors of their own learning by engaging in a cycle of experiences that fosters generative and strategic thinking in collaboration with peers and teachers.

These firsthand experiences with "reading to learn mathematics," or RLM, had a significant impact on the participants. Engaging in these experiences gave the participants insight into the educational value and potential use of specific reading activities and strategies, something that was necessary if they were interested in designing worthwhile RLM experiences for their own students in the future. Even more important, these unusual learning experiences prompted the participants to raise questions about reading, mathematics, teaching, and learning, which were made public in a shared class journal— a collection of photocopied journal entries written by and distributed to everyone in the seminar (including the instructors) each week. The conversations that flowed from these questions stimulated each individual in turn to think further about his or her own conceptions of these activities.

In the second half of the seminar, the focus shifted to experiences designed to prepare for the classroom action research phase of the project scheduled for the upcoming school year. Activities during this part of the seminar included a brief examination and analysis of a "pilot" unit that integrated several reading experiences into the study of numbers, led by the two members of the group who had developed and taught the unit the previous semester; a search by the participants for readings and activities that could be used in their classes, followed by opportunities to share and discuss the texts/activities they had found; reports of participants' initial attempts to include reading in their mathematics classes; research by the participants on their own strategies for reading various texts; and the development of research questions about RLM that the group (not just the principal investigators) was interested in pursuing.

This part of the course, though essentially successful and productive, revealed how difficult it is to create genuine collaboration between teachers and university researchers in educational research. Our efforts to challenge and transform the traditional role and authority of university researchers as outside experts often created uneasiness and tension, and occasionally even the impression that we were not using the available time effectively. Yet these tensions led to very productive discussions that revealed the participants' initial expectations for the project and their reasons for becoming involved. Gradually, a more collaborative spirit emerged and all involved began to take on greater ownership of the project itself. Valuable "products" also came out of this phase, including data on how mathematics teachers read different types of texts and how they conceive of reading; a plan for studying RLM experiences as teams the following year; ideas for specific reading activities that could be used in mathematics classes; and even a number of classroom reading experiences conducted by some of the participants in their own classrooms.

Collaborative Action Research

In the school year following the professional development seminar (1989–1990), four of the participating teachers volunteered to collaborate with us in planning and implementing some units involving reading experiences in at least one of their classes. In order to support each teacher in the design and documentation of RLM experiences in the target class, four "research teams" were formed. The idea of working as research teams had grown out of the planning done during the seminar and reflected the desire of most participants to remain involved in the project regardless of whether they were able to offer their classroom as a research site. Each team was comprised of the classroom teacher, the reading education researcher (Marjorie Siegel), one of the mathematics education researchers (i.e., either Raffaella Borasi or Constance Smith), and often another teacher who had participated in the seminar. Each research team met regularly to plan and discuss instructional experiences that would create the best learning opportunities possible for achieving the goals set for that unit or course. The priority of the research team, in short, was meaningful instruction. For this reason, team meetings were usually devoted to thinking about the unit as a whole and the contribution that various texts and reading strategies might make. Since collaboration of this kind requires negotiation in relation to each teacher's particular situation, each research team developed a distinctive approach to the classroom research. In most cases, the teams worked jointly to develop units that addressed topics that were part of the existing curriculum (e.g., logic, probability, geometry), although one team worked in a more consultive way to support the classroom teacher's own curricular plan (a semester-long course on mathematical connections). Despite these differences, team discussions tended to focus on making and revising instructional plans in response to specific problems that arose and understanding what was happening in the classroom.

This phase of the research was conceptualized as collaborative action research because the purpose of the project was to create and study new instructional possibilities in mathematics classrooms (Carr & Kemmis, 1986; Rudduck & Hopkins, 1985). In the words of Carr and Kemmis (1986), the research presented in this book was "not *on* or *about* education, . . . [but] *in* and *for* education" (p. 156, emphasis in original). This meant that in addition to documenting the ongoing classroom events in field notes, we participated in curriculum development and classroom learning experiences, always in an effort to both understand and support the teaching and learning enacted in particular classroom settings. Our participation took various forms, including contributing ideas and insights to the ongoing instructional planning, reflecting on what had occurred during the class with other team members, facilitating small-group activities with students, and, on some occasions, playing a role in the actual teaching. In short, we did not treat our research methods simply as neutral techniques for collecting data but as an expression of our commitment as educators to creating the best possible learning environment for students and for negotiating social relationships that were educative for all involved (Gitlin, Siegel, & Boru, 1989).

Follow-Up Studies and Decisions That Shaped This Book

Even as the collaborative phase of the RLM Project was concluding, two of the teachers—Judi Fonzi and Lisa Grasso Sanvidge—continued to integrate reading experiences in their classrooms independently. We regard these experiences as especially significant because they were initiated and carried out by the teachers without the level of support they had received earlier.

The analysis of the data collected during the collaborative phase of the RLM Project and these additional teacher-initiated experiences developed over several years as our understanding of reading, mathematics instruction, and their possible integration continued to develop in light of the theoretical perspectives summarized in Chapter 2 (see the Appendix for a more detailed discussion of the research questions and data analysis procedures developed in this part of our research). During this period of data analysis, we benefited from the collaboration of Constance Smith (who served as the research associate in the RLM Project) as well as Judi Fonzi. Judi's participation in the analysis of data was especially significant, as she brought her unique perspective as the classroom teacher in several of the experiences we were examining. A number of publications resulted from these collaborative efforts, some aimed at a research audience (Borasi & Siegel, 1992; Borasi, Siegel, Fonzi, & Smith, 1998; Siegel, Borasi, & Fonzi, 1998; Siegel, Borasi, Fonzi, & Smith, 1996; Siegel & Fonzi, 1995) and some at a teacher audience (Fonzi & Smith, 1998; Siegel, Borasi, Fonzi, Sanvidge, & Smith, 1996).

As we tried to synthesize and further elaborate what we had learned about integrating reading into mathematics instruction from these complementary studies, we chose to focus this book on the contributions reading experiences could make to *inquiry-oriented mathematics classrooms* (see Borasi, Siegel, Fonzi, & Smith, 1998, and Siegel, Borasi, Fonzi, & Smith, 1996, for a research report of RLM experiences in all four classrooms studied as part of the RLM Project). As the following sections show, both Judi and Lisa sought to instill an "attitude of inquiry" in their students as well as an understanding of mathematics as a human endeavor. Their own histories as students and teachers had made them wary of approaches to learning mathematics that emphasized memorizing and applying procedures in place of flexible and collaborative strategies for thinking and learning. As such, Judi and Lisa were the two classroom teachers we worked with who were the most interested in and open to the underlying ideas and values of the RLM Project. They were also the two teachers who were not limited by grade-level or state-level standardized assessments and who worked in schools in which the institutional norms and values supported their interest in exploring new practices and collaborating with university researchers.

Another choice that shaped this book was the decision to document and study only *one* of the classes Judi and Lisa taught during the year the classroom research phase of the RLM Project took place—a decision we made prior to collecting data in these classrooms so we would be able to make the extensive classroom visits we felt necessary to construct an in-depth account of the ways Judi and Lisa used reading in their teaching. Therefore, although both Lisa and Judi developed many other interesting experiences involving reading in their teaching, in the book we focus only on the instructional events that were part of Lisa's yearlong "Pre-Algebra" course, Judi's fall 1989 "Math Connections B" course, and Judi's spring 1990 course on "Alternative Geometries." Note that this list includes some of the instructional experiences that Judi and Lisa designed and taught independently as an unanticipated follow-up to the collaborative action research phase of the project.

In the remaining sections of this chapter, we introduce the two teachers featured in this book and their classrooms so as to better orient the reader to the specific instructional experiences examined in later chapters.

A First-Year Teacher in a Rural/Suburban Middle School

Lisa and Her Research Team

Lisa Grasso Sanvidge was essentially a first-year teacher when she joined the RLM Project. After earning a B.A. degree in mathematics from Ithaca College (Ithaca, NY), she enrolled at the University of Rochester—where the co-authors were teaching at the time—for a master's degree in education leading to New York State certification to teach mathematics in secondary schools. While still completing her master's degree, she held a temporary teaching position at a Catholic school for a few months, and was then hired by a rural/suburban middle school to teach in their remediation program, working with small groups of students experiencing difficulties in mathematics. The next year, Lisa was offered the opportunity to teach a pre-algebra course in the same school, and she immediately offered this class as a possible site for the classroom research component of the RLM Project.

Lisa's openness to and growing appreciation of inquiry-oriented mathematics instruction was evident throughout her experiences in the master's program and the RLM seminar, and once she had a class of her own, she was enthusiastic about teaching from this perspective. This openness to new ways of teaching was fueled, in part, by her dissatisfaction with what she called the "comfort" of transmission-oriented instruction, something she expressed in the writing she did early in the seminar when the participants were asked to write their "pedagogical creeds." In her brief essay, Lisa reflected on this approach to instruction and challenged herself to continue asking what it meant to teach and learn mathematics:

> Students all too easily fall into the passive role of accepting new information from teachers. For the students it is an easy exchange. Some can master this type of learning and proceed to do quite well in school. These students generally memorize well. Their capacity for taking in new information is slowly expanded through their school years. They are takers, and can only return what is given to them. A regurgitation of sorts. I was this type of learner. It was comfortable learning. It is comfortable for teachers too. Teachers have so much to give, and share. There is never time enough to give it all. With students ready to take, the teacher can feel quite successful. Someone receives the information. It is easily accountable for. Is this really learning? Is this really teaching?
>
> As a teacher I keep asking myself these questions. If I give more information, if I present it better, are the students learning more? Am I a better teacher? I continually rethink teaching Math. I think I have one main goal and that is to get the students in my class to think. I believe that the best way to accomplish this goal is to have the students be exposed to a variety of experiences. They must actively interact in their learning. All kids respond to different things. Always I prefer to use a mixture

of hands-on activities and class discussions. I try to encourage the use of different problem solving strategies, as well as incorporate cooperative learning experiences.

Lisa's reflective stance toward teaching and her commitment to fostering high-level mathematical thinking was evident in all the journal entries she was asked to write early in the seminar. Although eager to learn teaching strategies that could help students think mathematically and not just memorize techniques, Lisa looked critically at each "new" approach she encountered:

> With every method or approach I use in teaching I must constantly ask myself how will this achieve my goal? How will this help these students to think, to be good thinkers? Well, to be a good thinker I believe you must be able to apply your current knowledge to the situation and then draw conclusions (knowledge) from the information presented to you.

At the conclusion of the seminar, Lisa's written reflections suggested that she continued to struggle over her beliefs about both the nature of mathematics and the goals for mathematics instruction, despite her conviction that transmission-oriented mathematics instruction was not the direction to take. She wrote:

> I think that my conceptions regarding mathematics and what should be taught in the classroom is constantly changing. It remains my continuing question, what is substantial mathematics? I keep reformulating my reply. This course helped me to realize that Reading could be looked at similarly.

As the concluding statement in Lisa's reflections indicates, her participation in the RLM seminar also encouraged her to reexamine her views of reading and to see its potential for mathematics instruction. In the following excerpts from her RLM seminar journal entries, we get a sense of the connections between reading and mathematics she had begun to make as well as her questions about what it might mean in practice:

- Reading should enhance the development of the student's ability to visualize mentally the key components of a problem. I would hope that through reading, students might relate numbers to their own experiences and also create extensions of those experiences. I see reading useful to engage my students in some real *exploration* in [a] more enjoyable approach to math. I would want to get away from the drill, and focus on comprehension and understanding of content. I see so many students now that don't have any difficulty with the process, but the processes are [devoid] of meaning. Reading should lend naturally to promoting reasoning skills and problem solving strategies.

- I believe a good thinker has much in common with a good reader. Just as you can do math without thinking, you can read without any understanding. To be a good reader is to apply yourself as a good thinker would.

- I continue to force myself to become aware of my reading process. . . . Reading can create pictures or paint a scene for me to become a part. Reading can involve me in conversation, as if I was speaking or being spoken to. Words can touch my mind and heart, bring me to suspense, fear, sadness or joy. My "pleasure reading" (if well chosen) always brings all these senses alive. . . . Reading a "technical piece" is more often than not, a struggle. . . . I am usually guided by a purpose—to look for words, thoughts to commit to memory. I usually just "experience" pleasure reading. What tends to happen with "technical reading" is that I re-re-re-read paragraphs. I don't experience anything and time passes.

- At the beginning of this [seminar] we agreed that using reading to learn mathematics covered all levels of math and all children. Still I sit in class and I wonder, was our answer idealistic or realistic? All the materials that I keep finding include too much high level mathematics.

- It's harder for me, when I think about the level of math that I teach at 7th and 8th grade, to see how I can use anything we have read. . . . I don't know what's out there, I guess, to try to achieve those [content] goals.

Despite these reservations, Lisa remained open to the contributions that new approaches to integrating reading in mathematics instruction might offer her students. As the following excerpt from her final journal entry shows, Lisa's initial concerns about how she might actually use reading in her classroom were gradually replaced by a renewed sense of possibilities after she had tried out some of the strategies introduced in the seminar.

My eyes are now more open to the possibilities of allowing the students to generate text. I hadn't thought of this as falling

under the category of reading but I now appreciate the possibilities. I have tried with my students to generate text as review for
a unit on rational numbers. The experiment had good points
but I don't feel that I carried it out to a point where I could
evaluate its true effectiveness.

I had thought I was going to walk away [from the seminar]
with interesting stories like *The Phantom Tollbooth*. Cute attention grabbers that were also packed with concepts and ideas in a
way that was more interesting, related different areas and
provoked conversation. I have, but I have also come away with
an open view of what could be considered reading. New sources
were introduced to me. Where I found a lack of resources
initially, I now feel overwhelmed.

I was able to take reading material to my classroom. I was
able to experiment with different techniques, such as "cloning
the author" and "say something." I did this only as a review of
material. I never incorporated techniques into initial lessons.

These feelings and early efforts to try out instructional innovations were
instrumental in Lisa's decision to volunteer for the classroom research
phase of the project, even though she did not have her own classroom
at the time! Openness to new perspectives and approaches was evident
in all Lisa's interactions with her research team; she genuinely wel-
comed the input and support the team provided throughout this challenging undertaking. In addition to Lisa herself, the research team
consisted of Raffaella Borasi (mathematics education researcher) and
Ken Steffen (another certified secondary school mathematics teacher
who had participated in the RLM seminar but did not have a class of
his own that year), with Marjorie Siegel (reading education researcher)
participating in a consulting role.

Lisa's School

During the 1989–1990 school year, Lisa was teaching at a rural/
suburban school located in a small town in the vicinity of Rochester,
New York. The school enrolled about 500 6th- through 8th-grade students, the majority of whom were European American, representing a
range of socioeconomic backgrounds. This school was fairly typical of
middle schools of similar size and serving this student population and,
unlike some urban middle schools, was not known to have any special
commitment to innovative curriculum and teaching approaches or
affiliations with national reform coalitions. Nevertheless, Lisa found

this a supportive context within which to work. She had developed a good relationship with her colleagues during her first year at the school, and the principal readily supported her interest and participation in a research project designed to introduce and study innovations in her mathematics classroom.

As noted earlier, Lisa was working as a remedial mathematics teacher when she accepted the additional assignment of teaching a pre-algebra course to 8th-grade students. As with any middle school mathematics course in New York State, the curriculum for the pre-algebra course Lisa was to teach was quite flexible. Lisa's freedom in designing learning experiences for this course was further supported by the absence of any statewide or school-wide final exam for such a course or the need to "keep up" with teachers in the school who were teaching other sections of the same course. As a result, Lisa felt free to introduce innovative learning experiences in her class.

The Geometry Unit

In fall 1989, the research team joined Lisa in developing a unit on geometry that would cover most of the geometry topics included in the pre-algebra course curriculum while at the same time introducing generative reading experiences. Prior to this unit (during the first 9 weeks of the school year), Lisa had worked to establish a good rapport with the 21 students in her class and help them feel comfortable with classroom routines that included frequent small-group work and class discussions.

As Lisa got ready to plan the geometry unit, she met several times with her research team to articulate the main goals for the unit and identify some "math-related texts" that could be used to introduce and explore some of the topics included in the course curriculum, inspire some significant applications of these topics, or offer information about the historical development of geometry. The team also began to brainstorm ideas about worthwhile learning activities that could be organized around these texts in order to fully tap their instructional potential.

As a result of these preliminary meetings, the research team agreed on the following goals for the unit:

1. Introduce students to basic properties of triangles (especially criteria of congruence) and appreciate their importance and implications.
2. Introduce the students to some basic properties of polygons and polyhedra (e.g., relationship between number of sides, vertices,

and faces [for solids]; relationship between number of sides and sum of interior angles; subclasses of polygons such as regular and convex polygons; perimeter, areas, and volumes [for solids] of specific figures).
3. Have students experience genuine discovery and problem solving in mathematics—including generating and evaluating questions/properties worth pursuing.
4. Provide students with a sense of the role and importance of observation, classification, and definitions in geometry through the study of polygons and polyhedra.
5. Have students recognize that geometry (and mathematics more generally) has a connection with the real world.
6. Make reading and writing an integral part of students' mathematical experience.

On the basis of these goals, the team selected the following texts (most of which had been recommended by Ken Steffen) as catalysts for key activities in the unit:

- A chapter on the origins of geometry from the book *The Whole Craft of Numbers* (Campbell, 1976).
- An essay entitled "Adventures of an Egg Man" (Hoffman, 1988) that discussed the uses of geometry in a recent real-life situation.
- Excerpts from the mathematical novel *Flatland* (Abbott, 1952), which describes a world in two dimensions whose inhabitants were regular polygons.
- Excerpts from Plato's *Mineaus*, which describes the five regular polyhedra and explains how he associated them with fire, air, water, earth, and the universe.

In addition, Lisa proposed that, as a culminating activity, the class construct a city made of Platonic solids, an idea she had drawn from an article in the *Arithmetic Teacher*, "Build a City" (Reynolds, 1985).

As the geometry unit evolved, these plans were further developed and refined by Lisa, with the continuous support of the research team. Raffaella Borasi, and often Ken Steffen as well, participated in all the pre-algebra class meetings throughout the geometry unit as observers and occasionally as assistants to the teacher. Informal meetings in which the teacher and the observer(s) reflected critically on what had happened in class and planned for the next day's class usually occurred immediately after the lesson. Although this daily collaboration made it possible for the team to plan the geometry unit jointly with Lisa,

Lisa remained the person ultimately responsible for making instructional decisions and carrying them out in class.

The geometry unit experience was thoroughly documented; observers took field notes in addition to audio- and videotaping each class, and the teacher collected all her students' work along with her plans and reflections. In addition, nearly all team meetings were audiotaped, and interviews with students that team members conducted at the conclusion of the unit were audiotaped.

The unit developed over a 6-week period during November and December 1989 and consisted of 24 daily lessons of 39 minutes each. The main components of the unit can be summarized as follows:

- *Gaining a sense of the origins of geometry and its practical uses*: To help gain an appreciation of the history and practical value of geometry, students read several essays and snippets from essays about the origins of geometry and applications of geometry in solving real-life problems (such as constructing a giant egg-shaped monument).
- *Learning about congruence of triangles*: One of the readings described earlier presented students with the problem of how to reproduce a triangle *exactly*, knowing the measure of only certain of its sides and/ or angles as a means of computing distances that could not be measured directly. This led the class to explore and eventually discover established criteria for the congruence of triangles.
- *Learning about plane geometric figures*: Building on the readings described above as well as their prior knowledge, students were asked to identify all the plane geometric figures they knew and then select a few for further study. For each of the selected figures, each student was asked to contribute examples and properties that the class would then critically examine and organize in a poster.
- *Understanding perimeter and area*: Strategies for computing the perimeter and area of various geometric shapes were developed by the class *after* students discussed the meaning and use of these important math concepts. The creation and reading of pictures and diagrams played a key role in this component.
- *Constructing a city of Platonic solids*: The activity of actually constructing a city whose buildings were made of Platonic solids (i.e., the five regular polyhedra: tetrahedron, octahedron, icosahedron, cube, and dodecahedron) was introduced to provide students with some concrete experiences in working with three-dimensional geometry, and also to give them a chance to use their creativity and find enjoyment while doing mathematics. Several readings were introduced to provide ideas helpful in naming buildings and planning the city's con-

struction and presentation. These included selections from the mathematical novel *Flatland*, an excerpt from Plato's *Mineaus*, and a brief overview of the history of Platonic solids and how they exist in nature (e.g., in the structure of some crystals).

One of the episodes in this unit is described in greater detail in Chapter 4.

Overall, Lisa was quite pleased with the outcomes of this unit, despite several students' complaints, at times, about the extent and nature of the reading experiences. In the end, she found that her students had come to see geometry in a different way and that she had done so as well:

> I never thought . . . Geometry could be taught with so much discovery and involvement of the students. I had never been exposed to its history or considered it[s] practical value. As a young student, Geometry had meant to me the ingesting of new vocabulary and memorization of formulas that although I could apply them, were meaningless. It was proofs and shapes. It seemed remotely related to math sometimes. Through teaching Geometry, I finally began to put together the pieces of an interesting puzzle.

The "Census" Unit

Although the research team meetings and support ended with the conclusion of the geometry unit, Lisa continued to develop units that were similar in approach to the geometry unit and to occasionally include reading experiences in her plans as she felt appropriate. Lisa also continued to share her teaching experiences informally with the RLM Project staff. One of these units, developed around the 1990 U.S. National Census, seemed especially worth documenting and studying because it both represented an excellent example of an "inquiry experience" and made extensive use of reading. We therefore asked Lisa to supplement the documentation she had already shared with us (consisting of copies of all the instructional materials used in the unit, including all the texts read, and a sample of the students' work) with a detailed oral account of the experience (audiotaped and later transcribed). The narrative of the "Census" unit reported later in Chapter 6 was constructed from these data and was read by Lisa to see if we had indeed captured this instructional experience accurately, at least from her viewpoint.

Because a detailed account of this unit can be found in Chapter 6, we only note here that this unit developed over a period of 3 weeks and was designed so as to introduce students to the basic statistics concepts included in the course curriculum (e.g., mean, median, and mode; multiple ways of representing data) in a meaningful context. The students thus became involved in "taking a census" of their own school inspired by the concurrent U.S. Census.

A Veteran Teacher in an Alternative Urban High School

Judi and Her Research Team

Judi Fonzi joined the RLM Project as a veteran teacher with 14 years of experience teaching mathematics in various settings—a rural high school, a state college, and a public urban alternative high school, where she had been teaching and coordinating the mathematics program for the previous 5 years. Judi had received a B.S. in mathematics and provisional certification as an elementary school teacher from the State University of New York at Brockport, and later received an M.A. in mathematics from the same institution, which also enabled her to become permanently certified to teach mathematics K–12 in New York State.

During her years as a mathematics teacher, Judi had developed a distinctive philosophy and approach to teaching mathematics. This was evident in the "pedagogical creed" Judi wrote at the beginning of the seminar, in which she summarized her goals as a teacher:

- To develop, or pique interest and curiosity in mathematics.
- To help people learn how to learn and want to learn.
- To convey the message "everyone is entitled to their opinion—challenge it, learn from it."
- To teach people to work together, to be responsible to self and to others.

Regardless of whether the setting was a rural K–12 school or a Learning Skills Math Program at a state college, Judi worked tirelessly to create the kind of learning environment she regarded as conducive to students' development as mathematical thinkers and learners. This often meant challenging the status quo of the institution where she taught, but it was a challenge she was usually willing to undertake. In 1984, Judi was offered the position of mathematics coordinator at the

School Without Walls, a public alternative high school in the Rochester (NY) City School District. As she wrote in her autobiography, this was a position that she "could only describe as utopia in the world of education." She credited Lew Marks, the founder and first director of the School Without Walls, with much of her own growth in understanding the learning process as well as her ability to translate her beliefs and values into classroom practices. Early in the RLM seminar, Judi shared the entire text of the graduation speech Marks had given the night he retired, which expressed many of Judi's fundamental conceptions of teaching and learning, especially her belief in the value of using students' questions as the starting point for learning and the need for engaging students in making important decisions about what and how they should learn. Judi also believed that if students were to benefit fully from a collaborative approach to teaching and curriculum, they needed to understand their own approaches to learning. Discussions of both the content and the process of students' learning were therefore characteristic of her teaching, so that students could explicitly reflect on what and how they had learned from such experiences.

Judi's emphasis on reflection was a result of her belief in the importance of helping students learn how to learn. A critical part of learning how to learn was learning to accept the struggle involved when a group worked collaboratively to pose problems and make decisions about what directions to pursue. As part of the seminar, the participants had been invited to collaborate *as learners* in deciding what and how to learn about the concept of infinity. But although RLM seminar participants were able to generate many worthwhile questions, they experienced great difficulty deciding on a joint project. When the group became frustrated, Judi drew on her experiences in helping students learn how to learn and assured them that their struggles were an expected part of the process and not a sign that the teachers (in this case Raffaella and Margie, the seminar leaders) needed to take control and provide a direction.

> When you try to do curriculum development and lesson planning . . . with kids and it happens the same way [as what the group was experiencing]. Ultimately, somebody will say, "Let's go back and take a vote on something." Somebody will finally take a stand, and the kids they just—they start rallying around something and they start to support an idea or they decide to break up into two ideas of whatever. . . . But the one thing that I believe and that I hear again here is: This is exactly how you teach somebody how to learn. Because this is exactly what you

have to do if you want to learn something—you have to decide what it is you want to learn! And I don't think any of us realizes how difficult that is until you try to do it aloud in a group.

In her final reflections on the RLM seminar, Judi reiterated her belief that if "learning how to learn" was the instructional goal, then teachers had to conceptualize teaching in ways that were radically different from those with which they were most familiar and comfortable.

> Using a discussion/discovery approach to learning puts more responsibility on the "teacher." Instead of preparing a nice clean lesson prior to meeting the kids, it's the teacher's job to help find and encourage the thinking and learning while it's happening. One can only learn this by doing and can only be successful if one believes in the process and recognizes the power of the participants.

Judi combined these pedagogical beliefs and practices with a humanistic view of mathematics to design mathematics courses that differed significantly from most school mathematics with regard to instructional goals, content, and learning experiences. For example, Judi was the first teacher at the School Without Walls (SWW) to design and offer an interdisciplinary course dealing with mathematics, computers, and science (MacScience) for which students could receive mathematics credit toward graduation; previously, all interdisciplinary courses had focused on the humanities. This course was described as follows in the School Without Walls catalogue of courses, which was published every semester:

> How does this work? What makes it go? How come we have to learn this stuff? What's this good for? Why does that happen? If I do this what will happen to that? What if nobody asked these questions?

> This course encourages you to ask and explore answers to questions like these through discovery. We will break down the artificial walls traditional classes have built between science and mathematics and focus on how the two really rely on each other. This course will be primarily a "hands-on" experience which will include extensive use of SWW science equipment, computers, community resources, writing, and discussions as tools.

> This course is a science and mathematics extended class and as such will require journals, conferences, decision making, and community involvement. The group will discuss and identify the actual topics to be explored. Jim [another SWW teacher] and Judi will be working with this class together, not as two separate units but as one unit with two resource teachers.
>
> One does not have to be a math or science whiz to be successful in this course but you MUST have an interest in the subjects.

Thus the "Math Connections" and "Alternative Geometries" courses, described in a later section and featured throughout the book, were quite representative of Judi's courses, however different from traditional mathematics they might be.

Judi also came to the RLM Project with some experience using a variety of math-related texts in her mathematics courses. This was evident in a journal entry she wrote early in the seminar, in which she responded to a request to reflect on the role of reading in a mathematics class:

> I can only tell you what role reading does play in my mathematics classes (and it's not used enough). Technical (or textbook) reading is used to acquire specific technical information and "how to" methods. Non-technical reading—that's where the fun is—it's used with discussions and activities—can be concept related or opinion related. It's used to humanize the idea of "mathematics," it helps to "soften" its edges by allowing for talk. Reading allows for the use of art, poetry, prose, letters to the editor, historical pieces, people (current and biographies), all of which, by their nature, dispel the idea of right and wrong answers.
>
> For the average person the "how to" needs are filled with arithmetic. Readings and discussion can help people develop an appreciation for the ideas, instead of an all too common fearful respect of the mechanical process. In an age of electronic technology we need to develop more thinkers not number shovers. Humanizing the sciences should encourage more learning and thus develop a better informed society with more socially responsible scientists. At least that's what I'm aiming for!

Despite the fact that Judi already used math-related texts in her teaching and valued the thinking they inspired, she felt much was to be gained from exploring the role of reading in mathematics classrooms more fully.

In short, Judi brought to the RLM project a set of beliefs and practices that resonated with an inquiry perspective on mathematics instruction as well as an appreciation for the contributions that math-related texts other than math textbooks could make to students' learning. At the same time, the RLM seminar provided her with some additional reading materials and with new strategies that could help students gain more from the reading of such texts. More important, however, the seminar introduced Judi to some specific theories that gave her the language she felt she needed to better articulate her beliefs and their implications for mathematics instruction.

When the collaborative action research phase of the RLM Project began, a research team formed around Judi, consisting of Marjorie Siegel, Constance Smith, and John Sheedy (a mathematics teacher who had participated in the RLM seminar but could not implement RLM experiences in his class that year, because of the nature of his teaching assignment), with Raffaella Borasi occasionally attending meetings to keep informed on the unfolding experience. This team met biweekly throughout the first semester of the 1989–1990 school year (September–January). On all these occasions, the team worked in a consultative role to support Judi's own curricular plan and goals for her course. Marjorie Siegel and Constance Smith also participated in almost every meeting of the class chosen as the "target" class by the research team, with each of them taking on a variety of roles to be explained later.

The School Without Walls

The School Without Walls provided a supportive institutional context for Judi's teaching and, by extension, for the classroom research component of the RLM Project. As noted earlier, the School Without Walls is a public urban alternative high school in the Rochester (NY) City School District that was created by a group of students and teachers in 1971 with the goal of developing independent learners by focusing on learning how to learn. The school was built on the philosophy that students should take control of their own learning, thus recognizing students as individuals with interests and needs, people who should be encouraged to let curiosity guide their learning. Officially a magnet school in the Rochester City School District, the School Without Walls chooses its students from a pool of applicants through an interview process; however, the school's student population must represent the city composite of race, gender, and academic achievement. This is important, for although Judi felt that her students were special, they were representative of the student body in this urban school district.

The school's name is reflective of the original intentions of the founders to break down the boundaries that exist between school and community, students and teachers, classrooms and the outside world. Interdisciplinary courses (such as Judi's MacScience course), a required community service component, extensive use of community resources (both people and institutions), biweekly teacher/student conferences, reflective journal writing, and independent study are just some of the ways the School Without Walls community works toward their goals. There are two types of classes at the school: extended classes and more typical content-area classes. The majority of school time is devoted to extended classes, which are held 4 days a week for 2½ hours. Those classes provide students with opportunities to explore different interesting topics (e.g., cultures or media) in an interdisciplinary way. These classes are determined through a process in which input from both students and teachers is sought before courses are designed and advertised in the course schedule.

This democratic model of school governance can also be seen in the weekly "town meetings." The entire school community participates in these meetings, which provide occasions for open discussion and shared decision making regarding school policies and practices. In addition, members of the faculty set aside one morning each week when regular classes do not meet so they can discuss what is happening in their classrooms and in the school as a whole. Among other things, teachers share their successes and ask for help with the problems they encounter.

One final dimension of the School Without Walls that sets it off from most urban high schools is its assessment practices. From its earliest days, the teachers felt that assessment practices should be consistent with the school's learning goals, and for this reason students are not graded in the usual sense. Instead, every 10 weeks the school sets aside a week in order for students and teachers to work together on assessment. The forms used in this process reflect the school's emphasis on learning how to learn, and hence students are evaluated on such things as problem solving, coping with frustration, and communication skills. Rather than simply filling in these forms and sending them home, teachers meet with students in individual conferences to discuss and evaluate each student's learning, making assessment week an intense time. This process results in a completed evaluation form and a brief narrative describing the student's progress; at the end of the conference, both the teacher and the student must sign the form to indicate they have discussed the evaluation.

The "Math Connections B" Course

In fall 1989, Judi offered three sections of a course called "Math Connections," which was designed to help students explore the way that art, music, literature, science, and so on could be used to understand mathematics, and vice versa, with the goal of broadening students' conceptions of mathematics beyond the commonly held belief that mathematics deals primarily with operations on numbers. This course was advertised to potential students by means of the following description in the school's course catalogue:

Math Connections
Judi Fonzi
.50 Math Credit

This class will run for three different groups and is a 1 semester class. Please check with your advisor to find the group you should be in.

This class will focus on math as an interdisciplinary subject. This means: how art, music, literature, creative writing, history, science, geography, . . . can be used to understand or make meaning of mathematics, AND how mathematics can be used to understand or make meaning of art, music, literature, creative writing, history, science, geography, [etc.]

The primary emphasis of this class will be posing questions and searching for creative solutions or explanations. Problem solving, reasoning, communicating, and developing an appreciation of mathematics are the goals of this course. Computation is but A tool to be used in SOME situations, and hence does not play a major role in this class.

Because Judi approached the teaching of the course in a manner similar to the way she had taught other interdisciplinary courses, "Math Connections" was designed to involve students in a series of investigations that would be determined in collaboration with the students enrolled in each section. Hence, after a common beginning, the three sections of the course developed in quite different ways. All three sections involved interesting inquiry experiences and uses of reading, but in this book we focus on only one of these sections—"Math Connections B"—because it was the one chosen by the research team as their "target" class and was thus the only one fully documented throughout the semester.

The "Math Connections B" class met three times a week for an hour, from September 1989 to January 1990, for a total of 47 sessions. Fourteen students representing a mix of first-, second-, and third-year students enrolled in this course. Five males and nine females were enrolled, although one young woman rarely attended the class. Although African American, Hispanic, and Asian American students were well represented in the school as a whole and in the other sections of "Math Connections," only 3 of the 14 students in Section B were students of color. Both Marjorie Siegel and Constance Smith were present at nearly every class meeting and became full participants in this learning community. Thus, in addition to documenting ongoing classroom events, they often participated in small-group experiences, working alongside students as learners and facilitators, and occasionally taking on some teaching roles. As was the custom in this school, students were on a first-name basis with both university researchers (as well as the teacher) and came to regard them as members of the learning community.

Extensive data were collected throughout the whole semester so as to document this instructional experience in its entirety. In addition to the observers' field notes, audiotapes were made of every class meeting and, in the second half of the semester, videotapes as well. Biweekly meetings of the research team were also audiotaped. In addition, Judi kept a file of her daily plans and other relevant documents, and all students' work and instructional materials were photocopied. At the conclusion of the course, students were interviewed by one of the researchers, either individually or in pairs, to gain their perspective on the experience; these interviews were audiotaped as well.

Because this course is described in detail in Chapters 4 and 5, here we note only that the course can be thought of as consisting of five major segments: (a) introducing students to the concept of math connections and the School Without Walls' values about learning; (b) deciding on a project through which to explore math connections; (c) carrying out this project, consisting of an inquiry into the math connections of racing; (d) learning new ways of sharing information in order to be more successful in carrying out future inquiries (this involved explicitly teaching selected reading strategies, using these strategies to share information, and using them in the context of doing mathematical work); and (e) demonstrating what was learned about learning through individual projects.

The "Alternative Geometries" Course

Broadening students' conceptions of mathematics was not an isolated goal for Judi; rather, she intended the experiences in all of the sections of "Math Connections" to set the stage for learning technical mathematics concepts, though not necessarily conceptualized in traditional ways. Therefore, in the semester that followed, Judi offered four courses that she hoped would give students opportunities to engage with more technical mathematical topics in the same spirit of inquiry that characterized the "Math Connections" courses. These courses were "Conquering Innumeracy," inspired by and based on the best-selling book *Innumeracy* (Paulos, 1988); "Mathematics History: Why and How," which addressed basic arithmetic concepts and procedures from a historical perspective; "Mathematics of Relationships," which introduced algebraic concepts in everyday situations; and, finally, "Alternative Geometries." Judi developed these courses without the support of the research team, because at this point the planned collaborative action research phase of the RLM Project had ended. However, in all four courses, Judi continued to use reading as an integral part of the students' learning experience and to document some key instructional events.

To illustrate the nature and roles of these reading experiences, we have chosen to focus on the "Alternative Geometries" course, because it was the best documented of the four courses Judi taught the semester following the "Math Connections" course. The database for this course consisted of Judi's written plans, copies of all instructional materials used and most of the work students produced, anecdotal records of what had occurred during selected lessons, and occasional audio- or videotape recordings of classroom experiences. In addition, Judi participated in a series of meetings with members of her research team in order to reconstruct the course and reflect on classroom events that took place during the "Alternative Geometries" course; these meetings were recorded on audiotape.

"Alternative Geometries" was advertised in the original course description as involving:

Exploring the geometry of such surfaces as a sphere or ellipse, or the properties of one, two, three, four dimensional space. Taxigeometry, non-Euclidean and Fractal geometry are all possibilities for investigation as well as unique student-defined geometries. The concept of proof and the many types of mathematical proof will play an important part in this investigation.

Thirteen 2nd-, 3rd-, and 4th-year students enrolled in this course, most of whom had participated in one of the sections of the "Math Connections" course offered the previous semester.

The first 10 weeks of this semester-long course focused on taxigeometry (e.g., Krause, 1986; Papy, 1974). This is a geometry describing a "grid" surface where only vertical and horizontal movements along the "lines" are allowed—in other words, geometry as experienced by a taxicab driver in a regularly patterned city like Manhattan. In the second part of the "Alternative Geometries" course, the class moved on to explore other surfaces besides the "grid," starting with a sphere.

At the conclusion of this course, Judi felt it had been very successful, as all the students who actively participated in the class meetings and did the required assignments achieved the main goals of the course, which she described in a letter to parents as "to learn to explore mathematics, to learn how to create mathematically sound systems in mathematics, and to become aware of the importance of the work of Euclid and the significance of the creation of alternative geometries." We return to this course in Chapter 6 when we describe a "math inquiry cycle" on taxigeometry.

CHAPTER 4

The Potential of Reading Rich Mathematical Texts Generatively: A Transactional Perspective

As Chapters 2 and 3 suggest, our first attempt at expanding the narrow view of reading mathematics we had encountered in the literature was the idea of "reading rich mathematical texts generatively." More specifically, we wanted to develop and analyze reading experiences that focused on a wide variety of what we called "rich mathematical texts"—such as essays, articles, and stories *about* mathematics. We believed students might gain new perspectives on learning and knowing mathematics by interacting with texts that showed how specific mathematical concepts or techniques are used in the real world, how professional mathematicians approach problems, how some of the results found in mathematics textbooks came about, and how people learn. However, a transactional perspective on reading had shown us that achieving the potential of such experiences would depend, in part, on *how* students read these texts. We therefore chose to design learning experiences around rich mathematical texts that incorporated reading strategies developed by researchers working from a transactional perspective.

In particular, we were interested in exploring the potential of the following transactional reading strategies:

- *Say Something* (Harste & Short, 1988): Readers select a partner and a text and talk their way through the text, stopping at reader-designated points to share their confusions, questions, and feelings, make connections to background knowledge and experience, put the text in their own words, or generate hypotheses. Rather than teach students a prescribed way to process the text (such as first summarizing, then formulating a question), this more open-ended approach is intended to allow readers to monitor their reading in whatever ways they choose and to reflect on and revise their meanings as the event unfolds.

- *Cloning an Author* (Harste & Short, 1988): Readers read a text individually and silently but are asked to stop reading whenever they choose and to write what they regard as important ideas on cards; after they have finished reading, they are asked to arrange their cards in such a way as to show the relationships among ideas; these "maps" can then be discussed with peers and can be revised in the course of that discussion, because the cards are easily rearranged to reflect new connections and relationships. Although the emphasis on creating a visual arrangement of their ideas may seem similar to instructional strategies that focus readers' attention on the structural relations among important ideas represented in text (i.e., semantic maps of text structure), Cloning an Author invites readers to take on or "clone" the *activities of an author*—the selection and organization of key ideas—rather than reproduce the *author's text structure*.

- *Sketch-to-Stretch* (Harste & Short, 1988; Siegel, 1984): This strategy takes the idea of transforming the text even further by inviting readers to draw their interpretations of the text. After reading a text, readers are asked to "draw what they made of or learned from the text" and then to share their sketches with other students. The assumption underlying this strategy is that by recasting meanings generated in one sign system (language) into another (pictorial), readers may reflect on their interpretations from a different perspective, a move that may produce new insights.

As a result of the RLM Project described in Chapter 3, 18 RLM Episodes (i.e., instructional experiences in which a variety of "rich" math texts were read employing some version or combination of the reading strategies described above) were collaboratively developed in the classrooms of four teachers and later analyzed (for a full report, see Borasi, Siegel, Fonzi, & Smith, 1998; Siegel, Borasi, Fonzi, & Smith, 1996). Because these reading experiences are probably unfamiliar to the reader, this chapter is designed to illustrate what we mean by "reading rich mathematical texts generatively," explore the learning potential of such experiences for inquiry-oriented mathematics instruction, and examine these experiences from the perspective of transactional reading theory. To do so, we have chosen to present and discuss detailed vignettes of only two RLM Episodes—one drawn from Judi Fonzi's "Math Connections" course and the other from Lisa Grasso Sanvidge's geometry unit—that we believe represent prototypical examples of "reading rich math texts generatively," involving different topics, reading strategies, and instructional contexts (see appendix in Siegel, Borasi, Fonzi, & Smith, 1996, for a brief description of the other RLM Episodes examined in the larger study).

The two vignettes offer complementary images of "reading rich math texts generatively" and were constructed in such a way as to show how the teacher orchestrated the instructional experience as well as how students took up the strategies introduced. The first vignette looks closely at two students' use of the Say Something and Sketch-to-Stretch strategies in the context of an instructional event designed to help students learn new ways of sharing information and expand their conceptions of mathematics as a discipline. To illustrate how the strategies encouraged a generative reading of the text, this vignette presents extended excerpts from the students' conversations with each other and with the class as a whole. The second vignette focuses, instead, on a series of lessons devoted to understanding some geometric concepts and applications through the reading of a text; students read the text using a variation of the Cloning an Author strategy the teacher had devised as well as a new strategy she spontaneously introduced to bring a difficult concept to life for the students—a strategy we later called Enacting a Text. Although some samples of individual student work are included in this vignette, the focus is more on showing how the teacher adapted the strategies so as to foster meaningful engagement and learning on the part of her students.

Narrative 2: "Math & War" Vignette— Exploring the Connections Between Mathematics and War Through Reading, Talking, and Drawing

This vignette illustrates two readings of the essay "Mathematics and War" (Davis & Hersh, 1981), both of which involved use of the Say Something and Sketch-to-Stretch strategies by students working in pairs or groups of three. The vignette focuses primarily on the reading experience of two students, Char and Jolea (who were joined by the reading education researcher, Margie), because their interactions offer an especially rich example of the negotiation and generation of meanings through social interaction, as well as a spontaneous evaluation by Jolea of the effectiveness of the Say Something strategy. Later in the vignette, we also make reference to two other students, Van and Shellie, in order to point out some similarities and differences between the reading experiences of these two groups of readers.

This reading experience took place in the context of the "Math Connections B" course (see Chapter 3 for a description of this instructional setting) after the students had planned and carried out their first inquiry into the math connections involved in various types of racing. This inquiry had culminated in a series of group presentations. Neither the students nor the teacher had been completely satisfied with these presentations, owing to the groups' limited success in integrating the findings of individual group members into a coherent presentation that could be understood by others. Working as a collaborative teaching team, Judi and two other members of her research team—Margie and Constance Smith (the other mathematics educator involved in the project)—therefore decided to introduce a variety of reading strategies to help students develop ways to solve this problem in future inquiries. Each of the strategies they chose, starting with Say Something, invited students to share their thinking with others and build connections between and among the ideas that were shared. So as to further students' understanding of math connections (the overall theme of the course), the team also decided to introduce and apply these strategies to a series of essays from *The Mathematical Experience* (Davis & Hersh, 1981), a book that discusses various aspects of the nature of mathematics, including its social, historical, and political dimensions. Therefore, while reading on, it is important to keep in mind that the key goals of reading these essays were defined in terms of gaining a better understanding of mathematics as a discipline as well as "learning how to learn" and not in terms of the acquisition of specific technical mathematical concepts or skills.

The team's plan for introducing the first reading strategy was to have students select and then read, using Say Something, one of two essays—"Mathematics in the Marketplace" and "Mathematics and War"—from the chapter "Underneath the Fig Leaf" (Davis & Hersh, 1981, pp. 90–92), after a whole-class demonstration of this unusual reading strategy.

Demonstrating the Say Something Strategy

To give the students an idea of what the Say Something strategy was all about, Margie asked them first to read silently the short paragraph that introduced the two essays:

> A number of aspects of mathematics are not much talked about in contemporary histories of mathematics. We have in mind business and commerce, war, number mysticism, astrology, and religion. In some instances

the basic information has not yet been assembled; in other instances, writers, hoping to assert for mathematics a noble parentage and a pure scientific existence, have turned away their eyes. Histories have been eager to put the case for science, but the Handmaiden of the Sciences has lived a far more raffish and interesting life than her historians allow.

The areas just mentioned have provided and some still provide stages on which great mathematical ideas have played. There is much generative power underneath the fig leaf. (Davis & Hersh, 1981, p. 89)

The class took about 2 minutes to read the paragraph to themselves and was immediately ready to "say something." Constance moved to the front of the room to record the students' responses on newsprint as the discussion slowly unfolded. "It reminds me of a Congressional Report—it's a bunch of bureaucratic mumble-jumble," said the first student. "I didn't understand it at all," added another. "Too many big words," agreed a third. Gradually, the students' questions and comments shifted to the intended audience and purpose of the piece: "Who'd they write it to?"; "What's the point?"; "Is this the whole thing or is there more to it?" Constance quickly recorded these responses on newsprint while Margie asked if someone could say something about the content of what they had read. One girl responded with more questions: "What are they trying to do in here? Are they trying to make some kind of connections between science and math?" Others focused on the title. "Under what fig leaf?" they wanted to know. Finally, a boy who had been rather quiet up to this point said, "I think I understand. It's supposed to be like what this class is about. Because it is talking about how people don't realize that math is related to other things."

Margie took this opportunity to stop and point out some of the important things that happened in their "say something" conversation, in an attempt to help the students value the process they had just experienced as well as identify other situations in which saying something to a partner while reading could be useful. Pointing to the specific comments Constance had recorded on newsprint, Margie showed the students how they had developed ideas of their own by listening to someone else, and explained that what might have felt initially like going off on a tangent actually ended up helping them understand the text. She concluded by reemphasizing how reading with someone else had provided the opportunity to voice and address their questions and concerns, and pointed out that doing so had paid off in a better understanding of the material read. As evidence for this, she showed them how their comments had begun with frustration over the language of the piece and how they had gradually built on one another's questions until the connection between the author's message and their own mathematics class had become clear.

Char and Jolea's "Say Something" Experience

The next time the class met, the students quickly paired up and chose one of the articles mentioned above. The pairs then moved to comfortable spots in the room and settled into the rhythm of reading and talking with their partners. Char and Jolea had selected "Mathematics and War" (a 3–page essay in nine paragraphs), and they agreed to let Margie participate in their "say something" conversation once she explained that she, too, had chosen the "Mathematics and War" article. (Note that Margie's role in this reading experience was intended to be that of a partner, although at times she also implicitly modeled for the other group members some ways of responding to the text, much as in teacher demonstrations of think-alouds.) The two students decided to proceed by reading paragraph by paragraph, just as in the whole-class demonstration, and started reading the first paragraph silently, though they found it hard at first to concentrate with another student reading aloud across the room. In addition, Char expressed some ambivalence toward the strategy on the basis of an experience the previous year, so Margie suggested that she and Jolea get started and Char could join in when she felt ready.

> Legend has it that Archimedes put his science at the service of warfare. He is reputed to have devised compound pulleys to launch galleys, to have invented a variety of catapults and military engines and most spectacularly to have focused the sun's rays on besieging ships by means of a paraboloidal mirror. All this for King Hieron of Syracuse who was the most brilliant scientist and mathematician of his age, but the achievements just listed, although they can be explained by the mathematical theories of mechanics and optics, do not appear to have involved mathematics at the basic level of application. (Davis & Hersch, 1981, p. 90)

Jolea: To me—I don't know much about the subject [war]. It is— I don't know. It's kind of mixed up. I don't know. It's— Maybe I'm just stupid.

Margie: [Responding to the last comment.] No. Well, I guess I was surprised that it went back that far. That connection between war and mathematics. I mean all the way back to— I mean that first sentence: "Legend has it that Archimedes put his science at the service of warfare." Even way back

then. [To Char, who could barely be heard.] What were you
saying?

Char: Well, the last of it said they did not appear to involve
mathematics in the basic level of application.

Margie: What do you think about that?

Char: Well, I don't know. Kind of like it happened but we
didn't think of it.

Margie: Yeah, I thought that was strange too. Because I
thought that it was pretty clear that catapults and adjust-
ing [a] paraboloidal mirror to get the sun's rays and reflect
that back—they seemed to involve mathematics. Maybe
I'm—just because I've been in this class I see that connection. But they seem to be saying that umm—that it doesn't
[involve mathematics]. So—What were you saying, Jolea,
before?

Jolea: I was just—I don't know—I didn't understand while you
were talking but now I understand. I guess a lot of the
words I didn't understand.

Char: I couldn't pronounce them. [They both laugh about the
difficult words, such as *Archimedes*.]

After a bit more discussion, they read the next paragraph:

What is the relationship between mathematics and war? In the beginning, the contribution was meager. A few mathematical scribes to take
the census and to arrange for induction into the army. A few bookkeep-
ers to keep track of ordnance and quartermaster. Perhaps a bit of survey-
ing and a bit of navigation. In their capacity as astrologers, the principal
contribution of the ancient mathematicians was probably to consult the
stars and to tell the kings what the future held in store. In other words,
military intelligence. (Davis & Hersh, 1981, p. 90)

Jolea: Hmmmm. Confusing.

Margie: Confusing.

Char: Well, yeah because it like goes from one thing to another.
It starts off—they're saying the relationship between math
and war was small. And only in a few places—the navigation and stuff like that. . . . And then it went on to talk
about consulting the stars and astrology. And it didn't feel
like it fit.

Jolea: Almost in the beginning they didn't—almost in the beginning they didn't use—like—mathematicians. So they were
forced to abandon their role. Do you know what I'm saying?

Margie: I see, yeah, they had a few roles for the mathematicians.

Jolea: So that—they didn't really [Jolea is interrupted by a classmate]. So they connected to—other things—just like in this class. How math connects to other things; they didn't have the capacity to look around.

Margie: Well, I was kind of laughing a little bit about that—as astrologers. . . . Maybe you can help me out—in terms of whether the mathematicians were also astrologers. It says, "In their capacity as astrologers"—maybe their only role was to help try to consult the stars—and then they say, "In other words military intelligence." I thought that was kind of funny.

Jolea: You know, now that I think about it, it's almost—I think of astrologers as a total scientist or something. They didn't know how to—

Char: I think of them as corny people that don't know what they're talking about that you read in the paper.

Margie: Now. But I think *then* it was something different.

Jolea: Seeing the stars. They do that kind of stuff; but it's almost as if they didn't have a title. A separation of titles like astrologer, oceanographer. [They're] all under scientist. All those are under scientist. But a mathematician is in reality the all. To be a scientist you have to have mathematical skills. No matter how they teach it. It doesn't seem to have that division [for] them. Like one person, as we know it today, that's not a mathematician to us, but then maybe it was. Maybe they did do astrology and—

Margie: I see. Okay. So they didn't have that divided up.

Here we can begin to see how Say Something supports the reading of a challenging text such as "Mathematics and War." The confusion Jolea initially expressed prompted Char and Margie to share their interpretations of what the paragraph had to say, resulting in a debate over what an astrologer was and what role astrologers played in ancient times. As the conversation proceeded, Jolea began to talk about the difficulty of separating mathematicians and scientists, a theme she continued to elaborate on over the course of this reading experience.

Modern warfare is considered by some authorities to have begun with Napoleon, and with Napoleon one begins to see an intensification of the mathematical involvement. The French Revolution found France supplied with a brilliant corps of mathematicians, perhaps the most brilliant in its history: Lagrange, Condorcet, Monge, Laplace, Legendre, Lazare Carnot. Condorect was a Minister of the Navy in 1792; Monge published a book on the manufacture of cannons. Under Napoleon, mathematicians continued to bloom. It is reported that Napoleon himself was fond of mathematics. Monge and Fourier accompanied Napoleon on his Italian and Egyptian campaigns, and if these men did not do anything directly mathematical during these army hitches (Monge supervised booty while Fourier wrote the *Description of Egypt*), one is left with the feeling that Napoleon thought that mathematicians were useful fellows to have around. (Davis & Hersh, 1981, p. 90)

Jolea: Umm—I was confused about this last part that I read. I cheated and I read it a couple of more times.

Margie: That's okay; that's really not cheating.

Jolea: But umm—then I understood it.

Char: I thought that—Neapole? Is that how you pronounce it?

Margie: Napoleon. [Jolea also comments.]

Char: I recognized it but I can't pronounce it. Umm—What was I going to say? Umm—He was like this—I felt like this paper was saying this was this great guy and he recognized all this and that's really good and that's all they had to say—that's all they were trying to get across.

Margie: Well, I thought it was—I see sort of a development here—going back to some of the other paragraphs that— Well, in the beginning there was some contribution, with Napoleon there was even more. And maybe partly because he was fond of mathematics himself. I mean he saw it [as] interesting. So that makes me wonder if ah—people will find more relationships and connections if they sort of have an interest and a knowledge themselves. I don't know. [Char has voiced agreement with Margie several times.]

Jolea: The last part of this—the last sentence? Where is it?

Char: About "the mathematicians were useful fellows to have around"?

Jolea: Yeah, personally for himself to have around him or just around everywhere?

Char: I took it as just around and like—building knowledge or— [Margie agrees] because they really didn't have any—kind of like people go to college or—

Margie: Well, and because one of them—it says up here— [Monge] was publishing a book on the manufacture of cannons. And so maybe he [Napoleon] saw that they would

> be useful in helping him win wars which is what Napoleon
> would be interested in.
>
> *Jolea:* Yeah, "and if these men"—which I assume were *these*
> because they worked with him—"did not do anything
> directly mathematical during the army hitches." I don't
> know?
>
> *Margie:* And even if they didn't do anything—oh, "one is left
> with the feeling that Napoleon thought that they were
> useful."
>
> *Jolea:* And I took it useful to him.

There was another 2-minute pause while the participants read the
next paragraph.

> Arriving at World War II, one finds mathematical and scientific talent in
> widespread use in the Army, Navy, and Air Force, in government research
> laboratories, in war industries, in governmental, social and business agen-
> cies. A brief list of the variety of things that mathematicians did would
> include aerodynamics, hydrodynamics, ballistics, development of radar and
> sonar, development of the atomic bomb, cryptography and intelligence,
> aerial photography, meteorology, operations research, development of
> computing machines, econometrics, rocketry, development of theories of
> feedback and control. Many professors of mathematics were directly in-
> volved in these things, as were many of their students. This writer was
> employed as a mathematician-physicist at NACA (later NASA), Langley
> Field, Virginia, with only a bachelor's degree to his credit, and many of his
> contemporaries at Langley Field subsequently occupied chairs of mathemat-
> ics throughout the country. (Davis & Hersh, 1981, pp. 90–91)

Interestingly, Char commented that the text was getting easier
for her to read, despite the use of such words as *cryptography* and
econometrics.

> *Char:* It was easier to read than the other three [paragraphs].
>
> *Margie:* It's getting easier, huh?
>
> *Char:* Yeah, I don't know if it was just the words or if I con-
> nected to it more. I felt like when they were going through
> the different umm—things—aerodynamics, da da da—every
> time I read another word it [was] like, "Yeah, that's related."
> And I [thought] how it was related and I would go on.
>
> *Jolea:* I saw it as a growth in math. They started to connect
> other things that they could do—other things that math
> was involved in. It went into careers.

Margie acknowledged Jolea's observation and expressed her interest in the fact that one of the authors had worked on a government-sponsored research project during World War II with only a bachelor's degree.

The group quickly moved on to the next paragraph.

> With the explosion of the atomic bomb over Japan and the subsequent development of more powerful bombs, atomic physicists who had hitherto lived ivory-tower academic existences experienced a sense of sin. This sense of sin spread simultaneously over the mathematical community. Individual mathematicians asked themselves in what way they, personally, had unleashed monsters on the world, and if they had, how they could reconcile it with whatever philosophic views of life they held. Mathematics, which had previously been conceived as a remote and Olympian doctrine, emerged suddenly as something capable of doing physical, social, and psychological damage. Some mathematicians began to compartmentalize their subject into a good part and a bad part. The good part: pure mathematics, the more abstract the better. The bad part: applied mathematics of all kinds. Some mathematicians and a rising generation of students left applications forever. Norman Wiener, who had been engaged in developing theories of prediction and feedback control, renounced government support of his work and devoted the remainder of his life to doing "good works" in biophysics and to propagandizing against the nonhuman use of human beings. (Davis & Hersh, 1981, p. 91)

Char: I understood the first inch of it, but then I must have got lost. [Margie asks, "Inch?"] Maybe the first five, six lines— for the rest of it—I like "Wow."

Jolea: I—I got lost up here but when you walked away, I just said well I've got time now, I'll just do it over again. And I got it and I understood it. And—I think it's something that we forget a lot of the time. So many times praising what the scientists come up with and learn the uses [of], that we forget about the bombs and stuff and that scientists—because of them and their knowledge—that's what comes out of it sometimes. The bad, just the bombs and—

·*Char:* Yeah, but we can't have the good without the bad.

Jolea: Right, exactly. But I don't think—I think it's more focused on other things and we forget. Yeah, we talk about nuclear war a lot but we forget what it comes from. I mean it's just not there. And to think so many people have that knowledge—it's scary. Some people could do so many horrible things with it.

Margie: I think to me this bottom part had to do with how mathematicians felt themselves about what you were saying.

Jolea: I got a little lost down there.

Margie: Yeah, umm—I think sometimes mathematicians felt guilty about it. And some of them said, "We're not going to do this application stuff anymore."

As the conversation continued, the group talked more about the guilt that mathematicians felt, but they also discussed the fact that it might be more dangerous for one country to have nuclear arms than for both to have them, implying that there was more than one way to think about the development of weapons. The group then went back to reading, and when Char walked away for a minute, Jolea offered a spontaneous evaluation of the Say Something strategy.

Jolea: I don't know if I should say this but—I don't think I'd be able to read from a book [like this] without reading and then talking about it.

Margie: Why do you think?

Jolea: Because I think I've tried reading some and I get so confused and—

Margie: You get confused? What's helping about this?

Jolea: That you only read part. You know, usually you have to read the whole thing, maybe you do it for homework and then the next day it's not as fresh and you forget the little things that— You remember a couple of things that confused you. But now it's—and you're doing it right away and something's right there.

Margie: Could you see a way to adapt this while you are doing some homework?

Jolea: Yeah, I think eventually you can. Yeah. That's another thing I was going to say, I think eventually if you do this enough to learn— Just like anything if you do something with someone enough you can usually go solo.

When Char rejoined the group, they continued discussing the value of the strategy before continuing to make sense of the next two paragraphs—one about the galvanizing effect *Sputnik* had on the relationship between mathematics and war, and the other about protests against the scientific institutions that housed military research during the Vietnam War. The paragraph describing how *Sputnik* had intensified the space race and the development of computers prompted Jolea to observe that "almost as if the paragraph before [on the moral consequences of mathematical research] was forgotten. The fear of it [war] and the bad feelings."

The group then turned to the final paragraph.

> One began to hear it said that World War I was the chemists' war, World War II was the physicists', World War III (may it never come) will be the mathematicians' war. With this, there entered into the general consciousness the full realization that mathematics is inevitably bound up in the general fabric of life, that mathematics is good or bad as people make it so, and that no activity of the human mind can be free from moral issues. (Davis & Hersh, 1981, p. 92)

As the conversation unfolded, Char tried to make sense of Jolea's concern with the moral dimensions of mathematics and war and Jolea continued to work on sorting out the relationship between science and mathematics—the themes that they had begun to explore in their discussions of previous paragraphs.

> *Jolea:* Umm—I was still stuck on seeing the guilt of the scientist.
> *Char:* I never saw that.
> *Margie:* The guilt?
> *Char:* Yeah.
> *Jolea:* Yeah—the guilty—but it seemed it [the guilty feelings] went to the people who weren't involved in science. They were—Once the guilt went away, so it seems, or maybe the people who did feel guilty just backed away and just said, "Forget it. [I'm not going to do] this type of science." But ahh—Just the—just started to condemn the ones that were doing it.
> *Margie:* Well, and that gets really complicated. Because on the one hand we don't want to get rid of science—[Jolea agrees] and mathematics. And yet on the other hand that's a dilemma. How do you use it in responsible ways?

Jolea noted that this dilemma was still with them and described a discussion in another class on Reagan's Star Wars proposal.

> *Jolea:* And yet this is still here today. And I just— Two weeks ago we had the same discussion in our class. [Jolea is trying

to remember the program the class had discussed and Char remembers that it's Ronald Reagan's space program.]

Margie: Oh, Star Wars.

Jolea: I think it was—yeah. It probably went up or something and we were just—we just said how it was affecting the environment. Obviously we can't do without the bad. We have to do that experimenting and we always have to be ready for the next step.

Char: You don't know if it's going to be good or bad until you're working on it. So it's hard to tell.

When Margie asked what they thought of the sentence that assigned each world war to a different scientific discipline, Char responded, "That's okay. But I feel—when I was reading it, I feel all of them were mathematicians' wars. . . . After reading it and [the authors] going through—and this is where math came in and more connecting it to all this and—it kind of surprised me that they separated it like that." The question Jolea was left thinking about was the division between science and mathematics. She wondered aloud, "I'm having trouble. I want to ask you this. Umm—try dividing mathematicians from the science world. What's the difference? [Char agrees.] Maybe a mathematician has the ability of the formulas but not the knowledge of how to use it to a scientific ability. . . . Science just seems to have a lot to do with math. And studying math is studying math. Scientists, you're studying math but a lot of things and—maybe not really seeing the math connection."

At this point, Margie gave Char and Jolea the directions for the Sketch-to-Stretch strategy, which they were to complete for homework. She asked them to make one sketch that showed what they had learned from the text.

Char and Jolea's Use of the Sketch-to-Stretch Strategy

At the next class meeting, students who had completed the sketching assignment were asked to explain their drawings to the rest of the class. Char and Jolea began by explaining that they had been unable to create one sketch because they had "disagreed too much," that is, each of them had come away from the reading experience with a different theme they wanted to further explore and represent through their sketch. There were similarities between their sketches in both form (both were divided into small boxes, some of which were further divided by a diagonal line, and used cartoonlike stick figures) and content (both represented the increasing use of mathematics for war and the moral questions it raised). When it was Char's turn to share, Judi wanted to pass her sketch around the class so everyone would have an idea of what she was talking about, but Char felt she needed it in her hands to explain it, so it remained in her hands as she spoke (see Figure 4.1).

> It started out with the catapult. . . . When I saw the catapult I see—strictly math as I guess I've always known, a lot of numbers and a lot of angles. And then having the scientists being . . . really proud of themselves but also the society being really proud of . . . a group of people being able to think that stuff up. And then it went on to like the atom bomb. And how the majority of the scientists . . . thought that was great, "Look what we can do now, look at the technology we have." But then there was a few of them that were kind of like, "Why am I doing this? All I'm doing is killing people." And society kind of started to ah—realize what was going on. There was a few of them around that didn't like the idea but the majority of them

Figure 4.1. Char's sketch of the "Mathematics and War" essay.

thought that was good. You know, "We bombed China. We did this." Now with nuclear war there's still a lot of scientists that [say], "Wow look at the technology of fusing atoms and everything." But there's more scientists now that feel that's wrong to just do this . . . research just to build more warheads to beat Russia. And in that case there's a lot more of society that feels it's wrong—for the scientists to be doing this because we are only killing people. But there's still a few that are, "Yeah, nuclear war is needed." And that's what my drawing shows.

Char's sketch thus went beyond the text and showed three aspects of the connection between mathematics and war that she had gained from her reading: The first column showed the actual product of the mathematicians' thinking at three different points in time (e.g., a catapult, a bomb, Star Wars); the second column showed the mathematicians' moral dilemma (between the intellectual challenge of doing the research and the effects on humankind); the third column showed society's response to the products of the mathematicians' research, both pro and con. At this point Char passed her sketch around.

After discussing Judi's questions about the comic strip motif, Jolea's sketch (see Figure 4.2) was sent around the class with a warning from her that it might look a lot like Char's but "the feeling behind it" was different. Upon hearing this, Judi reworded her directions to the class, suggesting that the students look more closely at the sketch to see the differences.

> *Jolea:* In the beginning I didn't look at it as really war. I looked at it as people then separating people, professions like scientists and mathematics. Not being able to connect mathematics to anything, really—they were very small, the connections, I think, very small. . . . And it seemed to be very science involved—science did not connect to math. And this is why in my second picture there was a dividing line and there was like a [black]board up here. This [the blackboard] means math and this [a lab table] means science and there's the dividing line [between them]. And then Napoleon came along and then he kind of brought those two together. From what I understood from the reading, he brought math and [science] more together but yet still . . . they still didn't connect very well. . . .
> *Judi:* So is that why the dividing line [in Square 3] is missing? [They looked at the sketch again.]

Figure 4.2. Jolea's sketch of the "Mathematics and War" essay.

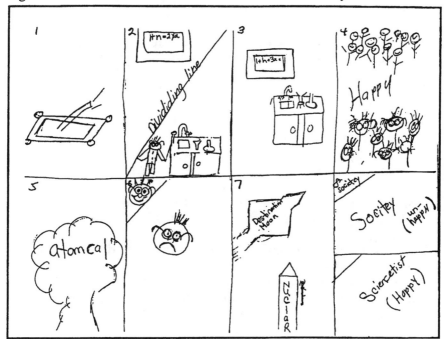

Jolea: And then more doors started opening up so everyone was happy. You know, they were coming up with new things and everyone was happy. And they also started working on the atomic bomb but when the bomb came along— The way I took [it] was after the atomic bomb scientists [felt guilty about this application of mathematics to war] . . . and you see my scale [of scientists who felt guilty about using science for destructive ends in comparison to those who did not feel this sense of guilt], there was to be a greater amount of scientists that knew what they had done [i.e., realized their complicity in the use of the bomb]—not only what they had done but what they were teaching other people? And maybe they are not as ethical.

Jolea seemed a bit unsure of herself as she talked about this part of her sketch. She then began to talk more about the process of reading and drawing. As she talked, it became clear that her sketch reflected her question regarding the dividing line between mathematics and science as well as the moral dilemmas that arose from the application of mathematics to the practice of warfare.

> Then—see, I split it up only because of the way I read it, I think. We read it paragraph by paragraph and discussed it. After each paragraph we discussed it and I think this is why I came up [with] these divisions. Because after it said that the scientists weren't thrilled with what they had done and then started to regret it, it went on to the next paragraph. It was like that was all forgotten. They didn't care what they did—they were getting money, you know. They were coming up with these things like that's all they cared about. That's where the nuclear comes in. . . . They just didn't care anymore but then society started to care and they started the protests. And that's were this picture comes in [Square 8]—society is unhappy and scientists are happy.

After some discussion of the difference between doing mathematics and using mathematics, other students began asking questions about the sketches and the "say something" experience. Gina's question was generative for both Jolea and Char, because it gave them a chance to reflect further on the experience.

> *Gina:* What did you learn about yourself?
> *Jolea:* That I can't separate math and science. That maybe there is no— Maybe not about myself; maybe something that I made myself realize. I liked the article. It was really something to think about.

Several people then asked Char the same question.

> Well, I guess I knew all these. I knew about the catapult. I knew about the atom bomb. I know about science and I know about society. But I never put the three of them together like a story. "This because of this then this and then this happened." But I knew them as little separate stories—I never like made one big thing out of it. So actually seeing it here—kind of like, WOW why didn't I think of that!

Van and Shellie's Reading of the "Mathematics and War" Essay

Van and Shellie's approach to the Say Something strategy was slightly different, but equally helpful in supporting their efforts to make sense of the same text. What was striking was the way Van and Shellie defined particular roles for themselves, Van reading aloud and Shellie interrupting to ask questions about what the text meant. Though at first glance this may make it seem as if Van was active and Shellie passive, that was not the case, as Shellie often responded to her own question with a possible interpretation or a connection that gave the ideas represented in the text more meaning. For example, when Shellie didn't understand what the word *catapult* meant, Van's explanation made Shellie think about an episode from the cartoon "The Smurfs," in which Smurfs had used a catapult. In another case, when they got to the section of the text that discussed the protests against the role of mathematicians in the Vietnam War, Van made a connection to the environmental organization Greenpeace and remembered an episode from a television show in which an abortion clinic had been bombed. Thus, by bringing their own background knowledge to bear on the text, Van and Shellie were able to develop a personal interpretation. Their discussion of the last paragraph (see page 75 for the text of the final paragraph) offers an especially good illustration of how these two students approached their "say something" and in particular of the way they built connections between the text and their own lives:

> *Van:* So, what do you want to discuss? . . . Not World War III because there is nothing [laughs]. I don't want to discuss World War III.
>
> *Shellie:* I want to know why they said World War I was the chemists' war, why they said World War II was the physics war.
>
> *Van:* I don't know! Okay, okay, let's go back—World War I—
>
> *Shellie:* Chemicals were used in World War I? Ohh. The gases— remember, Charles said the yellow gases? [She refers to information about mustard gases gathered in another class.] It was because—remember, because chemicals were used in World War I and it took a mathematician to mix the chemicals together? [In the meantime, Van is looking back through the article trying to find any reference to World War I.]
>
> *Van:* I don't remember having World War I in here. That's World War II. . . . No. I'm trying to find it in the back.
>
> *Shellie:* Oh, they never said anything about it.
>
> *Van:* Then, how are we supposed to figure out what chemist[ry] was involved besides the mustard. [They both laugh out loud.]

Shellie: Okay, let's say World War II then. How was it the physicists' war?

Van: They built the bomb.

Shellie: All right Vanny! Then why will [reading from the text] "World War III (may it never come)" be mathematics?

Van: 'Cause I think that it would take a lot of math and stuff to build something stronger than the atomic bomb.

Shellie: [Jokingly] Please we've got all the weapons— Man, we would like dog Russia—we would dog everybody. [They laugh. Then, more seriously, Shellie asks a question.] See, why would we need mathematicians? We've got all the [weapons] we need to blow up the world!

Van: No, because let's say—let me try to put this into cars. Okay. I'm going to do this for you. All right. World War I, your first car—is a Chevette. [At first Shellie makes fun of the analogy, saying that World War I should be a go-cart, but Van continues.] No, listen. World War I: Joe's brown car, the Buick Regal when he first got it. Now, he bought it like that—World War I, people did not have many ideas—it came like that. Now World War II—Joe got it black!

Shellie: He painted it and— [Both girls add details.]

Van: He hooked up [improved] a little bit of the engine. His seats were still brown, remember? So it's . . . got the tint, but he don't got the phone or nothing yet, okay? So World War II he hooked up a little. World War II they hooked it up a little [i.e., they improved the weapons].

Shellie: Okay.

Van: World War III—after the [Buick] Regal.

Shellie: The shifter, the phone [a few more car improvements are mentioned].

Van: But World War III, okay, after it's all hooked up—he's cruising, he's sporting it hard. Now he's thinking of more ideas . . . Like World War III, these people. Now, he wants to beat his Regal, okay, he wants something that is better than his Regal. They want something that is better than the atomic bomb. Because if Russia builds an atomic bomb that's better than us, then we have to think of something better than them—to keep up with the competition, okay?

The two students continue the conversation on these lines for a while, and finally Shellie concludes:

Shellie: That was a good example though, Van. That was really
    good.
Van: What, Joe's car? I knew you—
Shellie: I understand it. . . . We should tell someone about that.
Van: Yeah, we compared our math to Joe's car. I knew he was
    good for something in school.

When Van and Shellie created their sketch, they chose to represent the
analogy that Van had created between the increasing role of mathematics in warfare and the improvements their friend had made to his car
over time (see Figure 4.3). Sketching allowed them to develop this
analogy even further and generate the idea that, just as Joe could continue making improvements to his car, mathematics continues to develop as well. As they noted at the end of the presentation of their
sketch, "It's almost like a question, too, because there's like more things
that he can do with his car and there's more ways that math can be used."

Figure 4.3. Van and Shellie's sketch of the "Mathematics and War" essay.

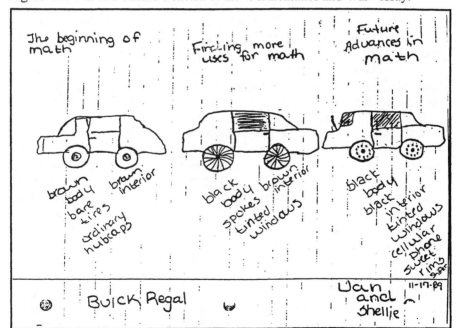

Notes on What Students Gained From This Instructional Episode

Before moving on to the second vignette, it may be helpful to pause and consider what students gained from this instructional episode. First, as the exchanges reported throughout this vignette demonstrate, a generative reading of the "Math and War" essay encouraged the students to reflect on aspects of mathematics that are rarely addressed in school—such as its relationship with science and real life, its evolution over time, and even its moral and ethical dimensions. As a result, several students came to recognize and value new connections between mathematics and life. The student's comment during the introductory activity ("I think I understand. It's supposed to be like what this class is about. Because it is talking about how people don't realize that math is related to other things"), the statements and questions Char and Jolea produced at several points in their conversation, and their two sketches demonstrate the students' growing appreciation of these connections. The "Math and War" essay also exposed students to information about how mathematics—specifically its use in the service of warfare—has evolved over time. This issue obviously intrigued several of the students, as Jolea and Char explicitly discussed it in their "say something" session and represented it in their sketches, and Van and Shellie chose to depict the very theme of "change" in their joint sketch. Indeed, one of the main insights gained by Jolea, Char, Van, and Shellie from this reading was the realization that mathematics is a field that continues to grow—quite a contrast to the common perception that "everything that could be discovered in mathematics has already been discovered" (Borasi, 1992). This realization seemed to come together with a new understanding of the idea of mathematics as the product of human activity, something that is especially evident during Char and Jolea's "say something" session when they discussed the social role of mathematicians (as "people") over time as well as the growing ethical and moral concerns some individual mathematicians felt regarding the use of their work for war purposes. Although this may seem not too surprising, because the "Math and War" essay explicitly tries to highlight "humanistic" dimensions of mathematics such as the moral and ethical issues that may arise from its use, the extent to which Char and Jolea were able to grasp and elaborate on these themes in their "say something" conversation and their sketches was remarkable. Although these students seem to have thought little about the ethical dimensions of mathematics before reading this essay, their exploration of this issue was quite sophisticated and added new insights and connections to what was presented in the text—an impressive achievement even for adult readers of the same text! And even if some of their classmates had overlooked this issue in their own reading of the text, Char and Jolea's sharing of their sketches gave the whole class an additional opportunity to appreciate the meaning and importance of ethical issues in mathematics.

When we consider these results in relation to our earlier discussion (see Chapter 2) of the assumptions and goals associated with inquiry-oriented mathematics instruction, it is evident that helping students become aware of the more "humanistic" elements of mathematics was a valuable outcome of this instructional episode. Not only did it lead students to question their views of mathematics and come to a better understanding of mathematics as a discipline—a most neglected area in traditional schooling—but also it contributed to the development of better attitudes toward and expectations for this discipline. Many of the students in this class had expressed a stronger affinity to the humanities than to mathematics and science; and, as Char stated during the sharing of the sketches when the class was discussing the ethical issues raised in the essay, "like humanities kind of things, I always felt like [mathematics] was different." Thus, recognizing that mathematics was more similar to the humanities than they had previously thought helped several students in this class begin to question their belief that "mathematics was not for them."

Because learning specific mathematical content was *not* among the instructional goals for this set of lessons, it would not be appropriate to look for gains in this area. Instead, the learning experiences described in this vignette were quite successful in helping the students develop strategies for effectively gathering information from texts and sharing this information with other inquirers, something they had failed to do in their previous inquiry. Recall that this series of lessons marked the introduction of two new reading strategies—Say Something and Sketch-to-Stretch—with the explicit goal of providing students with effective ways to make sense of texts, and to communicate their learning to other inquirers. The experiences described in the "Math & War" vignette amply demonstrate students' understanding of and ability to use these reading strategies for both purposes. Further, we observed that later in the same course several students continued to use Say Something and Sketch-to-Stretch in other experiences, and some even spontaneously chose to use a variation of these strategies to learn from challenging texts in inquiries carried out in subsequent courses. However, the goal of expanding students' repertoire of strategies for "learning how to learn" was not achieved only by acquiring new reading strategies. Van and Shellie's use of an analogy, for example, provided students with a powerful demonstration of how generative it can be to use familiar concepts and experiences when approaching a new problem or topic. Char, in particular, showed evidence of having internalized this as a problem-solving strategy later in the course (as illustrated, for instance, in the "Analog & Analytic" narrative reported in Chapter 1). Other students also seemed to have discovered the generative potential of sketching; the challenge of representing their ideas in images without a "dictionary" for doing so inspired several students to draw visual metaphors and analogies (Siegel, 1995). The individual and class reflections about the process that were part of this reading experience also contributed to students' understanding of their own learning processes, and point to the benefits of valuing reflection and making time for such discussions in a mathematics class.

In sum, the generative reading of the "Math and War" essay indeed proved to be an effective vehicle for achieving the main instructional goals set by the teacher for this experience. Although the choice of text was pivotal in this success, it is unlikely that students would have stayed engaged in the reading, developed and debated their interpretations, or reflected on their own learning processes without the teacher's orchestration of Say Something and Sketch-to-Stretch—a point we revisit in more depth later in the chapter.

Narrative 3: "Egg Man" Vignette—Investigating Technical Concepts and "Big Ideas" About Geometry Through Multiple Readings of an Essay

This vignette presents an interesting contrast to the previous one, because it shows how Lisa engaged her entire class in multiple readings of an essay that examines several important geometric concepts in the context of a contemporary real-life problem (see Chapter 3 for a description of Lisa's instructional setting and an overview of the geometry unit within which this episode occurred). Each reading of the essay was accomplished using a reading strategy adapted to fit the teacher's instructional purpose. As a result, this vignette illustrates a variation of the Cloning an Author strategy (which we came to regard as part of a larger category we called Using Cards) as well as an additional strategy we called Enacting the Text, which Lisa had spontaneously introduced in a previous class to help make more concrete some of the mathematical procedures described in the text.

Earlier in the geometry unit, the class had used Say Something, along with some form of Enacting the Text, to read a text describing the kind of geometry that so-called primitive people might have used. By the fourth day of the unit, Lisa felt that the class was ready to investigate some important geometric concepts in a contemporary situation. She wanted the students to realize that geometry is used in everyday life even today; at the same time, she hoped that the essay she had chosen would heighten students' awareness of and interest in the study of geometric figures—a topic that she planned to address more explicitly later in the unit.

Over Thanksgiving vacation, Lisa therefore assigned the reading of "Adventures of an Egg Man," a 20-page essay included in the book *Archimedes' Revenge* (Hoffman, 1988). This essay reports on the construction of an "egg-monument" three stories high. This "giant egg" had been commissioned in 1974 by a Canadian town and supported by a grant from the Royal Canadian Mounted Police. As the author shows, this project proved to be much more challenging than anyone had initially expected but was finally accomplished by a mathematics/computer science professor named R. D. Resch, who spent more than 18 months on the task. The essay very effectively portrays the struggles and creativity it took to solve the problem, as it explains the various approaches Resch tried and eventually abandoned (such as trying to design a method of construction based on the characteristic properties of an "ideal egg"—a shape that no mathematician had studied before!) before settling on constructing his "egg-surface" as a semiregular tridimensional tessellation made of more than 2,000 equilateral triangles and 500 equilateral 3-pointed stars. Throughout the essay, the author also presents a wealth of information about properties of various geometric figures and their construction, as well as other relevant mathematical facts and ideas, by means of nontechnical explanations often involving diagrams, so that the reader can get a better sense of the mathematics involved in the solution of this real-life problem. In addition, the essay also includes some information about Resch's life and career (including other interesting examples of applied-mathematics projects he had worked on), thus offering the reader some insights into him as a person and a mathematician.

Initial Individual Reading of the Essay Using Cards

To help the students make sense of such a long and difficult reading on their own, the teacher decided to use a variation of Cloning an Author—one of the transactional reading strategies described at the beginning of this chapter. Lisa introduced the strategy by talking about the connection between the Say Something strategy students had experienced in previous classes and the use of index cards in Cloning an Author:

> What we have done [so far] is to look at how people used geometry in primitive times, in the past. What I'd like to do [now] is give you a reading that shows you how geometry is used more currently. . . . Since you cannot work with your partner to do the reading over the vacation . . . I'm going to give you index cards. What I'd like you to do is write down some of your comments you would have made to your partner, had your partner been with you, on the index cards. . . . Just write one question . . . one thing on each index card.

Despite some initial complaints about the length of the reading and about having such a long homework assignment over a vacation, all but four students completed the assignment. With one exception, the students used at least 4 of the 10 index cards the teacher had given each of them. What they recorded on these cards varied considerably in content, as illustrated by the sample reproduced in Figure 4.4.

Though the great majority of the students chose to write their comments in the form of questions (96 out of the 118 cards produced overall), what they recorded on their cards varied considerably. Most cards were used to record specific points from the essay that the students had not understood (e.g., "How can [3–pointed] stars be hexagons?"; "I don't understand the densest known sphere packing"; "Why does an egg symbolize peace?") or to raise questions about more general issues discussed in the essay (e.g., "What does the tiling requirement have to do with the shape of the egg?"; "Why did he have to look at so many eggs to try and find a perfect one?"). Some students, however, also recorded their impressions of the reading (e.g., "I like the way they constructed the egglike shape with thread, thumbtacks and a pencil"; "I found that the reading was very confusing and hard to understand. Didn't you?") and, in just two cases, what they learned from it (e.g., "Kissing spheres. I learned a little about what they are"; "I didn't realize the construction of a circle went back that far"). In a few cases, the comments went beyond the reading as the student challenged what was reported in the text (e.g., "Why not making something easier?"; "If mathematicians are so great, why don't they find a formula to build an egg?"; "Shouldn't an egg be bigger if it weighs 3,000 pounds?") or, even more interestingly, raised some new questions (e.g., "What is the purpose of an Ellipse?"; "Even though an egg shape doesn't

Figure 4.4. Sample of students' cards.

Student 1:

What does an egg have to do with math?
How are you supposed to build an egg with material that doesn't bend?
Why does an egg symbolize peace?
If mathematicians are so great, why don't they find a formula to build an egg?

Student 2:

How does this talk of chickens and a three-story egg tie in with math?
Did you feel that the way they made the ellipses and circles in the diagrams were quite unique?
Is there a difference between an ellipse and an oval?
If Resch's "changing of paper into three-dimensional shapes is not origami," then what is it?
I think it is interesting that sometimes, no matter how hard a person applies pressure, he will not be able to break an egg. Don't you feel that it's interesting also?
I found that this reading was very confusing and hard to understand. Didn't you?
At the end of the packet, it said that people wanted to blow up the egg. Why would they want to do that?
A few paragraphs talk about how an egg is formed inside a chicken. What does this have to do with math?
Why did everybody laugh at the idea of the egg?
Why would he be interested in changing paper into three-dimensional form for two whole decades?

Student 3:

Are the angles divided up so they always equal 360°?
Are all the shapes equal even though their angles are different?
Why does the "Banded Egg" need tiles?
Are two identical triangles equal to a square if they fit in it? [picture of two triangles, and then a square divided in half by a diagonal and forming the same triangles]
Are their angles the same? [picture of two sets of equal triangles]
Even though an egg shape doesn't have an angle, could you find out the degrees of its top? [picture of the egg construction, a square with an angle marked, and an egg with the top marked as an angle]
How do you find the area of a circle or sphere?
How can the shape of an egg contribute to its strength?
Why did they do this? [picture of two pins and a string attached to them forming an ellipse]
The story was hard to understand. Some of the words were hard, but it wasn't that interesting.

have an angle, could you find the degrees of its top?"). Interestingly, 8 out of the 21 students also raised the question, "What does an egg have to do with math/this class?"—despite all the mathematical facts and explanations reported in the essay!

A First Follow-Up to the Reading Experience

Although the first reading of the article occurred at home, about two class periods of 40 minutes each were devoted to follow-up activities related to the reading of the essay. First of all, Lisa asked for some volunteers to briefly state what the story was about and what they thought about it—to remind everyone, and especially the few students who had not done the reading at home, of the story's content. A few students immediately volunteered, though most of them chose to relate their impressions of the reading, rather than to summarize the content, pointing out that, in their opinion, a lot of the information was not relevant or related to mathematics.

Within this initial conversation, Lisa also invited the students to comment on how they did the reading and how they used the index cards. This elicited some interesting reactions and discussions. In particular, in response to a student's observation that there were "a lot of big words," Lisa tried to help the students appreciate that it is not always necessary to understand every single word in a reading. As she asked students to share what they did when they found words they did not know, several students agreed that they did not need to look them up in the dictionary, because in most cases they could make sense of the reading even if they skipped them, or they could figure them out by looking at the surrounding words.

A student's question about what they were supposed to do with the cards they had written provided a natural opening for Lisa to introduce the small-group activity she had planned so as to engage the students more actively in a discussion of the reading. The following instructions were written on the board (because in the past few lessons the students had seemed to have a difficult time paying attention to instructions once they were in their small groups) and briefly explained by the teacher:

- Read index cards.
- Arrange similar cards together.
- Discuss what are the most interesting and important cards; choose four or five to discuss in your group.
- Report to the class.

This group activity developed for about 15 minutes, and during this time most of the students seemed quite engaged and interested, although few groups got beyond the stage of classifying the cards and none managed to discuss the cards selected as most interesting (mostly because of lack of time). There was also no time left in this lesson to share the results of this group work, so Lisa decided to collect all the index cards, asking each group to mark those they had selected as most important.

The lesson concluded with the distribution of an assignment sheet asking the students to "Look at the reading on Archimedes' Revenge [the essay they had just read] and your textbook; list the names of as many shapes as possible." This assignment was planned so as to prepare the students for the next part of the geometry unit, in which Lisa had planned to have the class select a few geometric figures for systematic study from a compilation of the individual lists created for this homework assignment.

Revisiting Key Sections of the Essay in Class by Using Cards and Enacting

As she read the index cards she had collected, Lisa was pleasantly surprised by the variety and quality of the students' comments and questions—which told her that most students had seriously tried to understand the reading and had gotten a lot from it, in contrast to the somewhat negative reactions she had gathered from the previous day's conversation in class. Thus she thought that everybody would benefit from further follow-up activities based on the cards. Because she had concerns about the small groups' ability to do these activities on their own, she decided to try a different approach. First, she compiled a list of all the cards the groups had selected as "most interesting" (for the groups who had not made the selection, she herself chose what she thought were the five most interesting cards) and formulated a homework assignment (see Figure 4.5) asking students to choose and further pursue one of these questions. This assignment sheet was handed out at the beginning of the next class, with the following explanation:

> I had a chance to go through all your cards, and can I just say at this moment that I was really impressed by some of your questions. I thought that they were very good. I really . . . I am truly amazed by some of the things that you're writing down. So I just wanted to let you know that, okay? . . . Now part of your

Figure 4.5. Homework assignment with a sample of students' cards.

Below are listed some questions from Archimedes' Revenge; choose ONE question and find an answer to respond to the best of your ability to your classmate. (Questions with a "*" before them are questions group members felt were the most interesting.)

* How can the shape of an egg contribute to its strength? (K.K.)
* Why won't an egg break when squeezed on the ends? (J.D.)
* Even though an egg shape doesn't have an angle could you find out the degrees of its top? (K.K.)
* Are 2 identical triangles equal to a square if they fit in it? (K.K.)
* Won't the circle not come out right if you tilt the pencil the wrong way? (K.K.)
How can stars be hexagons? (K.B.)
What does the construction of a circle have to do with the myth about the egg? (M.S.)
What does the tiling requirement have to do with the shape of the egg? (M.S.)
What uses is there for a shape similar to an egg? (D.M.)
What is the purpose of ellipses? (D.M.)
How is the making of a real egg going to help him? (D.D.)
* How does 5 hexagons equal 7 circles? (C.G.)
* Why didn't anybody use eggs in Geometry? (C.G.)
* How do you construct an egg out of equilateral triangles and three pointed stars? (M.C.)
Isn't an ellipse just like an oval? (R.V.)
How does this talk of chickens and a three-story egg tie in with Math? (T.D.)
Were the way they made the ellipses and circles in the diagrams quite unique? (T.D.)

homework assignment will be to pick one of these questions and try, to the best of your ability . . . to give a good answer to one of those. Now you might have to look up some information. You might already know some information. Just try. Put down as much as you can to help answer one of these questions.

In order to provide a model for this activity, Lisa had planned to address two of these questions in class: "Won't the circle not come out right if you tilt the pencil the wrong way?" and "What does the construction of a circle have to do with the myth about the egg?" These particular questions were also selected with the goal of helping the students appreciate some key points of the essay that were especially relevant to the geometry unit (i.e., the characteristic properties of geometric figures and their relationship with methods of construction) as well as learn some properties of circles and ellipses included in the curriculum the teacher was expected to cover in the course.

While Lisa set up all the material needed for this lesson and handed out the homework assignment, she asked the students to locate and reread on their own the section of the essay in which the author presents the construction of a circle and an ellipse as a preliminary to discussing the challenge presented by trying to come up with similar constructions for an "egg-shape."

> Resch soon found, however, that there was no formula in the literature for an ideal chicken egg. For many shapes that have a name, the literature contains not only an algebraic formula, but also a method of construction. Take the circle. It is simply the set of points in a plane that are equidistant from a given point in that plane. To construct a circle, tie one end of a length of string around a pencil and anchor the other end with a thumbtack to a piece of paper. With the string pulled taut and the pencil point held against the paper, rotate the pencil around the thumbtack; the result is a circle. [Figure of a pencil drawing the circle.] At some point, a twisted wag even turned this simple construction process into a sick joke, which I learned from the mathematician Martin Gardner: "Mommy, mommy, why do I always go 'round in circles?" "Shut up, kid, or I'll nail your other foot to the floor." It's an easy step from a circle to a sphere—imagine the kid's foot (or the string's end) nailed to a point in three-dimensional space, swing the kid's rigid body (or the pencil at the end of the taut string) every which way and observe the shape the kid's head (or the pencil point) traces out. Alternatively, you can think of a sphere as the shape swept out by a pirouetting circle.
>
> A chicken egg, of course, is closer to an ellipsoid—the shape swept out by a pirouetting ellipse—than to a sphere. Even the most demented mathematician wouldn't be able to generate an ellipse by twirling a child but could do so easily with the aid of a pencil and a loose string anchored by thumbtacks at both ends. [Picture of a pencil drawing an ellipse.] (Hoffman, 1988, pp. 90–91)

Lisa then engaged the class in a concrete interpretation and testing of the first method of construction described in the excerpt by asking the students to help her actually draw a circle following the procedure involving pencil and string explained in the reading. As they did so, she initiated a discussion about the relationship of this method to known properties of circles:

Lisa: Well, they show you how to make a circle here, and what do they say about circles on that page? What's listed in that very first paragraph? What does it say? Can somebody just kind of summarize it for me? [Dave starts to explain.] Dave?

Dave: All the equal distances around one point will make a circle.

Lisa: Okay, so if you wanted to construct your own circle, you picked a center on the board here, and if you got a tight string—I'm going to need some help. Jessica, can you hold this for me? [The teacher has gotten a portable bulletin board and has set it on Jessica's desk. She is pointing to the board and showing the students exactly what she is doing to construct this circle.] I picked the center here, all right, I got the string—

Lisa tied a pencil to the string and then started tracing with it on the bulletin board, while the class watched with great interest. There were comments like, "Neato!" "Cool." "Ohh." "Interesting." "It's just like a compass."

Lisa: It's just like a compass. What happened here?
Class: A circle!
Lisa: Pretty good-looking circle too, wouldn't you say, Rick? [He agrees, as does much of the rest of the class.] What could I say is characteristic about circles? What kind of property? How are circles special, that allow me to do this?

Though several students started to answer this question, their contributions soon revealed that most of them had not yet made a clear connection between this construction of the circle and the defining property that "all points of a circle are at the same distance from the center":

Kathy: They don't have any angles or—
Jessica: It's perfectly round, you don't have to, like, change. You can do it the same length away.
Lisa: What do you mean, "same length away"?

To help the students come to a clearer understanding that it is really the circle's "equidistance" property that makes this construction possible, Lisa then suggested that they verify with a ruler that the distance to the center of each point of the circle they just drew was the same. The students seemed quite interested and engaged in this demonstration. Lisa also took the opportunity to review some vocabulary about circles during this discussion.

Lisa then explicitly revisited Kim's question ("Won't the circle not come out right if you tilt the pencil the wrong way?") by asking the student herself to demonstrate what she meant. Using the pencil the teacher had tied to the pin on the bulletin board, Kim began to trace a new "circle," but tilting the pencil differently as she moved around, while commenting, "Like, if you tilted it like this, it would come out all weird [pointing out to the rest of the class how the beginning and end of her figure did not even meet]. Like this."

Lisa tried to help the students see the significance of this result and its connection with the previous discussion:

> *Lisa:* Okay, notice. What did tilting this pencil do? What happened to the string? Did you notice when she was—
> [One student says that it made an ellipse.]
> *Ron:* It moved up on the pen.
> *Lisa:* It moved up on the pen, which changed this distance, didn't it?
> *Ron:* Yeah.
> *Lisa:* It changed it—it almost made it shorter so that you didn't have a perfect circle, so that they weren't always an equal distance.

Lisa now moved to reproducing the construction of the ellipse—a figure the students had not studied before—as suggested in the reading (which, in this case, provided a picture with only little verbal explanation to illustrate this construction). This time, a student was asked to perform the construction on the bulletin board, and he eventually succeeded, despite some trouble at the beginning with moving the pencil around without upsetting the string. Lisa then invited the class to come up with a characterizing property for this ellipse—as they had done before with the circle—though this time the information was not in the reading nor was it known to these students. The students had considerable difficulty addressing this question until Lisa suggested that they once again measure the distance from each point of the ellipse to the two central pins. Several students were asked to measure these distances for a point of their choice, and these results were recorded by the teacher on the board in the form of a table. With some prompting on Lisa's part, the class then noticed that the sum of these distances was always the same number. Lisa concluded this activity by articulating the characterizing property of an ellipse.

At this point Lisa moved the focus of the discussion to the key issue of the relationship between the properties of a figure and its method of construction; she also helped the students see how looking at the construction of familiar figures can help with the construction of new ones, and in this way implicitly addressed the second student's question ("What has the drawing of the circle have to do with the myth of the egg?"). It is worth noting that the discussion that followed also addressed, albeit indirectly, some other questions various students had written on their cards—especially the ones challenging what the essay had to do with mathematics and this course in particular.

> *Lisa:* All right, now, so what Resch said was that he thought this was interesting. This is an interesting property of ellipses, that the sum of those distances are always the same. And he thought that a special property of circles was that those points are always equal distance from that center point. Why did he mention this when he was mentioning the egg? What did he go on to say in those paragraphs? Look at page 92. Read!

The students took some time to look back at this section of the essay:

> Unlike an ellipse, a chicken egg is blunter at one end than the other, but this asymmetry doesn't mean it can't be represented mathematically. Indeed, back in the seventeenth century, the French man of letters René Descartes ("I think; therefore, I am") explored the algebraic formula for egg-shaped curves. Two centuries later, the Scottish mathematical physicist James Clerk Maxwell, best known for his quantitative demonstration that electricity and magnetism are part of the same phenomenon, extended Descartes' efforts. Maxwell was merely fifteen at the time, and he sent off a paper on egg shapes to the Royal Society of Edinburgh, Scotland's premiere scientific society. The paper was warmly received, but the august society refused to let such a pip-squeak address them on the subject. It missed an arresting demonstration that egg-shaped curves can be constructed with pencil, thread, thumbtacks, and a little ingenuity. [Picture of Maxwell's construction with some explanations.] Resch's main problem was that if you have seen one chicken egg, you haven't seen them all. They do vary slightly in shape, and it was up to him to discern the ideal form. In a fit of frustration, he called up the agriculture department and had it airfreight him an egg-grading manual. "I thought," says Resch, "that the manual would surely include a definition of chicken egg. But all I found were photographs labeled A, AA, B and BB. Finally, I came to an image called the ideal egg. So I had it photographed and then digitized in my computer program." For six months, Resch and two graduate students worked day and night to turn his folded-sheet structures into an egg, but all they got was negative results. "We did not know what was

wrong—our program, our geometry, or our mathematics." Resch ended up throwing out his computer program, setting aside the folded sheets that had served him so well for two decades, and starting over from scratch. His plan was to construct the egg out of numerous flat tiles joined together at slight angles, treating the egg as if it were a three-dimensional jig-saw puzzle. (Hoffman, 1988, pp. 92–93)

Lisa: All right, what was he saying? . . . They said that there's things that we know about circles. There's properties that have already been studied and explored that we know about circles and ellipses. What did he say about eggs?

Dave: They don't have a similar property.

Lisa: They don't have a similar property and what else?

Dave: They don't have any properties.

Lisa: They really haven't been studied before. He found this very frustrating probably. If you wanted to build something and there was nothing to help you, wouldn't you find that a little frustrating? Don't you think that he'd have to do some work to find out some properties? And that's what he did. What did he go ahead and do? How did he try to find some properties about eggs? What did he do? [One student says, "Experiments!"]

Ron: He drew it first.

Lisa: [Pointing to Ron] He tried drawing it, but what did he do before he tried to draw it?

Ron: He looked up the different shapes.

Lisa: Where did he look them up? . . . He got some different eggs, didn't he, together to just try and look and see visually what he could see. Just as if I brought in a whole bunch of circles and looked at them all first, maybe saw what was similar about them.

The conversation continued in this vein for a while, as Lisa tried to help the students understand the significance of Resch's story as an example of how mathematicians go about "discovering" the properties of a shape and using them for some purpose.

Despite the modeling that went on in class and the students' genuine interest in some of the questions and issues raised by the classmates and reported on the homework sheet, most students still had difficulty when they tried to address some of these questions on their own for homework. Although some of their answers were sketchy, several were quite clever and insightful, as the examples reported in Figure 4.6 demonstrate.

Figure 4.6. Examples of students' homework.

Example 1

Question: What uses is there for a shape similar to the egg?

Answer: A similar shape is an ellipse. It is the shape in which the planets move, to describe stuff.

Example 2

Question: Why didn't anyone use eggs in geometry?

Answer: I think maybe no one used eggs in Geometry or found a formula for it because maybe no one had really thought it was considered a shape. Maybe they just thought of it as an egg we eat. Or something in which a baby chick is hatched from.

Notes on What Students Gained From This Instructional Episode

This vignette presents a portrait of students as they take up the challenge of understanding some fundamental ideas in geometry through a generative reading of a unique essay. Indeed, the "Egg Man" essay could be considered a wonderful introduction to the very "essence" of classical geometry. It illustrates the importance that studying geometric figures has for practical as well as mathematical applications, and it identifies some of the key elements of this study, such as deciding which shapes are worth studying, defining each shape precisely, identifying characteristic properties (by sorting out what is common across many examples of the same shape), and developing methods of constructing and/or reproducing the shapes, or both. That most students were not able to appreciate this message in their first reading of the essay shows that understanding what geometry is all about is not easy for middle school students to grasp. In addition, the questions students raised about the relevance of this reading to their mathematics class supports our earlier claim that students are rarely expected to appreciate the nature and scope of the branches of mathematics they study in school. As noted in Chapter 2, the mathematics education community has grown concerned with students' limited awareness of the big picture and is beginning to give increased recognition to the importance of understanding core mathematical ideas such as those outlined above. It is also worth noting that, although the essay explicitly describes what it means to develop a method of construction for a given geometric figure, it was only when the students worked as a class to reproduce the methods for constructing a circle and an ellipse, *and* when they explicitly discussed the connection between these methods and the characterizing properties of the figure in question, that they gained a better understanding of these important issues. As in the first vignette, we think this only confirms the idea that texts are meaning potentials and that understanding a text requires the active construction and negotiation of meaning by the reader.

In the process of making sense of the "big" ideas described above, the students also learned some specific math facts and techniques (such as the definitions of *circle* and *ellipse* and specific methods for constructing these figures precisely). These notions had been neither previously mastered nor understood by most of the students in this class, as the dialogue reported in the vignette indicates. But later in the unit, the teacher remarked on how well the students seemed to have retained a solid understanding of circles and how they were able to apply it in a different context. Although no formal testing of these facts and techniques was carried out, the teacher's observation suggests that the students were genuinely engaged in learning during the "Egg Man" episode.

Reading the "Egg Man" essay may have contributed to the students' awareness that mathematics is often motivated by the need to solve specific problems and is valued, in part, because of its practical applications. It is more difficult to find concrete evidence to support this hypothesis, because the class discussion did not explicitly address these issues, and few students' cards focused on this theme. However, we think this essay is rich with possibilities for dealing with students' conceptions of mathematics as a discipline and a practice. For example, reading about how building the egg monument took several years and the concerted effort of several people could initiate a discussion challenging the belief that solving math problems should take 5 minutes or less (a belief that is quite common among students, as Schoenfeld [1989, 1992] has shown). Similarly, realizing that a professional mathematician *today* found it necessary to identify on his own the properties of a shape no mathematician had studied before might have challenged another widespread belief—that "everything that has to be discovered in mathematics has already been discovered" (Borasi, 1992). That this was surprising for many students (as revealed by some of their cards) suggests that it might not have been difficult to engage them in a conversation on this point in relation to their own beliefs about mathematics.

Finally, we would like to point out how reading this essay at the very least *exposed* students to other valuable mathematical facts, processes, and connections—even if they were not expected to pay explicit attention and "understand" these technical details at this point in time. For example, because Resch's final solution employed a three-dimensional tessellation, the article provides some simple and clear explanations (often supported by very informative diagrams) about which regular polygons tessellate and why. The essay also touches upon mathematical problems, such as "packing spheres efficiently," that have both a mathematical and a practical interest and, in some cases, have not yet been fully solved. Lastly, the account of how Resch approached the problem of building his giant egg concretely illustrates some important elements of mathematical problem solving—such as the importance of problem definition and its relationship to the practical constraints one is working with, the kind of solutions sought (i.e., trying to determine a method of construction for egg shapes versus figuring out what tiles could be used to build an egglike surface), and the use of similar but simpler problems as "stepping stones" to a resolution of the problem (such as looking first at the construction of circles and ellipses to gain some ideas about how to construct an egg). Despite the fact that many students may have overlooked or simply ignored these interesting points while reading the essay, we think there is some benefit to having encountered them in the context of discussing the solution of real-life problems; at the very least, students may have gained a sense of the potential uses of mathematics and might remember being exposed to some of these ideas should they encounter them again in future mathematical studies. In fact, a few students' cards suggest they were intrigued by and tried to make sense of some of these technical mathematical details—as illustrated by questions like, "How can stars be hexagons?" or comments such as, "Kissing spheres. I learned a bit about them."

In this discussion of what students gained from the reading experiences described in the vignette, we have pointed to the "big ideas" and specific concepts students learned. But we have also chosen to highlight the *potential* of an essay such as "Adventures of an Egg Man" (Hoffman, 1988) to serve as a catalyst for learning about many worthwhile mathematical concepts and processes as well as issues related to the nature of mathematics. Even if only some of this potential was tapped in the "Egg Man" vignette, we do not consider this a limitation of the instructional episode because another reading of the essay could be orchestrated yet again, but with other purposes in mind. Instead, we think the learning experiences that grew out of the reading of this text clearly show how the interplay of instructional goals and student perspectives shapes the use made of any text in a specific mathematics class and, thus, what students gain from it.

Understanding and Tapping the Potential of Transactional Reading Strategies in Mathematics Classrooms

The vignettes presented in the previous section offer good illustrations of new and varied ways that reading can engage students in meaningful mathematics. In this section, we return to transactional reading theory to explain the vignettes in theoretical terms and, in doing so, show why this perspective on reading may be useful to mathematics educators. At the same time, we want to point out some dimensions of these instructional episodes that emerged from our research and may be critical if teachers want to tap into the learning potential of generative reading in mathematics classrooms.

What Transactional Reading Theory Can Tell Us About the Vignettes

Though at first Rosenblatt's transactional theory of reading, described in Chapter 2, may have seemed a strange choice for understanding reading in mathematics classrooms, the two vignettes presented earlier provide striking examples of Rosenblatt's theory in practice and suggest that a transactional perspective may indeed have something to offer mathematics educators.

Rosenblatt (1978) defined the reading transaction as a unique event—a coming together of particular readers and particular texts in particular situations such that each element shapes and is shaped by the total situation. From this perspective, each of the reading episodes presented earlier was a unique, dynamic event, so that to change any one element (the readers, the texts, the social relations among the participants, the purposes) would be to create a new event.

In the "Math & War" vignette, for example, the invitation to share tentative meanings with peers as they talked their way through a text, the particular text selected, the link to ongoing course discussions about math connections and ways of learning, and the background and interests characterizing the students in each pair, all contributed to create a unique event. The uniqueness of each reading transaction becomes especially evident when we compare Char and Jolea's reading event with that of Van and Shellie. Though the same text was read within the same instructional context, each group did so in different ways, drew on different knowledge and experience, and thus produced different interpretations. For example, Van's personal knowledge of the evolution of her friend's car led her and her partner to a unique analogy that helped them better understand the growing relation between mathematics and war over time.

The multiple readings of "Adventures of an Egg Man" (Hoffman, 1988) described in the second vignette also illustrate the concept of a transaction among reader, text, and context in which each element shapes and is shaped by the others. In the first transaction—when each individual student read the text at home, recording comments or questions on index cards—students approached the text with some prior understanding of the history of geometry and with the idea that they would learn something about contemporary uses of geometry from this text. Unlike the "Math & War" vignette, in which students were trying out a new strategy for sharing information, the focus here was primarily on exploring the ideas represented in the text so as to expand students' understanding of geometry—although this did not mean that students were expected to learn "everything" they encountered in the text. The range of questions and comments students recorded on cards suggests that they did treat this reading as an occasion for making personal meanings and not as an attempt to reproduce the text or arrive at the authoritative (read: teacher's) meaning of the text. Still, the fact that 8 of the 21 students raised the question of what an egg had to do with math shows that they were definitely reading in light of a particular setting (their mathematics class) and brought their histories as mathematics students and expectations for that setting to the reading. The homework assignment that required students to identify names of shapes mentioned in the essay produced a very different reading of the same text; this time the reading experience was defined as a search for specific information rather than an open-ended meaning-making experience, a shift that shows quite clearly how even the reading of the same text by the same reader can become a completely different event when guided by a different purpose. During the next class period, the students had yet another opportunity to read the "Egg Man" essay. This time, however, the focus was on developing shared understandings of those parts of the text related to the mathematical concepts the teacher wanted to pursue in more depth. Yet this did not become an event in which the teacher delivered the content of the text to the students through either a directed reading or an oral summary of the points. Instead, she used several of the students' own questions to revisit the text and, for the first question, had them literally "act out" what the text described. The decision to concentrate only on certain sections of the text further shows how this final reading of the essay was influenced by the teacher's instructional goals.

Implicit in the above discussion is another tenet of transactional reading theory, namely, that readers' interpretations are not fixed by a text but instead vary across readers and situations. Where Jolea saw the "Math and War" text as an essay about the progressive differentiation of the work of scientists and mathematicians, Van and Shellie saw it as an essay about mathematics as a growing discipline with new questions to be explored; moreover, none of the moral questions that were central to Char and Jolea's "say something" were represented in Van and Shellie's sketch of the text. Similarly, when students read the "Egg Man" essay using the card strategy, the variety of questions they produced reflected a range of concerns and interests, which served as the starting point for their investigation of concepts central to understanding geometry.

Another key aspect of Rosenblatt's transactional theory of reading is the idea that readers generate and revise meanings throughout the reading event. Interpretations do not spring ready-made from the text, even when each word is read accurately, but grow and change as readers propose tentative meanings and reconsider them in light of further reading, thinking, and dialogue. This point is illustrated in each vignette.

The "Math and War" vignette shows how readers put forward tentative meanings and built off one another's thinking to arrive at an interpretation that made sense to them. In Char and Jolea's "say something" experience, for example, readers used the opportunity to stop and "say something" to express their confusions and surprises, summarize the text in their own words, interpret particular sentences and arguments, and make connections to their prior knowledge and experience as well as to earlier segments of the text. These comments were not a series of monologues but built off one another, allowing each reader to construct, elaborate, or rethink her own hypothesis by considering the ideas of others. Char's interpretation of the article, in particular, shows how meanings can grow and change through dialogue and reflection, as it was only through her discussions with Jolea and Margie that she came to appreciate the moral issues that had concerned Jolea.

The idea that meaning grows and changes through dialogue and reflection is also evident in the "Egg Man" vignette, though in this case the growth in understanding was achieved through multiple readings of the same text, each of which encouraged the students to take a different perspective. The first reading encouraged students to think about the essay (through questions and comments) in whatever ways made sense to them; only after the students had made their varied responses public did the teacher initiate a second reading, which guided the students toward a particular interpretation of the essay (the connection between the construction of specific geometric shapes and their properties). By grounding this subsequent reading in the students' initial responses, the teacher helped them refine their understanding of the specific examples being considered (i.e., construction of a circle and ellipse) and grasp the significance of these examples for the essay as a whole ("What has the drawing of the circle have to do with the myth of the egg?"). This cycle of generating and refining meanings did not end at this point; instead, the opportunity to select one of the questions their peers had formulated and research it launched yet another cycle of meaning-making.

What the Vignettes Can Tell Us About Tapping the Potential of Transactional Reading Strategies in Mathematics Classrooms

As we have noted in earlier chapters, we began the RLM Project with the belief that transactional reading strategies drawn from the reading instruction literature could offer mathematics students heuristics for approaching "rich" math texts as generative readers. The experiences reported in the two vignettes lend support to this initial belief; more important, however, the vignettes can help us better understand how transactional reading strategies contribute to mathematics instruction, and what other instructional supports need to be present in order to tap this potential fully.

The transactional reading strategies portrayed in the vignettes were Say Something, Sketch-to-Stretch, variations of Cloning an Author that we chose to consider as part of a larger category we named Using Cards, and a new strategy—Enacting the Text—that was not derived from the reading instruction literature. Each of these strategies invited students to transform the author's meanings into the reader's meanings by symbolizing (e.g., talking, drawing, writing) or acting out the text. As such, the strategies not only offered students support for active thinking and reflection but also resulted in the production of artifacts (sketches, cards, diagrams) or experiences (conversations or actions) that could be made public and further negotiated in light of particular instructional goals.

Yet each strategy supported students' learning in a unique way. For instance, Say Something provided a structure for talking while reading that encouraged students to share insights and reactions, bring to bear relevant information, restate or summarize what was read, identify points needing clarification and begin to make sense of them with their partners' help, state hypotheses and interpretations that could be checked and revised, raise and begin to address new questions, and even express feelings of confusion or frustration. As such, this reading strategy provided students with a constructive way to deal with the challenges presented by a difficult text and an opportunity to benefit immediately from the perspectives of another reader.

Writing cards while reading a text also supported students' engagement with a difficult text by helping them articulate their difficulties and interpretations—as illustrated in the "Egg Man" vignette, in which students used their cards to record points they had not understood, share their impressions of the reading, and even raise questions that moved beyond the text. Much of the value of Using Cards, however, depends on how the cards students create are organized and shared, as this allows students to benefit from the multiple perspectives and interpretations generated in the individual readings. Although the original Cloning an Author strategy involved a visual mapping of the cards, the experiences developed in Lisa's class show that this is only *one* of the possible ways students' cards can be used to achieve this goal.

Sketch-to-Stretch presented students with the unique challenge of recasting their understanding of the text in a new medium without the benefit of a ready-made code for doing so. As the "Math & War" vignette clearly demonstrates, the students took up this challenge and used Sketch-to-Stretch to both synthesize and elaborate the interpretations generated during their "say something" experience. It is worth noting that many students in this class commented on how drawing the sketch had added something new to what they had gained from their previous reading, perhaps because it required them to find their own way to represent their understanding. But it was the *sharing* of these sketches that proved most valuable in the "Math & War" vignette, as it led to a rich discussion about several aspects of mathematics as a discipline that the teacher had hoped to address through this experience.

A fourth strategy, Enacting the Text, was used by Lisa quite spontaneously during the last part of the "Egg Man" episode. This strategy seemed to come from the practice—common among advanced mathematics learners—of "working out on one's own" the techniques or procedures described in a technical math text, yet we were struck by the way this practice resonated with transactional reading theory. Notice, for instance, that in the "Egg Man" vignette students not only "acted out" the construction of the circle as described in the text in order to gain a personal understanding of the procedure described by the author but also developed on their own another construction (ellipse) that had only been partially sketched in the text. Moreover, Lisa encouraged the students to extend their understanding by actually testing the consequences of violating some of the conditions assumed in the text, as suggested by one of the student's cards ("Won't the circle not come out right if you tilt the pencil the wrong way?"). In this case, enacting was not a matter of simply recreating the author's message but of using the text as a catalyst for further mathematical investigations.

The vignettes demonstrate that these reading strategies can be thought of as complementary to one another owing to their unique features. The teachers we worked with recognized the value of combining strategies and often chose to use more than one strategy to read a given text. We also observed that the teachers treated the strategies as flexible heuristics and readily adapted them in whatever ways they felt would enhance the students' engagement and learning. Finally, we think it important to notice that combining strategies meant that students would sometimes *reread* a text—a practice that is extremely worthwhile, especially when the texts are as challenging as those used in the vignettes (as Jolea discovered during the "say something" experience).

The sophisticated quality of the texts used in the vignettes made the use of one or more of the strategies an important factor in the students' engagement with and understanding of the texts they read. Although far from the typical technical mathematics texts, both essays presented students with considerable challenges as they dealt with complex issues, and both had originally been written with an adult audience in mind. Indeed, this was one of the first things students commented on when they began reading. Remember, for example, how the middle school students complained about the "big words" encountered in the "Egg Man" essay, and the "Math Connections B" students characterized the introductory paragraph to the "Math and War" essay as "bureaucratic mumble-jumble." But in both vignettes, the strategies made it possible for the students to express whatever feelings they had about the difficulties they met with while reading. This, in turn, allowed their peers and teachers to respond to those concerns and ultimately helped students get beyond their initial frustrations and begin to generate and share tentative interpretations.

Up to this point, we have focused on the contribution transactional reading strategies can make to students' meaning-making and discussions. But we have also found that the extent to which the strategies actually achieve this potential depends on other instructional practices used in conjunction with the reading strategies. First, an important characteristic of the reading experiences featured in the two vignettes, regardless of the reading strategy employed, was the whole-class session that followed the initial reading of the chosen text. In both cases, these follow-up sessions were planned by the teachers to ensure that students took full advantage of what each text could offer them as students in a particular mathematics class. Two kinds of follow-up sessions can be identified from these examples: (a) sessions in which students share their interpretations of the text(s) read with the entire class (as in the "Math & War" vignette); and (b) sessions in which the teacher plans some mathematical activities that extend the reading experience in ways that help students make sense of and pursue further the specific mathematical ideas being explored (as in the "Egg Man" vignette). We have observed that both kinds of follow-up sessions are important, because they allow teachers to hear students' thinking, encourage students to grapple with the perspectives of their peers, and invite the entire class to work collaboratively to pursue the mathematical ideas introduced through the reading experiences. Finally, follow-up sessions are valuable because the experiences of revising, expanding, confirming, and stimulating students' thinking through collective exploration of meanings and feelings can effectively demonstrate to students that mathematical knowledge is socially constructed within a community of practice (Lampert, 1990; Lave & Wenger, 1991).

Another instructional practice that seems crucial to the success of instructional experiences involving the "generative reading of rich math texts" is the teachers' willingness to devote considerable class time to the actual reading of the text or to activities that center on making sense of the text. As both vignettes make clear, peer interaction around a text or set of texts is time-consuming but necessary if students are to experience the struggle of negotiating meanings and not have this experience short-circuited. Students in both vignettes had a chance to see that meanings are made, not given, that there are multiple meanings, that these differences have value, and that meanings (and readers!) grow and change. Making time for such experiences demonstrates to students that reading is genuinely valued as an integral part of the learning taking place in a particular mathematics classroom. This seems especially important given that students are likely to respond negatively, at least initially, to the idea of reading in a mathematics class—as was the case at the beginning of the "Egg Man" vignette.

Students' expectations for reading in mathematics classes, which are shaped through years of schooling, will in fact need to be addressed up front if generative reading experiences are to be productive. This means paying explicit attention to these expectations by talking with students about their beliefs and strategies for reading, as Lisa did when students complained about the "big words" in the "Egg Man" essay, and by clearly articulating the rationale for each reading experience (especially when a new reading strategy is introduced), as both Judi and Lisa consistently did. Judi also helped students reconsider their expectations for reading in a mathematics class by involving them in individual and whole-class reflections on their experiences with reading strategies. This was an especially important dimension of Judi's instructional practice given that a goal of all her teaching was "learning how to learn." As shown in Chapter 5, Judi used several distinctive practices to help students become aware of and appreciate the value of the reading experiences and, indeed, all the learning experiences in her classes. Although we had never conceptualized the reading strategies as techniques that could "work" no matter what the norms and values of the classroom might be, our collaboration with Judi and Lisa helped us understand more fully how crucial the instructional practices outlined here would be to the success of these experiences.

Summary and Conclusions

This chapter has examined what it means to "read rich math texts generatively" in practice and in theory; at the same time it has pointed to some critical instructional practices that teachers would want to consider when planning such reading experiences. In summarizing this discussion, we call attention to the characteristics of a transactional perspective on reading mathematics that have the most importance for its use in classrooms. First, "reading rich math texts generatively" does not mean separating reading from other meaningful mathematical activities or using it as a way to introduce or finish off traditional instructional units on various topics. Instead, the classroom examples indicate that when fully integrated into ongoing instructional activities, a generative approach to reading mathematics can contribute to students' learning in significant ways. Students learned mathematical content (including "big ideas" about particular mathematical topics, technical facts, concepts, and procedures), learned about the nature of mathematics (including awareness of different branches of mathematics, humanistic aspects of mathematics, connections between mathematics and other fields, real-life applications, history of mathematics), and learned about processes and strategies (including strategies for problem solving, making sense of texts, sharing one's thinking with others, and learning how to learn).

Integrating reading into classroom learning activities produced instructional episodes that were diverse and complex. Even just the two examples reported in this chapter illustrate quite clearly that "reading rich math texts generatively" can appear quite different, depending on the teacher's instructional purposes. In each case, the choice of text was never made without considering the instructional purpose it would serve and the kind of reading strategy that would promote such a goal. For this reason, mathematics teachers may want to become aware of the wide range of materials (including excerpts from novels, newspaper and magazine articles, and texts consisting of figures or directions) that teachers in the RLM Project incorporated into their teaching (see Siegel, Borasi, Fonzi, & Smith, 1996, for descriptions of texts used in other RLM Episodes). In addition, they may find it helpful to become familiar with the kinds of transactional strategies described in this chapter and to make explicit their own intuitive strategies for reading mathematics, such as the "enacting" strategy the teacher spontaneously invoked in the "Egg Man" vignette.

Despite variations in instructional purposes, the kind of texts that can be thought of as "rich" mathematical texts, and strategies for reading them, what distinguishes a generative approach to reading mathematics from other interpretations is the belief that meanings grow and change as learners act on and act out texts. This perspective on reading mathematics suggests that what is thought of as "learning from text" requires active engagement on the part of readers, so they can transform an author's meanings into their own. The artifacts that result from transforming texts in these ways are especially important to tapping the learning potential of generative reading experiences, as they enable learners to make their thinking public and open the way to negotiating their meanings with others. As we have noted, this public negotiation of texts—the process of making and remaking meanings— is central to a generative approach to reading mathematics, because it allows students to examine and further develop their understandings of mathematical concepts, processes, and perspectives. In addition to providing occasions for publicly negotiating meanings, the "sharing sessions" in Judi and Lisa's classrooms were times for students to reflect explicitly on their learning processes and to learn how to act like members of a community of practice. In these classrooms, this meant, among other things, learning to participate in a dialogue, to value and learn from the ideas and experiences of others, to rethink one's own ideas, and to appreciate the complexity and power of constructing knowledge together. Sharing sessions can thus multiply the ways that transactional reading strategies can contribute to meaningful mathematics instruction.

Although none of the texts employed in the RLM Episodes we studied was a typical "technical math text," introducing similar reading strategies might reduce many of the negative reactions students tend to have toward these difficult texts. The instructional activities typically recommended in the literature on reading mathematics, such as strategies for learning technical vocabulary and interpreting the syntax and overall organization characteristic of word problems and textbook explanations (e.g., Shuard & Rothery, 1984), tend to focus students' attention on features of the text. Although such strategies may be useful, they are not sufficient in and of themselves, because making sense of texts is influenced by what readers bring to a text as well as the situation within which a text is read. Moreover, because the purpose of such strategies is to enable students to read and solve the problem accurately, instruction devoted to teaching and using them rarely involves sharing sessions, making it less likely that students will benefit from the ideas and experiences of their peers. Introducing transactional reading strategies may thus expand students' repertoires for dealing constructively with technical mathematics texts.

This chapter has tried to show that a transactional perspective on reading mathematics has much to contribute to the teaching and learning of mathematics, especially at a time when educators are searching for ways to make mathematics learning more meaningful, challenging, and worthwhile for all learners. Yet the more we examined the RLM Project experiences we had documented, the more we began to see that a transactional perspective was not the *only* valuable way of conceptualizing reading in mathematics instruction. In the next two chapters, we turn to the subsequent studies we conducted and introduce two other ways to think about reading mathematics that emerged from our analysis of experiences in Judi's and Lisa's classrooms.

CHAPTER 5

Reading Practices in an Inquiry-Oriented Mathematics Classroom: A Social Practice Perspective

As we examined RLM Episodes such as those discussed in the previous chapter, we began to realize that the "generative reading of rich math texts" we had initially regarded as our "new integration" of reading and mathematics was but *one* of the ways students read in these instructional experiences. In the "Math & War" vignette, for example, students not only read the essay (using Say Something and Sketch-to-Stretch) but also the newsprint on which one of the instructors recorded students' responses during the introductory demonstration of Say Something. Although this reading occurred quite spontaneously and almost invisibly, and did not involve the use of an explicit reading strategy, it nevertheless played an important role in the ongoing instructional activity. Recording and reading the students' responses demonstrated the value the teacher placed on students' thinking and simultaneously served as a means for the teacher and the class, together, to review what they had done, reflect on the nature and significance of the learning activity they had engaged in, and set the stage for the next activity. In the same vignette, another kind of reading we initially took for granted occurred as students looked at the sketches their classmates had created (see Figures 4.1, 4.2, and 4.3) and tried to make sense of them in light of the explanations provided by the artists. Similarly, in the "Egg Man" vignette, we noticed several cases in which the students read directions written by the teacher for class activities or homework assignments; the students read these teacher-generated texts to understand what they were expected to do rather than to generate new meanings or start new conversations. In some cases, even texts we had initially defined as "rich math texts" were not read in a way that could be considered very "generative," as when students were asked to re-read the essay "Adventures of an Egg Man" (Hoffman, 1988), searching for all the geometric figures described in the essay in preparation for further class investigations of these figures.

Examples such as these prompted us to look beyond our initial approach to integrating reading into mathematics instruction and consider further the varieties of reading we had noticed in Judi's and Lisa's classrooms. Rather than dismiss these examples as simply "instrumental" or "efferent" modes of reading with little apparent relevance to our research, we began to question what may in fact "count" as reading in inquiry-oriented mathematics classes where creating a community of practice and constructing and negotiating meanings as a community are a priority. Because the "Math Connections B" course represented such an environment, and had been thoroughly documented (as described in Chapter 3), we felt it offered a unique opportunity to systematically examine the nature of reading in an inquiry-oriented mathematics classroom.

Such a study, however, required an analysis of the classroom data that was grounded in a theoretical perspective on reading different from the transactional perspective that guided our initial conception of reading in mathematics instruction. Rather than assuming that reading was, a priori, a generative act, we approached the narrative of "Math Connections B" with the question "What counts as reading in this classroom?" and set ourselves the task of identifying all the reading events that occurred in the context of the course, not just those involving the generative reading of what we considered "rich" mathematics texts. To support this analysis, we drew on the emerging conceptualization of reading as a social practice (summarized in Chapter 2) that treats reading as an embodied and situated activity so bound up with the life of a community (such as the "Math Connections B" class) that what counts as reading comes to be defined by the social practices of the community. In this way, we attempted to move beyond our initial theoretical framework and make sense of the complexities we encountered in this classroom. In practice, this meant that we had to locate all instances of reading in relation to the overall instructional activity of which they were a part, and then categorize and characterize these reading events with respect to the purpose they were intended to serve (see the Appendix for information on the units of analysis and the procedures employed in this analysis, and Siegel & Fonzi, 1995, for a research report of this study).

Somewhat to our surprise, this analysis revealed that some kind of reading was embedded in nearly every instructional activity that occurred in this course. The first three segments of the "Math Connections B" course (which led up to and included the students' inquiry into the mathematical connections of racing), described in the following narrative, clearly illustrate this finding and show that the boundaries separating classroom reading and mathematics activities begin to fade when conceptualized as social practices. To highlight the ways that reading was embedded in this complex instructional experience, we have chosen to accompany the narrative with commentaries that explicitly identify the various reading practices illustrated. These commentaries have been included in parentheses and printed in a different font so as to better distinguish them from the "story" of the instructional experience. We hope that this format will make evident how integral reading was to living and learning mathematics in this classroom and allow us to introduce "in context" the categories of reading practices we generated, after which we discuss their significance and implications.

Narrative 4: The "Racing" Project—Reading Practices at Work in an Inquiry-Oriented Mathematics Class

Before we begin our "commented" narrative, it may help the reader to have an overview of the three main segments constituting this instructional experience, which developed over the first 10 weeks of the "Math Connections B" course. During the first segment of the course (Days 1–4), the activities and experiences that Judi planned had multiple purposes. First, Judi wanted students to "learn how to learn"—the overarching goal of the School Without Walls and a core objective in all her classes. This included learning how to participate in class experiences and discussions, to share ideas, and to value the opinions of others; learning how to reflect on and change their opinions; and learning how to use a decision-making process and value the complexity of that process. The activities and experiences that occurred during this segment were thus designed to initiate new students into the social norms and values of the School Without Walls and reinforce these norms and values for returning students. A second focus of this first segment was introducing the idea of math connections—the theme of the course. Students engaged in a variety of experiences designed to encourage them to reflect on their conception of mathematics and to generate a bank of ideas from which to plan subsequent learning experiences. Judi felt that these ideas about the nature of mathematics and learning mathematics needed to come from the students, not from her, a belief that served as the basis for her instructional choices during this segment of the course.

During Segment 2 (Days 5–7), the class worked to decide on a collective project that would enable them to begin to explore math connections, a process that called on students to engage in the kind of generative thinking associated with posing questions. Specifically, Judi's goals for Segment 2 were to (a) help students reflect on all they had said in the first days of the class about math connections and learning mathematics, so that the choices about what to investigate and how to approach the project would be grounded in students' ideas and experiences; (b) engage students in a thinking process that would help them generate broad questions that could be explored in a class project; (c) begin to value their ability to engage in this kind of thinking process; and (d) continue learning to use a decision-making process and value the complexity of that process. In a sense, this segment was intended to help students see not only mathematics but also themselves a bit differently, as members of a community of learners capable of generating and planning their own inquiry process.

At the conclusion of Segment 2, the class decided to engage in a first "short" project investigating the "mathematics of racing," in order to learn what was involved in doing inquiries of this kind before pursuing a more in-depth study of math connections. Segment 3 (Days 8–24) of the course was then devoted to carrying out this inquiry, a process that took about 5 weeks instead of the 1 week the teacher had initially expected! The class inquiry into the mathematics of racing required considerable planning and decision making, gathering and making sense of relevant information, and sharing the insights thus gained both within and across small groups—all activities that were new to the students and turned out to be more problematic than expected. As a result, the outcomes of this project left much to be desired—in the eyes of the teacher as well as the students themselves. Nevertheless, this experience fulfilled its primary purpose, as it prompted important reflections on the *process* in which the class had engaged, which in turn enabled the students to identify important strategies they would need to develop in order to be more successful in future inquiries. Given the nature and length of this third section of the "Math Connections B" course, our narrative of it is not as detailed as that of the previous two segments but instead focuses on introducing learning experiences and reading practices not featured in the previous sections of the narrative.

Segment 1: Introducing the Concept of Math Connections and the School Without Walls Values About Learning

Judi began the course by prompting students to identify their own perceptions and attitudes about mathematics and mathematics instruction. Day 1 was devoted almost entirely to completing a mathematics questionnaire (see Figure 5.1).

Judi's expectation was that in the process of responding to the questionnaire, students would begin to raise questions about mathematics and mathematics instruction. The homework for that first day was to write a journal entry in response to the following prompt: "Look around you and identify at least one thing that can somehow be related to mathematics and tell how it can be related. It should be something in which you hadn't noticed the connection before or something you have been curious about." (*Both of the experiences described in this paragraph involved not only writing but also reading—the questions and the prompt; in the context of the overall instructional activity, these reading events were identified as examples of reading to generate an immediate written response*.)

On Day 2, the class watched a video that showed connections between mathematics and the real world ("The Wheel of Fortune," from James Burke's "Connections" series). Judi had students write down every implied reference to mathematics they could find so that they could remember enough about the connection to adequately explain it to others. (*Even if in this experience the text was not a written text, we still considered this a case of reading with a focus to extract specific information—in this case, finding examples of connections between math and the*

Figure 5.1. Mathematics questionnaire.

NAME:

MATHEMATICS QUESTIONNAIRE

1. Give two (or more) examples of activities which you consider characteristic of mathematics. Explain why they are characteristic.
2. Give two (or more) examples of worthwhile math activities to do in school. Explain why they are worthwhile.
3. If you could change any one thing about math class (which you have had in the past) what would it be? How would you change it?
4. Think of a good mathematician. What makes her/him a good mathematician?
5. Think of a good mathematics teacher. What makes her/him a good mathematics teacher?
6. Think of a good mathematics student. What makes her/him a good mathematics student?
7. How did you learn mathematics? What things helped you learn mathematics?
8. What is it you like about math? Do you enjoy doing mathematics?
9. What is it you don't like about math?
10. What would you like to do better as a result of your math education?

---

real world; note that here the teacher suggested a specific strategy for approaching this "reading"—i.e., taking notes for future reference.)

Day 3 began with the students reading aloud the journal entries on math connections they had written earlier for homework. A volunteer recorded a list of possible topics for investigation on the board as students read their journal entries and tried to make the connections more explicit, with the teacher's help. (*This is an example of a reading practice that was very typical of this class and that we have characterized as <u>reading a text representing individual thoughts to generate a shared text</u>; in this case, the "texts representing individual thoughts" were the students' journals, and the "shared text" produced was a list of possible topics of investigation the whole class could later examine and work with.*)

Van was the first to read:

> To know what it should consist of, the layout of the building and what should go where. The design of a building. It takes a lot of math to build and decide the structure of the building.

Shellie had noticed a different math connection:

> In the past I was never really curious about cars but recently I have been. I never thought about it before that it could be related to math. Take for instance the speedometer. When you travel 60 mph for 1 hour, you have gone 60 miles. Or, if you go 60 mph for 30 minutes, you have traveled 30 miles. I wouldn't think while I was driving that it could be related to mathematics.

Later, Melissa read a part of her entry:

> I've been curious about the writing of music. It has been bothering me for a long time. I found out last week that the writing of music is related to math. You have to count spaces, lines, and the number of beats.

When most students had read their journal entries and their ideas had been added to the growing list of potential math connections, Judi read aloud selected student responses to Questions 1 and 2 from the questionnaire, and these ideas were added to the list so that students would have input into both the content and the process of their learning. (*This is another example of the same reading practice—i.e., <u>reading a text representing individual thoughts to generate a shared text</u>—using different texts, i.e., selected responses to the questionnaires, which allowed the* *class to produce a shared list of ways to learn mathematics.*) Responses to these questions included the following: to do projects; to have fun, math is not just textbooks and homework, group activities; board activities and card games, sum of dice, playing for money, hockey can be indirectly characteristic of math, do by learning, not memorizing, to learn is to understand; puzzles; having sales, the most you'll spend and how much you'll get out of it, probability and graphing; individual projects and group activities; working on a computer and bingo; thinking, unanswered questions. The students reacted to this last response.

Jake: Judi, you wrote that one!
Judi: No, I didn't! Are you impressed? You should be!

Once the students' connections and perspectives had been shared publicly, Judi shared some examples of math connections that students might not have thought of, especially connections between mathematics and literature. She read aloud an excerpt from *The Phantom Tollbooth* (Juster, 1961) and invited students to think about whether the story was an example of using mathematics to understand literature or literature to understand mathematics. Although she had planned to read just a few pages of *How Much Is a Million?* (Schwartz, 1985), the class was drawn into its predictable structure and read along with Judi, in the tradition of shared reading! She also showed them a book on spherical geometry, *Here's Looking at Euclid (and not looking at Euclid)* (Petit, n.d.), written in comic-book style. Judi concluded her examples by showing the class a project completed by a former student. This student was a talented artist and had used her strength to connect to mathematics by illustrating a logic problem. Judi talked about the student and then showed the class the drawings she had created, hoping to demonstrate that they too could find a way into mathematics. She also wanted them to see that they were not being used as guinea pigs in what seemed a "weird" math class, as she had encouraged nontraditional approaches to learning mathematics in previous courses. (*All of the instances of reading described in this paragraph can be considered examples of pointing to a text to show an example of something, because in each of these cases the focus was not on understanding the content of the text per se but instead on showing the students examples of unusual pieces of literature involving mathematics; accordingly, in each case only selected pieces of the text itself were read or shown to illustrate various ways of making math connections that the teacher wanted students to become aware of.*)

The first homework assignment for that night was to bring in a magazine that the students themselves read so they could continue building a collective list of ideas about math connections. A second journal entry was also assigned: "React to what has been said and done so far; begin to identify the ideas which interest you most" (*another experience involving* <u>*reading to generate an immediate written response*</u>).

Day 4 began with a discussion of the RLM research project and the implications that participating in it had for students. As consent forms were distributed and read by the students, a more general discussion of the RLM Project and its potential effect on the class took place, prompted by one student's questions and concerns. (*We categorized the reading of these consent forms as an example of* <u>*reading critically and reflectively to make a decision that impacts your life*</u>, *because before signing these consent forms the students would want to fully understand the information contained in this text and what it might mean for them*). Judi assured the class a curriculum developed by "outsiders" would not be forced on them, and the consent form was then filled in by the students.

The class then continued its examination of connections between math and their world by breaking into small groups and looking for math connections in the magazines the students had brought in. In this activity, the students skimmed through the magazines looking for references to math as well as examples of how the magazines used math (*a more "typical" example of* <u>*reading with a focus to extract specific information*</u>).

Each group recorded its findings on a sheet of newsprint, and the posters thus created were shared by each group with the rest of the class along with some reflections on what they had found (*an example of* <u>*reading to support a presentation*</u>, *because here presenters read aloud or even simply pointed to selected sections of the posters they had created to focus the audience's attention on the relevant text segment*).

Segment 2: Deciding on a Project to Begin to Explore Math Connections

Up to this point, Judi had organized the class so as to offer demonstrations of math connections (examples of what math connections looked like) and experiences that engaged students in making math connections in their own lives (cf. Rowe & Harste, 1986). In doing so, she hoped students would begin to see that math could involve more than numbers. By Day 5, however, Judi began to shift the students' attention to making a decision about the focus and approach they would take in their first investigation of math connections. Hence, even though some of the activities looked the same as those used to introduce students to the concept of math connections (e.g., holding up examples of math connections and talking about them, reading students' journal entries, reading students' responses to the questionnaire), the purpose was quite different. And Judi explicitly marked this difference at the beginning of Day 5 by explaining to the class that she had a list of things the class could do to reach a decision about the focus of their joint inquiry.

When Judi asked the class what they wanted to do first to find a focus, several students suggested Judi share more of the examples in her box. "Any more groovy stories?" one boy wanted to know. She had not brought any more examples of literature, but she pulled out a copy of a suburban newspaper that contained the fall school bus schedule (*another example of _pointing to a text to show an example of something_*).

> *Judi:* Why are bus schedules math related?
> *Students:* Route—[you] have to make calculations to stay on route. How far you live from the route.
> *Judi:* What else makes it math related?
> *Students:* How many kids fit? How many buses the school district needs? Decisions about how far a kid lives to decide if you need to take a bus. What about safety on school buses?
> *Judi:* Any other parts of making up a bus schedule that are mathematical?
> *Students:* Need to consider gas mileage. How much to pay bus drivers? How many gallons of yellow paint to paint school buses.
> *Colin:* [to Judi] What else? You tell us some things. You keep asking what else but I thought you knew all these things and were just asking us.
> *Judi:* No.
> *Tim:* Judi learns with us.

After Judi held up several more examples, the students suggested she read their second journal entries (regarding what had been said and done in class so far) aloud without identifying the author so they could guess who had written the journal response. Judi had thought that reading the reflective journal entries aloud might give students some ideas about their next steps, and students were intrigued with whether they knew one another well enough yet to identify individuals' perspectives. (*Although on this occasion the teacher read aloud students' journal entries and responses to a questionnaire, as she had done earlier during Segment 1, we chose to code these experiences as _reading to convey meaning_*

rather than "reading a text representing individual thoughts to generate a shared text" because in this case no shared list was constructed, as students were only expected to hear how their peers had reacted to the class so far.)
Among the entries Judi read was Char's:

> It's really different. It's not math as I've experienced it. It's going to be a challenge. Right now because it's all so new I'm not sure what direction I'd like to move in.

Melissa had reconsidered her interest in music:

> My reaction to what has been said and done so far is that I didn't realize that there could be so many connections to mathematics. The speedometer on a car interests me most because of all the technical things that make it work and how it's related to math.

Judi followed this up by reading aloud selected responses to Questions 7 and 8 from the mathematics questionnaire, which led to a spontaneous discussion of why there was no textbook for this course. The students concluded that a textbook would be too limiting because someone would have already decided on the math connections to make, although one student noted that new students might need a math textbook if they were unfamiliar with this approach to learning.

When Judi finished reading the responses, she passed out copies of her notes for the day and called students' attention to the paragraph she had written under "homework."

> Look over these lists and begin to identify some common general ways math is being used, the kinds of questions it is answering. Also look at the things all of you said about quality activities in math, what helped, and what you like about math—and start writing down some ideas about what this class or you as an individual would find valuable experiences.

(We chose to characterize what the students were expected to do in this homework assignment as <u>reading to generate a reflective written response</u>—in contrast to "reading to generate an immediate response"—because responding to this prompt required students to look back at what they had done so far in class and try to make sense of those experiences.)
In the 2 days that followed, the class spent considerable time generating and expanding potential questions to explore in this first in-

vestigation. Although engaging in problem finding is rare in mathematics classes, Judi felt it crucial that the students do so in order to develop an appreciation for what is involved in defining worthwhile questions for inquiry and to learn some strategies for problem posing.

Day 6 began with some confusion over the homework; students felt it was similar to a previous journal entry, and Judi used this confusion to talk about the purpose of the homework assignment and to share the thinking she had done in response to her own assignment. Judi explained that she had found it hard to generate questions from the class list and so decided to walk them through the process she had used to generate questions related to bus schedules, which she had written down and duplicated for the students. As she read the different sets of questions, she emphasized her shift from questions with one-word answers (e.g., How many buses? How many kids?) to broader, deeper, more thought-provoking questions about the topic (e.g., Does the bus schedule impact the school day?); with each shift, Judi literally took a step and said, "And then I went *further*," using both her body and her voice to mark the difference in the scope of the questions. (*We considered the reading of this teacher-generated text a prototypical example of reading to demonstrate one's thinking*).

Judi then explained that they would be forming groups to generate questions from the lists because "my belief and the belief of the School Without Walls and the people who are here [Margie and Constance]—is that you learn best when you are raising your own questions and then answering or attempting to answer them." After some discussion of this point, Judi had students form their own groups on the basis of whom they felt comfortable working with but also made sure that at least one person in the group understood the task at hand.

Students worked in groups to generate questions based on the class list and the questions Judi had produced in her examples of bus scheduling and measurement. The last 10 minutes of class were spent having each group talk about its approach to the problem. For homework, students were then expected to take home the lists they had developed in their groups (the groups decided it would be good to photocopy all the lists) and continue thinking about the questions. The goal was to make their questions broader so they could look at them again as a group the next meeting. (*In the context of both small-group activities and follow-up homework described in this paragraph, this collection of texts was used by the students to expand their thinking about math connections and formulate questions worth exploring—a practice we have called reading a text to push something further.*)

Day 7 was a continuation of the process of generating broader questions. Judi began by asking several students to read what they had done for homework with the group lists, also inviting them to state questions when they had not done so. (*We consider this sharing to be another example of <u>reading a text representing individual thoughts to generate a shared text,</u> because the students' ideas continued to be added to the newsprint where math connections and questions worth pursuing were being recorded.*) Char's homework (see Figure 5.2) demonstrated that the questions the students had posed were indeed broader, bigger questions than the ones they took home with them, a point Judi made explicit after Char explained her thinking. Several other students shared their thinking about various topics (e.g., racing, buildings, knowledge) and

Figure 5.2. Char's process of generating questions, done for homework.

Measurement

Can we measure everything?

At first I said yes. I started to come up with idea after idea of things we do and can measure. To my surprise I came up with some I questioned.

+ feelings	+ pain
Love	Does one cut hurt more than the one yesterday
Hate	
Happiness	
Disappointment	

+ maturity	+ intelligence
Is one 16 year old "older" than another, if so how do you tell?	How do you measure who's smarter than who?

+Infinity

tangible and intangible

 ♦ Can all tangible things be measured?
 ♦ Can all intangible things be measured?

Just things

Tangible	*Intangible*
a yard stick	space distance?
my pen	Feelings
my house	person's self
my world	space "Does it go on forever?"

Judi confirmed that they had also engaged in the kind of thinking she had demonstrated the previous day.

When no new ideas were suggested, Judi asked the students to look back at the questions they had generated, but this time with the goal of identifying a topic that intrigued them all so they could begin to make a decision about where to go next. (*This kind of reading was quite different from that in the previous activity, even if the same texts were used; in this case, the students read the list the class had generated <u>to make a decision that would impact their life</u>—namely, what the focus of the next section of the course would be.*) Various ideas about how to proceed were discussed, but because none was preferred over others, Judi set out her plan for engaging as a class in a brief project (1 week) before committing to a bigger project. She emphasized that this would be an experiment in exploring a question and working in small groups, so they could reflect on what happened before moving on to another topic. The class agreed and decided to vote on the topic for such a project. The topic of racing won and, as class time ran out, Judi reminded the students that they were to come to the next class meeting with all the racing-related ideas they could think of and that the topic of racing need not be limited to car racing only.

Segment 3: Carrying Out the "Racing" Project

In order to help the students get started with their inquiry on racing, on Day 8 Judi handed out a plan she had developed to define the scope and schedule for this first project and asked students to read it before she briefly commented on it (*an activity involving <u>reading to convey meaning</u>*).

The class then immediately moved to the first activity listed in this plan: categorizing the questions on racing that each student had been asked to develop for homework. Judi invited the students to share their thinking, and several students did so by reading aloud what they had written for homework, while Judi recorded on newsprint questions about racing that students had generated (*another example of <u>reading a text representing individual thoughts to generate a shared text</u>*). In some cases, Judi engaged students in a dialogue about their questions to help them make their questions explicit. The questions students shared dealt with issues such as profit-making in horse racing and the mathematics of betting, the influence that engine size might have on an auto race, and factors that might affect the outcome of a race, whether the race involved Olympic runners or motorcycles.

As part of this sharing, students were encouraged to talk about the process they had followed in generating their questions (*another example of reading to demonstrate one's thinking*). Judi also contributed to this discussion by once again making her own thinking process public to demonstrate for the students the process of articulating broad questions and subquestions. Explaining how she had decided to read every racing-related newspaper item for 3 days, she held up an article about the controversy over the design of the boats entered in the America's Cup sailing race, wondering aloud if the mathematical differences between various designs might affect the racing speed.

At this point, one of the students asked Judi if they were on the right track. This gave Judi an opportunity to read her plan for the project aloud once again, this time so that the class could take stock of how far they had progressed and decide whether they wanted to suggest any modifications (*an example of reading to get feedback*). As the class discussed how much they had accomplished in relation to Judi's proposed list of activities, it became apparent that they had not gotten very far down the list and still needed to categorize their questions and form inquiry groups around specific questions before their work could proceed.

With 5 minutes remaining in the period, the students were eager to break into groups. However, Judi wanted to make sure that they had considered different ways of categorizing their questions before doing so. After some discussion of this issue, the class decided to categorize the questions generated so far in terms of "kind of racing"—such as car, motorcycle, horse, and human racing—and to form groups around these categories.

The lesson concluded with an assignment that directed students to complete the next several items on Judi's written plan—choose a category to explore, make a written list of possible resources, have an idea for a question to explore that related to a specific kind of racing, and look at Judi's list to make any necessary changes. (*Completing this assignment required students to look at Judi's plan in yet another way, as in this case they read it to understand and follow directions.*)

During the next couple of class meetings, the students compiled a list of possible resources for their inquiry, and then each group discussed the questions to focus on and planned the next research steps. Keeping minutes of these group meetings and reviewing such minutes at the beginning of the next meeting were instrumental in keeping the groups focused. (*Reviewing both lists and minutes at the beginning of a group session are examples of reading to set the stage for the next activity.*)

At this point, each small group went to the local public library in order to find materials that could help them address their questions. Locating these materials by itself posed something of a challenge and required two quite specialized ways of reading:

1. Looking through the card catalogue to find appropriate books (*another example of <u>reading with a focus to extract specific information</u>*).
2. Skimming through the books thus identified, as well as others students noticed in the same section, to see if they might have relevant information and be worth checking out (*an example of <u>skimming a text to make a decision</u>—in this case, about what books were worth reading*).

Before proceeding further, the teacher thought it would be important for the class to reflect on their experience with the inquiry thus far. To support this reflection, Judi engaged the class in the creation of a "What did I learn?" list—an activity typical of her classes. Judi began by asking for everyone's attention and for everyone to be thinking; she then invited those students most familiar with this practice to explain it to new students:

Judi: What goes on a "What did I learn?" list?
Tim: What you discovered about yourself and what you discovered about other people.
Jolea: Personal insights.
Judi: Okay, what other kinds of things go on a "What did I learn?" list?
Jolea: Accomplishments.
Tim: Umm—your thoughts. Your thoughts on your approach.
Jolea: Just not what you learned but how you think you got there. [Tim agreed.]
Judi: When we as a class do a "What did I learn?" list, sometimes what I learned might be very personal to me, in other words, I might have learned it even if the rest of the group didn't. Does it still go on the list?

Jolea responded that it did and Judi confirmed her answer, explaining that everything went on the list and that the "I" meant individuals as well as the collective.

After briefly reviewing what had gone on in the course so far, Judi moved to a piece of newsprint she had taped to the blackboard so that she could record all these individual contributions for future reference. (*Recording the students' statements on newsprint for all to see and read made it more likely that they would not be forgotten. Throughout the discussion that followed, the text on newsprint also served as a site for valuing students' perspectives and experiences, as reading these statements was a way to take note of the ideas offered and register them in the collective memory of the class. We decided to name this rather unusual reading practice <u>reading reflective statements written on newsprint to value the meaning.</u>*) Judi then opened the floor to students' comments:

> *Jolea:* When we first started out, you know, saying what goes with math and did all those things where we were supposed to think how math relates to certain things, I was really—I didn't understand that until we started like one thing and we stuck to one thing. Like the day we did the magazines. That was the first day I saw light. So I guess it was easier to deal with something that was right there and be able to see it. Actually being able to relate to it—I don't know. But then how easy it came! It came really easy after that. I mean it just spilled right out. It was amazing.
>
> *Judi:* So maybe one of the things that you've learned is sometimes if you have concrete—"concrete" meaning "real"—examples, it's easier to understand?

Jolea nodded in agreement as Judi wrote on the newsprint, "Sometimes concrete examples help me to understand vague concepts."

> *Judi:* I just put some words in your mouth here. [Judi reads aloud what she has just written.] Is that [it]?
>
> *Jolea:* Yeah.

Later, Gina, a first-year student, offered her thoughts.

> *Gina:* How different it is to find ways to connect math—to connect things to math than it is doing it. Like if I was to take basic [math] I would be doing math problems. It's different from doing math problems. Is that anything you want?
>
> *Judi:* You've learned how it's different—
>
> *Gina:* —from basic math
>
> *Tim:* Math isn't always computing and figuring and solving.
>
> *Shellie:* No, I don't think it's that. Because she said something about making the math connections with other stuff.

Judi: Yeah. Gina, could you say it again and ... try?

Gina: The difference ... how it is different from connecting things to math—is how it is different from doing math, actually adding and subtracting and multiplying and other stuff.

Judi wrote Gina's statement on newsprint and this process continued for the remainder of the class period and was then further updated after the group presentations so as to produce the "What did I learn?" list reproduced in Figure 5.3.

After this reflection, the students negotiated more time to complete their research, and Judi also allotted more class time to the small groups so they could prepare their presentations on what they had learned about racing.

The process of planning presentations was further supported by a class discussion in which Judi and the students generated and revised a written list of criteria (see Figure 5.4) that the students themselves would have to use to evaluate each of their peers' presentation (*an example of reading to revise a text*).

Several class periods were then devoted to the small-group presentations. Though presentations may call to mind an image of a formal

Figure 5.3. "What did I learn?" list compiled on newsprint.

What did I learn?

- sometimes concrete examples help me to understand vague concepts (Jolea)
- math isn't just always #s [numbers] (Shellie)
- don't like racing as much as I thought I did—cuz it's educational (Shellie)
- connecting things to math is different from "doing" math (adding, subtracting, etc.) (Gina)
- how math has to do with everyday life (Denise)
- one question leads to many questions (which need to be answered first) (Kathleen)
- math is reflected in every aspect of life (can't get away from it) (Jolea)
- you may not find all the answers (info) in one [place]—have to look in many (Colin)
- Tim isn't very dependable (Melissa)
- more than one way to solve a question (not just be frustrated & quiet) (Lori)
- it's hard to work with the flu (Craig)
- math is very boring no matter what kind you take (Jake)
- "easier" to work alone after class discussions (Jolea)
- advantage to working in "responsible" group—get things done faster (Gina)
- we will think about math class if there is a connection to something else in our life (Judi)
- sometimes have to re-think the question being asked to find/use information available (Margie)
- sometimes we have to collect info & integrate the ideas (Mark)

Figure 5.4. Class-generated criteria for group presentations.

Quality of work
- Did they answer the questions they were looking for clearly?
- State their goal (question, objective) [and] tell us what they found, what they learned from analyzing the info, and what you still need to learn.

Presentation—How Presented
- Creativity
- Awareness of topic—give some evidence you know what you're talking about.
- Speaking clearly, loudly, physical presentation of self (body language)

Personal Gain—Having Fun
- Could you do it alone?
- Would you do the same topic again?
- What would you do differently?

Additional Comments

transmission of information from expert to novice, presentations in Judi's classes were always interactive, with everyone actively working to make sense of the information. The audience was always expected to ask questions and challenge the information, and the presenters were expected to defend their statements and explain what they knew. Anyone who could help with the explanation was always expected to do so. In this way, presentations were treated as generative learning experiences rather than as a test.

During these presentations, instances of reading could be observed on many occasions: The presenters often pointed to figures and diagrams they had created or read from notes they had taken, and the audience tried to make sense of the visual prompts offered to them. (*In these cases, we categorized the use of texts made by the presenters as reading to make a presentation, whereas we considered the reading done by the audience—given the presenters' use of visual supports—an example of reading to make sense of graphic/visual texts.*)

As a result of the evaluations the student–audience completed for each presenter, as well as the critical reflection that followed these presentations, neither the teacher nor the students were very satisfied with the outcomes of their inquiry on racing. These reflections made it possible for Judi and the class to plan experiences for the next part of the course that would address these problems and thus offer the students the information and strategies they would need to make future inquiries successful.

Finally, because the first quarter of the semester was coming to a close, marking the week devoted to a school-wide evaluation of students' progress during that 10-week period, Judi devoted class time to a set of activities she typically used to help students make sense of course experiences, evaluate their growth during this quarter, and set the stage for course experiences to follow. As was her practice, Judi began by inviting the students to compose a group letter to their parents that would explain what they accomplished during the course thus far.

To prepare for this activity, Judi first engaged the students in a "Walk Down Memory Lane," suggesting that they look at the trace of their journey recorded on the newsprint hanging all around the room on the walls, and then try to recall and reflect on the most salient of the experiences in which the class had participated. (*In this case, reading the newsprint can be considered an example of reading to set the stage for the next activity.*)

The process of writing the letter for the parents was facilitated by a student, Van, following an approach decided upon by the class as a whole. Each student first wrote an individual letter and read aloud to the rest of the class his or her favorite parts, which Van recorded on a piece of newsprint labeled "suggestions." Once all the suggestions were listed, students began to propose sentences for the actual letter, and this process of composing and revising continued until the letter was completed. (*The reading involved in composing this letter provides another example of reading individual thoughts to create a shared text, followed by reading to revise a text.*)

While the class engaged in this activity, Judi met individually with students to discuss their progress on those items from the school-wide evaluation form that the class had selected as appropriate items to be evaluated on in the 10-week period just concluded. (*Because the evaluation conferences had an important effect on students' academic standing, here students read the school-wide evaluation form critically and reflectively to make a decision that would impact their life.*)

Discussion

Although it is difficult to convey the complexity of such a dynamic and interactive classroom and at the same time provide an overview of the unfolding instruction, we hope the previous narrative has succeeded in both offering an image of the multiple ways that reading was part of this inquiry-oriented mathematics classroom and describing the distinctive nature of this learning environment. This narrative, along with those featuring other parts of the "Math Connections B" course in previous chapters, clearly challenges both the narrow view of reading mathematics found in most of the literature on this topic and our own initial conception of "reading to learn mathematics," and invites mathematics educators to expand their understanding of what could count as "reading" in an inquiry-oriented mathematics class. More specifically, our analysis of this instructional experience demonstrates the wide variety of reading practices students engaged in as participants in this classroom, as well as the need for an expanded definition of "text" in order to explain why some activities were considered "reading events." In what follows, we discuss each of these two points in greater detail before exploring the contribution a broader perspective on reading and text might make to understanding and tapping the potential of reading in mathematics instruction.

Varieties of Reading Practices in "Math Connections B"

As the narrative presented in the previous section demonstrates, we had to adopt a much broader interpretation of "reading" to fully understand the potential of integrating reading in mathematics instruction. Hence, the reading practices identified in our commentary went beyond our original focus on transactional strategies in an attempt to capture the way reading was actually used in the "Math Connections B" course. Because this initial focus had emphasized generative and reflective reading, we had anticipated neither the amount nor the variety and complexity of the reading practices in an inquiry-oriented mathematics classroom. Only when we began to identify a unit of analysis did we realize that our first problem was to locate reading in the narrative of instruction in "Math Connections B." Rather than restrict our definition of reading to "reading rich mathematical texts generatively," we looked at each instructional use of written language in relation to the course goals (broadening students' conceptions of mathematics and learning how to learn). For example, reading and responding to journal prompts and questionnaires was counted as reading, even though this kind of reading was largely instrumental—a means to an end; in the same vein, reading various texts aloud was included, as was the reading of student- and class-generated notes. As these examples suggest, it quickly became apparent that we could not look at reading separate from writing, talking, and other modes of communication. As a result of this approach, we began to see how the values central to Judi's teaching were expressed through reading experiences.

As the analysis proceeded, it became clear that reading was so bound up with the social and intellectual life of this classroom that only 2 of the 42 instructional events we identified in the "Math Connections B" course had no reading component. The cases of instructional events that had no reading components are significant for several reasons. First, they show that the 23 ways of reading identified in Figure 5.5 represented ordinary practice in this classroom. Second, these cases point to the limitations of thinking about reading only in terms of strategies students use to make sense of written texts and the need to reconceptualize so-called instrumental uses of texts in classrooms as social practices, a point we return to later in this chapter. As the narrative clearly shows, the reading practices were not done in addition to or as a preliminary to learning and doing mathematics; rather, ways of reading constituted ways to learn and do mathematics in this class. As the course unfolded, Judi and the students negotiated a particular image of what it meant to learn and do mathematics in this classroom, and in almost every case this was accomplished through some kind of reading experience. It is this interrelationship of reading and mathematics, not the sheer number of reading practices alone, that shows how central reading was in this inquiry-oriented mathematics class.

Once we adopted this new conceptual framework for reading, the embedded nature of reading in this mathematics class became visible. This is evident in the segments of the "Math Connections B" course we chose to portray, which allowed us to introduce—in the context of use—18 of the 23 different reading practices we identified. A complete list of these reading practices has been reproduced in Figure 5.5, organized in five broad categories that highlight the major ways reading was used to do and learn mathematics by members of the classroom community: reading to make public; reading to comprehend; reading to get an example; reading to generate something new; and reading to remember. In what follows, we examine the nature and significance of each of these major categories further, as we believe that, taken together, they can expand mathematics teachers' repertoire of ways to integrate reading into mathematics instruction. (For a more detailed description of each of the 23 reading practices and their occurrence throughout the entire "Math Connections B" course, see Siegel & Fonzi, 1995).

Category 1: Reading to Make Public

The reading practices grouped under this heading all shared the characteristic of reading a text to make meanings, thoughts, or information public. Usually, this meant reading aloud, though there were

Figure 5.5. Categories of reading practices in an inquiry-oriented mathematics classroom.

Category 1: Reading to make public
a. Reading to convey meaning
b. Reading to value students' meanings
c. Reading to get feedback
d. Reading to make a presentation
e. Reading to demonstrate one's thinking
Category 2: Reading to comprehend
a. Reading to understand and follow directions
b. Reading the teacher's comments to get the message
c. Reading with a focus to extract specific information
d. Skimming to make a decision
e. Reading critically and reflectively to make a decision that impacts your life
f. Reading generatively to make sense of text
g. Reading to make sense of graphic/visual text
Category 3: Reading to get an example
a. Pointing to a text to show an example of something
b. Reading a text to learn how to do something the text does
Category 4: Reading to generate something new
a. Reading to generate an immediate response
b. Reading to generate a reflective written response
c. Reading to revise a text
d. Reading a text representing individuals' thoughts to generate a shared text
e. Reading to push something further
f. Reading to spark an idea
g. Reading to set the stage for the next activity
Category 5: Reading to remember
a. Reading to copy from the board
b. Reading reflective statements written on newsprint to value the meanings

a few reading components in which that was not the case. In addition, "reading" could mean word-for-word reading of the text, selective reading in which the text was more "talked through" than read, or pointing to and explaining a text. In each case, however, the listener's role was never meant to be passive; rather, all texts were treated as potentials for which students had to actively construct meaning, which meant that raising questions about these texts was not only accepted but also expected and encouraged.

What differentiates the various reading practices identified within this group from one another is the purpose for making a particular text public. As the narrative shows, these purposes were not separate from the ongoing instructional activity of which reading was a part but, instead, flowed from those activities such that reading became the very means through which the particular activity was enacted. Of the reading components that fell into this category, we have identified examples that focused on the following:

- *Conveying the ideas written by a student or the teacher to others*—here a text was read aloud simply so the ideas would be made public and taken in, as when Judi read students' journal entries aloud so all could hear the ideas.
- *Valuing students' meanings*—here student-generated texts were read aloud not only to convey students' meanings but to place value on the ideas or experiences students had recorded, as when Judi read aloud selections from the students' written reflections on the racing project that exemplified emergent key themes so that students would reflect on the significance of their ideas and those of their peers.
- *Getting feedback on one's ideas*—here the text was read aloud expressly to invite feedback, as when Judi read her plan for the "Racing" project aloud so that students would take stock of their progress and plan their next steps.
- *Making a formal presentation*—here texts were read, talked through, pointed at, and elaborated on so as to share what had been learned and extend it through further questions and discussions, as when students presented what they had learned about the connections between math and racing at the end of the "Racing" project.
- *Demonstrating one's thinking process*—here students or the teacher read or talked their way through a text to make their thinking process public, as when Judi demonstrated how she had read various newspaper articles to generate questions for the "Racing" project.

As this list suggests, "reading to make public" played a variety of important roles in the "Math Connections B" course, most of which seemed to contribute to the creation of a community in which participants made their thinking public, listened to one another, engaged in discussion and debate over ideas, and explicitly valued students' voices and perspectives. Although we do not want to suggest that all these reading practices are unique to inquiry-oriented mathematics classrooms or even to schools, we think the frequency of these practices in the "Math Connections B" class (30 of the 126 reading events identified in this semester-long instructional experience were categorized as "reading to make public") and the absence of oral reading in most traditional-content-area classrooms (Alvermann & Moore, 1991) suggests that something different was happening here. Our sense of what was different is that reading was embedded in social practices associated with the construction and negotiation of meetings and forms of life within a community of inquirers. Given the emphasis Judi placed on taking up the practices of such a community, it is not surprising that social practices such as discussing future directions for a class to take or learning how to be a member of a community by listening to and valuing students' ideas were common in this classroom.

Category 2: Reading to Comprehend

The reading practices grouped under this broad category all focused on understanding a text. Though we took it for granted that all reading practices we identified required some sort of comprehension of the text read, comprehension was the express focus of the reading practices in this category. As with the presentations in the category above, comprehension was not thought of as "mining" (Pimm, 1987) the text—a passive, text-bound act involving the transfer of meaning from text to reader. Instead, comprehension was conceptualized in relation to the ongoing instruction activity; at times, this meant understanding directions so they could be followed, searching a text for particular information, skimming to decide whether to read further, or generating personal meanings, connections, and questions to be discussed with others. This meant that in some cases class members were expected to share an interpretation of a particular text, whereas in others personal interpretations were the starting point for negotiating a shared interpretation.

The reading practices in this category can thus be distinguished from one another by the nature of the interpretive work required to accomplish the activity the text was part of. More specifically, in this group we identified examples in which:

- *The text* (usually produced by the teacher) *was read to understand and follow directions*—as in the case of written homework assignments Judi prepared.
- *A text was read with a focus on extracting specific information*—as when students approached a text knowing what they were looking for rather than in an exploratory, generative way.
- *Several texts were skimmed to decide whether to further pursue their reading or to make a decision of some sort*—as when looking through books that were potentially related to their "Racing" project in order to decide which ones were worth checking out of the library.

- *A text was read very carefully when students had to use the information it could provide in order to make an important decision*—as when they had to decide whether to sign the consent form that would involve them in the research project, because in this case they needed not only to understand the information conveyed by such a text but also to critically reflect on the implications that text could have for them.
- *A complex text was read in a generative mode* (often using one of the transactional reading strategies discussed in Chapter 4) to find potential connections with or generate ideas about a topic/problem the class was working on—a reading practice closely related to the "generative reading of rich math texts" discussed in Chapter 4.

In addition, we found it helpful to distinguish cases in which *the needed information was provided by nonverbal texts* (such as tables, figures, or diagrams), because graphic and visual texts often require a kind of reading that is nonlinear and frequently mediated by the surrounding discourse or the array of texts that may be part of the instructional activity (e.g. Curcio, 1987; Curcio & Artzt, 1998).

The reading practices identified within this category make it clear that "reading to comprehend" is not as straightforward and unproblematic as many mathematics teachers might think; rather, it may involve quite different ways of approaching the text and quite different outcomes, depending on the nature of the text read and the ongoing activity. As with the "reading to make public" category, we do not want to suggest that the reading practices categorized as "reading to comprehend" are unique either to inquiry-oriented mathematics classrooms or to schools, as most of them (e.g., reading directions, searching for particular information, reading carefully to make a decision) are common to everyday life in and out of school. However, when we notice how they are bound up with social practices involved in doing inquiry that they seem to take on new significance.

Category 3: Reading to Get an Example

This category highlights a kind of reading in which the focus is *not* on understanding the text on its own terms but rather on using it as an illustration of something, as when Judi read aloud an excerpt from a novel to show students a connection between mathematics and literature, or as a demonstration for how to do something, as when students read several theorems in a mathematics textbook to see how theorems were written in the "Analog & Analytic" vignette. In each of these cases the text was read very selectively—sometimes even just holding up or pointing to the text, as Judi did when introducing the various examples of math connections she had collected! Although the texts read in this way were clearly selected because of their relevance to the topic or problem at hand, the focus was either on the text as a whole (e.g., this book is an example of a math/literature connection) or on the form of the text (e.g., this is how to write a theorem) rather than on engaging with the text in the manner its author may have expected. Thus the critical dimension of these reading practices was their relation to the task the students were about to undertake, yet with the expectation that the text served as a resource for understanding rather than as a model to be copied.

Category 4: Reading to Generate Something New

The reading practices in this category all involved reading to get somewhere else; that is, it was assumed that students needed to understand the text but that their understanding served as a means to an end rather than as an end in itself. Examples within this group presented interesting variation with regard to what was produced—an immediate response, a revised text, a shared list of ideas—and the kind of thinking it inspired—being prompted to think about something in a new way, getting an idea about how to proceed, building on and negotiating with others to identify new possibilities or frame new questions. More specifically, we identified cases when a text was read to:

- *To generate a written response*—as when students were asked to respond individually to a questionnaire or journal prompt, whether that required reflection on or synthesis of prior experiences, or invoked a more spontaneous response about a new topic or idea.
- *To revise a text itself in the course of the composing process*—as when students read the list of sentences they themselves had suggested in the process of composing a joint letter to parents about the math connections course or when students wrote and revised a theorem.
- *To create a shared text out of the written contributions of individual students, which were read aloud and negotiated further by the teacher and the class*—as when Judi read aloud students' journal entries regarding math connections they had noticed, out of which a shared list of such connections was created, or when students shared their broad questions for investigating the mathematics of racing and these were recorded on the board and further developed by Judi and the class.

- *To help the students move further in their thinking about a certain topic or problem*—as when students read the initial set of questions their peers and Judi had generated to form even broader questions early in the "Racing" project.
- *To spark an idea or set the stage for another activity*—as when students read a list of area formulas to get an idea of how to begin developing a theorem about two figures that have the same area, or when students reviewed minutes from a previous small-group meeting to plan the next steps in their study of math connections to racing.

Of all the categories presented thus far, the reading practices within this category seem unique to an inquiry-oriented mathematics classroom because generating ideas worth pursuing is critical to framing problems and raising questions (Brown & Walter, 1990). In this classroom, the practice of reading to "generate something new" also reflected Judi's beliefs about learning and teaching as well as her growing appreciation of the transactional notion of reading as exploration. So, although none of the reading practices identified within this group involved the "generative reading of rich math texts" as we had originally conceived it, the reading events that occurred in the first three segments of the "Math Connections B" course were generative of new connections, questions, understandings, and perspectives.

Category 5: Reading to Remember

Although it may at first seem obvious to point out the connection between reading and remembering in content-area classrooms, our analysis suggests that this connection may play out quite differently in inquiry-oriented mathematics classrooms than in traditional ones. In traditional math classrooms, it is often assumed that the central purpose of reading is to transmit information so that students can remember and later display what they have "learned" on tests; this is exemplified by the practice of copying the teacher's notes from the board—so common that the response is almost automatic when the teacher signals the onset of this activity by calling out, "Notes!" (cf. Lemke, 1990). In contrast, we observed only one example of this kind of reading in the "Math Connections B" class when, toward the end of the course, students were asked to copy some information written on the board onto their evaluation forms. Instead, reading to remember took a different form and served a different purpose in this class. Two reading events that recurred in Judi's classes—taking a "Walk Down Memory Lane" and creating "What did I learn?" lists—were unique to

Judi's teaching and emblematic of her belief that learning how to learn requires occasions in which learners can review and make sense of their experiences with an eye toward future learning and inquiry. Hence, reading the newsprint record of students' insights and concerns, which remained posted on the classroom walls throughout the course, played a very important role in this mathematics class because it served not only as a memory aid, but also as a concrete demonstration of the value Judi placed on students' voices and reflections.

To summarize thus far, our examination of reading in the "Math Connections B" course shows that reading was embedded in nearly every aspect of classroom activity and was richly varied. Ironically, the very embeddedness of reading in this class rendered it somewhat invisible, given our initial focus on strategies for making sense of text. Throughout our discussion of the reading practices identified in the "Math Connections B" course, we have proposed that this variety is related to the fact that teaching and learning in this mathematics classroom were conceptualized as inquiry and, thus, students participated in instructional activities designed to create a community of inquirers.

Rethinking the Definition of Text in Mathematics Classes

Implicit in the reading experiences described in the previous narrative and discussed above is evidence that multiple kinds of texts were used throughout the "Math Connections B" course (see Figure 5.6 for a comprehensive list). This great variety suggested the need to rethink our understanding of the kind of texts that are relevant to teaching and learning mathematics and in so doing reconsider our initial definition of "rich" mathematical texts. We quickly realized that neither textbooks nor "rich" mathematical texts alone were enough to support the development of a learning community or students' engagement in mathematical inquiries. We noticed, for example, that of the 40 kinds of texts that were used in this class, 22 were generated by either students, the teacher, small groups, or the class as a whole. These community-generated texts seemed especially important as they provided participants with multiple opportunities to publicly negotiate what it meant to learn and do mathematics in this classroom.

We also noticed that neither "rich" mathematical texts (e.g., cartoons, essays, stories and novels, comic books) nor textbooks were used in typical ways. On numerous occasions throughout the course, but

Figure 5.6. Texts used in "Math Connections B."

- Teacher-generated questionnaire
- Teacher-generated journal prompts
- Videos
- Student-generated notes
- Teacher-generated notes
- Class-generated lists
- Children's literature incorporating mathematics
- Student-generated drawings and graphic representations
- Cartoons
- Mathematical comic book
- Written plan for proposed commercial business
- Research consent letter
- Magazines (general)
- Student-generated posters
- Students' written responses to journal prompts
- Students' written responses to questionnaire
- Teacher-generated questions
- Student-generated questions and idea wheels
- Small-group-generated notes
- Pamphlet from public library
- Card catalogue at public library
- Library books (including reference books) on aspects of racing
- Magazine articles on aspects of racing
- Teacher-generated plan for inquiry
- Student- and teacher-generated form for evaluating presentations
- Student- and small-group-generated essays, theorems, and stories
- Teacher-generated diagrams and graphs
- Teacher-generated lists
- Newspaper articles
- Professionally prepared charts
- School Without Walls evaluation form
- Student-generated letters (to parents, guest speakers)
- Essays on aspects of mathematical connections
- Student-generated conceptual maps
- Teacher-prepared list of formulas for computing area of various geometric figures
- Ruler
- Mathematics textbooks
- Teacher-prepared handout containing excerpts on historical aspects of the Pythagorean Theorem
- Directions for paper folding and making origami ornaments
- Student-produced demonstration showing how two figures had the same area

primarily in the first 2 weeks, many examples of what we had called "rich" mathematical texts were held up, looked at, pointed to, and talked about to show how many different math connections were possible. Only when students identified their need to learn strategies for sharing information with peers were a series of essays on mathematical connections read in the ways we had initially associated with a generative approach to reading mathematics (as illustrated in the "Math & War" vignette reported in Chapter 4). Similarly, mathematics textbooks were not absent in this course but played a specialized role—such as demonstrating how to write a theorem or providing a springboard for generating "thinking questions" that individual students might choose to research.

Furthermore, the list of texts reported in Figure 5.6 includes several texts prepared for purposes unrelated to mathematics instruction. General-interest magazines, a plan for a proposed commercial business, commercially prepared charts on engines, newspaper articles, resources available at the public library, and directions for making origami ornaments all became relevant texts because Judi wanted to show students how mathematics was already part of their worlds and intimately connected to everyday life. The texts that fell into this category suggest that no text is a "mathematical" text in and of itself but becomes so by virtue of its relevance to the activities that constitute learning and doing mathematics in a particular classroom.

Our analysis of reading practices in an inquiry-oriented mathematics class also indicated a need for a broader definition of text than is usually found in the literature on reading in the content areas or even the one that framed our analysis of reading practices (any symbolic representation that had the potential to be interpreted). For example, at two points in the course, students watched a video; in the first case, they wrote down examples of math connections they noticed, and in the second, they recorded various approaches to doing mathematics they had previously read about. Although videos do not fall within the common definition of *text*, we nonetheless regarded them as such because in this classroom students made sense of them using a strategy employed when reading written texts. The other case in which we extended our definition of *text* beyond its initial boundaries was when students worked in groups to develop a theorem about two figures that had the same area (see the "Analog & Analytic" narrative included in Chapter 1). Students had been asked to prove their theorem using both analog and analytic approaches, and one group not only used a variety of diagrams but cut pieces of cardboard to fit the dimensions of one figure (a rectangle) and placed these pieces over the other figure (a square) to show that their two figures did indeed have the same area. Because reading this demonstration was critical to the development of an analog proof of their theorem, we chose to treat this demonstration as a text to be interpreted. These decisions resonate with a social-practice perspective on reading, which suggests the need to examine how texts are defined by the community of practice rather than by a definition of text adopted and privileged a priori. The conclusion we draw from the wide range of texts used in "Math Connections B" and the varied ways in which they were incorporated into classroom learning is that both our initial definition of "rich" as texts representing the humanistic dimensions of mathematics and even the broader definition we used to analyze the reading practices were too narrow. There is nothing inherent in a particular text that makes it "rich" for mathematics learning; therefore it is too limiting to decide what texts might be "rich" with learning potential without knowing how mathematics and mathematics learning are practiced within a particular setting.

Finally, we would like to highlight the finding that many instructional events in the "Math Connections B" course involved reading of multiple texts and, moreover, that instructional events were often linked to one another by these texts. A good example can be found in the early part of the course described in Segment 1 when Judi initiated the course by creating texts (e.g., mathematics questionnaire, journal prompt) that elicited students' individual responses; those responses were later read aloud, resulting in the construction of a shared text (e.g., list of math connections and approaches to learning mathematics). Several class sessions later, after students had seen more examples of math connections and searched for their own math connections in magazines, Judi again prepared a journal prompt that asked students to reflect on all that had been said and done thus far. These too were read aloud so all could hear how students were responding to the conceptions of mathematics and learning mathematics they were experiencing in this class. In this case, not only were written and oral texts treated as texts; previous instructional activities also became "texts" to be read and reflected upon. Researchers working from a social-practice perspective on reading have used the concept of intertextuality to show that juxtaposing texts within and across instructional events in the ways described above is a means through which a particular set of classroom beliefs, or ideology, is constructed (Bloome & Egan-Robertson, 1993; Brilliant-Mills, 1994; Green & Meyer, 1991). This concept offers a way to interpret the significance of linkages among written, oral, and visual texts in the "Math Connections B" class, as it suggests that these connections contributed to construction of a community in which doing and learning mathematics meant becoming inquirers.

Summary and Conclusions

The findings in this chapter present a picture of integrating reading in mathematics instruction very different from the one we had initially proposed. Our analysis makes visible the wide range of reading practices and texts used and shows how they were integral rather than supplemental to teaching and learning mathematics in this classroom. Noticing these different kinds of reading and texts is important for several reasons. First, it points to the many roles reading can play in mathematics instruction and thus offers teachers a broader view of how reading can be incorporated into their teaching along with specific practices to add to their instructional repertoire. But even more important than identifying the range of texts and reading is the finding that these practices contributed to a particular understanding of what it meant to do and learn mathematics in this class, one that required a set of social norms and values that would sustain a community engaged in open-ended learning experiences such as inquiry. These goals were not invisible in Judi's class, as she indicated on many occasions. What is striking, however, is the extent to which those goals were accomplished through reading, writing, talking, and other text-related interactions. As noted earlier, the reading practices grouped under the categories "reading to make public" and "reading to generate something new" seemed especially good examples of reading practices through which a community of practice was developed. In short, the reading practices identified in this classroom differed greatly from those observed in more procedurally oriented mathematics classes, and this difference reflects the fact that in this classroom the possibility of producing knowledge was taken seriously, suggesting a different ideology at work.

The idea that students were reading, writing, and talking their way into mathematical inquiry may not be how most mathematics teachers would describe the events presented in the narrative; from their perspective, what students were doing may not have been reading, writing, or talking but rather filling out questionnaires, watching videos, seeing examples of math connections, making posters, formulating questions, investigating those questions, making presentations, and so on. And we would agree! Students rarely read to "get" what was "in the text"; they read to "get" somewhere else. This kind of reading is what researchers who study reading in content-area classrooms have characterized as "instrumental" reading. Although these researchers have recognized the existence of instrumental reading in content-area classrooms, they have tended to attach little importance to it, focusing instead on strategies for learning from text (Alvermann & Moore, 1991). Yet the study presented in this chapter suggests that there is more to content-area reading than learning from text and that what is usually considered "instrumental" reading is fundamental to such classrooms because it contributes to the development of a particular classroom ideology about what it means to know and learn a discipline.

Taken as a whole, the findings of the study presented in this chapter show that it is more powerful to conceptualize content-area reading as a matter of learning *with* and *through* text rather than learning *from* text alone. In making this distinction, we wish to move beyond the concern for strategies and techniques for reading in content-area classrooms and call attention to the ways in which reading both expresses and constructs specific values about learning and knowing.

CHAPTER 6

The Role of Reading in Mathematics Inquiry Cycles: A Functional Perspective

The finding that reading was a pervasive way of learning and doing mathematics in the "Math Connections B" course (as discussed in Chapter 5) suggested a follow-up study aimed at understanding not so much what *kinds* of reading occurred when students engaged in mathematical inquiries but what different *functions* that reading, in combination with writing and talking, played in such inquiries (see Siegel, Borasi, & Fonzi, 1998, for a research report of this study). Our research was further defined by the decision to focus only on what we called "math inquiry cycles"—that is, instructional episodes designed to support student engagement in a cycle of inquiry involving problem sensing, problem formation, search, and resolution (Dewey, 1933; Peirce, 1877/1982).

Though little has been published in this regard with respect to mathematics specifically, several descriptions of an inquiry cycle, which identify key phases or components in the cycle, have been presented in the whole language literature (e.g., Burke & Harste, 1992; Richards, 1990; Wells & Chang-Wells, 1992). Our work builds on the description offered by Burke and Harste (1992), who used their earlier work on authoring cycles (Harste & Short, 1988) as a starting point for conceptualizing inquiry cycles. Their model of an inquiry cycle begins with experiences from which students can develop perspectives to frame individual inquiry questions. Students then engage in the research they have planned to help answer their questions. The next step of the cycle involves sharing tentative findings in collaborative groups, followed by a return to individual inquiry with the goal of rethinking and refinement of "rough draft" (Barnes, 1976) thinking and writing. Inquirers then turn to an outside editor (either a student or a teacher may serve this function) to help prepare their documents for public sharing and possible publication within the classroom or school community. Once formal documents are shared, the entire community reflects on the experience and may identify various strategies needed to support their work during subsequent inquiry cycles. Finally, the teacher and students together plan and organize open-ended experiences that may serve as invitations for the next inquiry cycle.

Although in some sense the whole "Math Connections B" course could be considered one such cycle addressing the broad problem of "mathematical connections," we identified smaller and better-defined inquiry cycles within this course—such as the "Racing" project described in Chapter 5, the "Analog & Analytic" experience presented in Chapter 1, and each of the individual projects students pursued in the final segment of the course. Other examples of "math inquiry cycles" were also identified in the experiences developed independently by Judi Fonzi and Lisa Grasso Sanvidge after the collaborative classroom research had been completed. Out of all the math inquiry cycles thus identified, we chose to analyze in depth a subset of three that we believed represented an interesting variety with respect to topic, instructional context, and the kind of mathematical inquiry developed. These experiences were the following:

- The "Analog & Analytic" Inquiry Cycle described in Chapter 1, in which the unplanned controversy over the interpretation of analog and analytical thinking in mathematics in the context of the "Math Connections B" course led to an inquiry of 3 weeks duration into these aspects of the nature of mathematics.
- A 10-week exploration of taxicab geometry, which was part of the "Alternative Geometries" course Judi Fonzi taught to a subset of the same high school students who had just taken one of the "Math Connections" courses.
- A 3-week unit on "taking a census" that Lisa Grasso Sanvidge designed for her middle school students with the multiple goals of better understanding the mathematics involved in this real-life situation and learning the rudiments of statistics.

A preliminary analysis of these inquiry experiences suggested a modified version of Burke and Harste's (1992) inquiry cycle, one we felt was more appropriate for describing inquiries developed in secondary mathematics settings. This consisted of four "chronological phases" (setting the stage and focusing the inquiry; carrying out the inquiry; synthesizing and communicating the results of the inquiry; taking stock and looking ahead) and three other components "embedded" throughout these phases (gathering tools/strategies/resources for the inquiry; getting a model; collaborating with other inquirers)—as summarized in Figure 6.1.

We then used this characterization of key elements of a "math inquiry cycle" to inform our analysis of the functions reading played in the "Taxigeometry," "Census," and "Analog & Analytic" cycles. We therefore constructed the written narratives for these experiences around the four chronological phases identified above, as is evident in the two narratives that follow. As in Chapter 5, these narratives are accompanied by commentaries intended to highlight and name the various functions that reading played within the inquiry being described. Once again, we have used parentheses and a different font to distinguish these commentaries from the main text.

Narrative 5: The "Taxigeometry" Inquiry Cycle— Examining the Notions of "Definition," "Proof," and "Mathematical Truth" Through a Study of a Non-Euclidean Mathematical System

At the very beginning of the "Alternative Geometries" course, Judi focused her efforts on stimulating students' interest in exploring surfaces other than the familiar Euclidean plane and on challenging their notions of definition, formula, proof, and mathematical truth. To achieve these goals, Judi designed a variety of experiences intended to elicit the students' conceptions of geometry and to introduce them to the historical and affective dimensions of investigating non-Euclidean geometries. Reading and discussing essays on alternative geometries in various ways was a central feature of these instructional activities, and it was as a result of these experiences that students eventually decided to explore the taxi-surface. The students then engaged in a series of inquiries examining the effects that the constraints imposed in taxigeometry would have on familiar Euclidean figures (e.g., circle, square, triangle). After several weeks, the students pulled together the results of their inquiries through various culminating activities, some designed by Judi and some by the students themselves. Finally, as was typical of Judi's courses, the taxigeometry segment of the class ended with several activities that encouraged students to reflect on the impact this experience had on their beliefs about mathematics and their approaches to doing mathematics.

Figure 6.1. Description of chronological phases and embedded components of "math inquiry cycles."

Chronological Phases	Description
Setting the stage and focusing the inquiry	The problem to be resolved through the inquiry is identified, more precise questions are framed, and the approach to the inquiry is decided.
Carrying out the inquiry	The inquiry plan is put into practice (although this is rarely straightforward, but rather often involves revisiting and refining the original plan).
Synthesizing/ Communicating the inquiry	The results produced are reviewed and organized so that the inquirer might address the original problem or question, and share the results with an outside audience.
Taking stock and looking ahead	Together, the teacher and students explicitly reflect on the inquiry experiences to better understand what they learned, how they learned, and how they felt about their learning. Any difficulties they wish to address prior to the next inquiry are identified along with new questions they may decide to explore in future inquiries.
Embedded Components	
Gathering Tools/Strategies/ Resources for the inquiry	Across each phase of the cycle, students and the teacher may identify the need for a tool, strategy, or resource that would contribute to their inquiry, and then gather and use it. Occasionally, this may lead to identifying the need to learn something new.
Getting a model	Students may search for, or be offered, examples or demonstrations of an activity they are about to undertake, on the assumption that they may take different things from these examples. Hence, modeling is not synonymous with imitating or copying the example.
Collaborating with other inquirers	Throughout the inquiry, members of a community of practice engage in ongoing dialogue and interaction with peers and others who may serve as resources in order to negotiate meanings and offer support and encouragement.

Setting the Stage and Focusing the Inquiry

The "Alternative Geometries" course began with an activity intended to elicit students' initial thoughts about geometry, definitions, and proof and, in doing so, challenge some of their taken-for-granted beliefs about mathematics. The students spent a good part of their first class responding to the thought-provoking questionnaire about geometry reproduced in Figure 6.2. (*This is an example of how reading can contribute to the function that we have called eliciting and/or challenging students' initial conceptions and knowledge of the topic to be explored— because reading the questions on this questionnaire was intended to encourage the students to consider and reflect upon mathematical issues they might not ordinarily think about.*)

Several lessons were then devoted to the reading of an essay entitled "Beyond Straight Lines" (Sheedy, 1996). This text was written in the context of a mathematics education course by a graduate student who was known to the students and later visited the class to talk with them about their reading of his texts. The essay reports the results of the author's own inquiry into the history of non-Euclidean geometries and includes not only the information he had gathered on this topic but also his initial discomfort with the idea of alternative geometries, the reassuring discovery that even great mathematicians in the past shared a similar discomfort, and some reflections about how this experience challenged his own view of mathematics.

Reading this essay served multiple functions in this course. First, Judi wanted to help students become aware of the negative feelings that were likely to arise when the "truth" of the familiar Euclidean geometry was challenged and to address these feelings before they could interfere with the students' inquiry. She also chose this essay because it introduced technical information about alternative geometries that she thought might increase students' interest and knowledge of this topic in preparation for their own inquiry into taxigeometry. To achieve these specific goals and help the students make sense of this challenging text, Judi carefully orchestrated a series of activities around the

Figure 6.2. Alternative Geometries questionnaire.

1. Give examples of the kind of things you have studied in the past that were called geometry. (grade school, junior high, as well as high school)
2. Give some examples of uses of geometry.
3. Can geometry be useful in the real world. How? Why?
4. How do you convince someone of your results/ideas in general? (tell some specific approaches you use)
5. How do you convince someone of your results/ideas, in mathematics? (tell some specific approaches you use)
6. What are definitions and what do we need them for? (in general)
7. What are definitions and what do we need them for? (in mathematics)
8. What do YOU think geometry is all about?

reading of this text. (*The experiences Judi orchestrated around the reading of this essay—described in what follows—demonstrate how reading can contribute to <u>becoming aware of affective issues that could arise during the inquiry</u> and <u>generate interest, gain background knowledge, and plant seeds for the inquiry,</u> respectively. We invite the reader to pay explicit attention, while reading on, to how the way the text was read played a key role in achieving each of these goals.*)

Rather than asking students to read the entire essay at once, Judi divided the text into three sections. She handed out the first section (in which the author introduced the whole piece by drawing an analogy with his prior experience of radically changing his view about playing chess) in class and asked the students to read the text aloud, using the Say Something strategy as a class. She then assigned the second section (relating the author's initial disbelief and discomfort with the idea that mathematics was not as "straightforward and clear" as he had always thought) as homework, along with the task of writing a journal entry in response (to be shared in class the next day). The last and most challenging section of the essay (summarizing what the author found out about non-Euclidean geometries and their development, and then reporting the implications of these findings for the author's own view of mathematics) was then read in class. To help students make sense of the complex technical information and philosophical considerations dealt with in this part of the essay, Judi suggested that it be read in pairs in class, once again using the Say Something strategy but also recording the most important thoughts and ideas generated by this reading on index cards—thus combining Say Something with some elements of the Using Cards strategy.

The sets of cards produced by three students reported in Figure 6.3 are evidence of the richness of the thinking generated by this reading activity. The cards students wrote during their "say something" experience played an important role in the whole-class sharing and discussion that followed, as students frequently read them aloud and/or used them as a reference and support (*note how the reading of these student-generated texts enabled the class to <u>share ideas to generate a wider range of perspectives/possibilities</u> than could have been generated individually*). This final discussion demonstrated that most of the students clearly had made sense of the piece, because they were able to both talk about specific ideas and present a synthesis of the ideas explored in the essay.

Whereas the previous reading activities had dealt with the general topic of alternative geometries, the next text Judi introduced to the class focused on taxigeometry more specifically in an attempt to stimulate students' interest in exploring this particular geometry. This text

Figure 6.3. Examples of cards students prepared in response to the third
section of "Beyond Straight Lines."

From Jolea's cards:

Mathematicians had a hard time accepting and understanding other forms of geometry
other than Euclid's. For Euclid was realistic, it was formed around our world and
our senses, the others weren't.

Who is to determine the accuracy and what becomes law in math?

Euclidean geometry was thought of as accurate for so many years so other forms
invented afterwards were thought as unlawful.

Math is humane just like us in the respect that it changes because it is not always
complete and accurate.

From Char's cards:

Big questions. It's challenging what everyone thinks.

Just stating that each geometry has its purpose. I guess there is no generic one.

"Euclid's geometry is true" but as people learned more, their needs increased. So
ultimately they saw things where Euclid's geometry did not apply.

"Completeness and perfection are ideals" . . . that kind of struck me as really
interesting, because it is true now that I think of it, but never really realized it
before.

From Shellie's cards:

"The universe was an extension of our earthbound experience."

If there weren't people breaking the rules then people would just always believe what
already is and therefore people wouldn't be able to discover new concepts.

"Is mathematics merely the invention of human imagination and not a body of
universal truths based on common sense? Is reality merely the invention of the
mind?" WILD!!!!!

was a mathematical story ("Moving Around the City," by John Sheedy [in Borasi, Sheedy, & Siegel, 1990]) reporting the author's fictitious adventures as he tried to find his way around an unfamiliar "modern" city, making sense of the conventions used to name streets (as a result of the city's goal of eliminating the need for street maps) and figuring out the ideal location for his new home given certain specifications and constraints. Among other things, this story illustrates several of the nonintuitive consequences of taxigeometry, such as the fact that "all the points equidistant from two given points" do not lie on a straight line (perpendicular bisector). Once again, Judi carefully orchestrated the reading of this text so as to achieve her instructional goals. Most notably, in order to help the students recognize and experience firsthand the consequences of the grid-surface described in this story, Judi removed the figures that showed how the protagonist reasoned his way through the problems set in the story and asked the students, as they read the text in class in pairs using Say Something, to attempt to create each diagram themselves before looking at the author's diagram. (*Note that Sheedy's mathematical story was introduced by the teacher mainly to spark ideas for a specific inquiry, thus demonstrating yet another function that reading could serve at the very beginning of an inquiry cycle; the teacher's decision to remove the figures, however, also shows how she used this text to make things problematic to raise questions worth investigating.*)

For homework, the students were then asked to reflect on both the content and the process of this reading experience in a journal entry. The next day, various students shared their writing by either reading what they had written aloud or talking their way through their text (*another example of reading to share ideas to generate a wide range of perspectives/possibilities*).

In the context of this sharing, one student challenged the teacher's statement that taxigeometry constituted a new geometry with the comment, "That's not special—it's normal geometry . . . it's just the old game with a new rule added to it." Not wanting to miss an opportunity to capitalize on the student's genuine doubt and curiosity, the teacher recorded the question, "Are these just new rules or a whole new game?" on the board for all to see, and the class immediately engaged in a heated debate over this question. In the effort to prove that this was indeed a different geometry, another student said, "You can't even make a circle in [it]." This marked the class's implicit decision to engage in an investigation of taxigeometry, which began by studying how circles and other familiar figures would look in this context. (*Although in this example the students got ideas for and made decisions about a specific inquiry simultaneously and spontaneously, the reading of Sheedy's story and, even more, the sharing of their written reflections about that experience along with the recording—and reading—of key questions on the board played an important role in the process of making decisions about the focus, scope, and organization of the inquiry.*)

Carrying Out the Inquiry

The students' own inquiry into taxigeometry thus began by exploring whether or not a circle existed under the new rules the students had identified (and recorded on newsprint) as operating in the "city/grid."

Some of the students began immediately to draw diagrams on grid paper that they felt represented circles on this new surface. These diagrams were often shown to the rest of the class as supporting evidence for the student's conjecture and, as such, they were critically examined and discussed by the class as a whole. (*Here the reading of the students' diagrams played an important role with respect to <u>generating specific questions/conjectures</u> and <u>analyzing/making sense/using data to answer these questions/conjectures</u>; these nonverbal texts also provided this learning community with a concrete means to <u>share and build upon individual contributions to the ongoing inquiry</u>.*)

In the course of this discussion, some students hypothesized that if the grid were very small (i.e., infinitesimally small), the discrete points identified as equidistant from a given point would come to approximate the usual circle (rather than a diamond). This hypothesis prompted another heated debate among the students!

This prompted the teacher to raise the question, "What is a circle?" In response, several students spontaneously looked in a textbook and a dictionary to find an "official" definition of circle (*an illustration of how reading can contribute to <u>gathering tools/strategies/resources to carry out some aspects of the inquiry</u>*).

Once the students located, among the definitions thus gathered, one that could be used to draw and defend a diagram (i.e., "a circle is a set of points in a plane that are a given distance from a given point [the center of the circle] in the plane"), the teacher asked them to use such a definition as a way to verify whether the diagrams they had created did or not satisfy the conditions stated and, thus, could or could not be considered examples of circles. This apparently simple request created some controversy and engaged several students in a heated debate about what it meant to "follow the taxigeometry rules," as illustrated by the following excerpt from the dialogue:

Judi: I'm going to read the definition one more time and you are each going to show what you've got, okay? It's everybody else's job to determine whether it [your diagrams] meets the definition or not. Ready? The definition—this is the *book's* definition I might add—is "a circle is a set of points in a plane that are a given distance from a given point (the center of the circle) in the plane." Okay? Alex?

Alex: I went through and measured out 10 points each way and then I took and measured it and made a marker with that on another sheet of paper and moved it around—keeping one point here [the teacher tells him to show the class what he did, and Alex shows his drawing—see Figure 6.4]. Okay, I made this point [the teacher clarifies "So this is your center"]. So I just moved it around, rotated it until I found a point that was the same distance from the center.

Figure 6.4. Alex's first conjecture about a taxi-circle of radius 10.

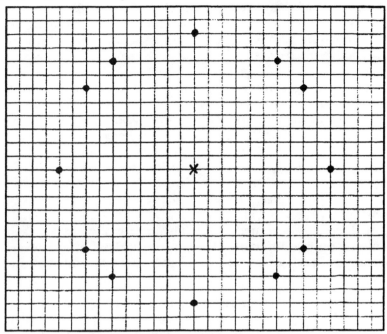

Nathan: But you're cutting across those lines.

Char: Yeah, you're cutting across the lines, see.

Alex: But . . . I'm not drawing any lines. A circle is the set of *points* a given distance—this is a given distance. . . . It doesn't say "connect the dots!"

Judi: What is the definition? Nathan and Char are challenging that you have not measured the distance correctly. . . . I want them [Char and Nathan] to talk to you about that.

Alex: (teasing) Tell me—how didn't I measure it correctly?

Char: Well, we were following the rules [the rules the students had agreed on and the teacher had recorded on newsprint]: "You can't go diagonally; you can't cut across; you can't go off lines."

Alex: When you're drawing actual *lines.*

Nathan: But this doesn't make a circle though.

Char: Okay, you're not drawing the lines but you're measuring the distance. . . . The way you are measuring spaces is by cutting across this line, right? It's by cutting across these squares?

Tom: But he's still taking it from the book.
Alex: [frustrated and yelling] Okay!
Judi: No, he has to use our rules. He doesn't have an option [meaning he has to stay within the constraints of the taxigeometry system].

(*The previous dialogue illustrates the important role played by the critical and interactive reading of three different texts—the textbook definition, the "rules" governing taxigeometry that had previously been recorded on the board, and the diagrams students had generated—in the process of generating specific questions/conjectures and analyzing/making sense/using data to answer these questions/conjectures. Notice, in particular, how the attempt to interpret the textbook definition in light of the rules for taxigeometry required students to literally see and experience firsthand what it meant to work within the constraints of this system.*)

The dialogue continued in this fashion for a while, with several students proposing different solutions, until Alex himself developed the sketch of a "taxi-circle" (illustrated in Figure 6.5), which ultimately

Figure 6.5. Alex's final drawing of a taxi-circle of radius 10.

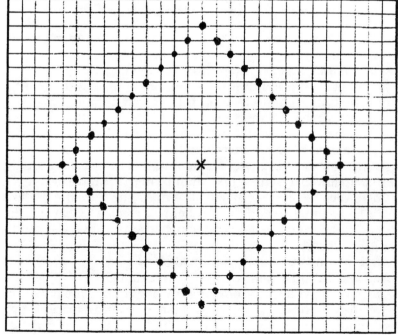

the class felt represented the "right" image and characteristics using the "taxi" definition of distance. The students were so excited by their decisions and discoveries that they posted their "findings" (the diagrams they had produced augmented by written explanations) on a wall in the classroom so that they could keep track of them and refer to them in the future.

This investigation forced the students to really think about the nature of definitions in mathematics. If one uses a definition of circle as "the set of all points a given distance from a given point" on a taxi-surface, the resulting figure is not round! Having identified the "diamond" shown in Figure 6.5 as the figure meeting both the criteria of the surface and the definition of a circle, the students still grappled with whether this figure could be called a "circle." At the same time, they began to question the story's definition of distance and speculated about other ways to define distance on a grid surface.

Once students came to grips with the idea that a definition describes a set of conditions and the resulting image is merely a consequence of those conditions when interpreted *in a given context*, they agreed to continue using the author's original definition of *taxi-distance* and began to wonder about other concepts related to circles (such as how circumference and area could be computed in taxigeometry) and how other figures (such as squares, rectangles, and triangles) would look in taxigeometry. Each of these explorations was developed along the lines of the one carried out for circles and thus depended heavily on the reading of students' tentative diagrams in conjunction with textbook definitions, student-generated definitions, or both, as described earlier (*another example of using reading to generate specific questions/hypotheses, analyze/make sense/use data to answer questions/test conjectures, gather tools/strategies/resources necessary to carry out the inquiry, and share and build upon individual contributions to the ongoing inquiry*).

In an effort to make explicit and validate both the process the students had followed up to that point in their exploration of taxigeometry and the results they had achieved, Judi decided now to assign the reading of selected sections of another graduate student's paper, which documented her own exploration of taxigeometry (Kort, 1989). In this paper, the graduate student articulated the decisions she had made and the drawings she had produced as she systematically considered the following issues in the context of taxigeometry: definitions of distance, triangles, perimeter, area, angles; the form and types of triangles, angles; how to measure perimeter and area; and circumscribing rectangles and circles around taxi-triangles.

So as not to "spoil" their ongoing exploration, the students were initially given only the sections discussing issues the class had explored up to that point—that is, the section on choosing a definition for distance and triangle, and the sections on the form and types of taxi-triangles (*a use of a technical math text that illustrates the potential role reading can play in <u>verifying and/or validating the process/results of one's inquiry in light of an outside source</u>*). Judi was very explicit about her rationale for using the reading in this way.

As students shared their reactions to this reading, the discussion brought them back to a question they had raised earlier about taxi-angles and how to measure them. Judi hoped to push them to grapple with possible ways to measure angles, because this seemed a place where they could experiment with different criteria and systems. In order to achieve this, she assigned yet another section of Kort's (1989) paper for students to read and react to. This time, however, her goal was to introduce some new ideas and perspectives that might help the students move beyond what they had already found on their own (*an example of using the same text for yet another function—reading to <u>stimulate deeper inquiry</u>*). The students' reaction to this reading was quite surprising; they were actually angry with the author! Kort concludes the section with the statement, "Because of all the problems and contradictions, the subject of angles is not worthwhile pursuing in taxi-geometry at this time. There are so many other interesting ideas than the notion of angle, that this aspect of taxi-geometry will not be further explored in this paper" (p. 7). The students felt the author had bailed out! Their response clearly shows that they had read the text critically and were beginning to see that mathematics is not a collection of "pre-established truths" and that even the mathematical thinking of "advanced" mathematics students could be challenged. This realization actually led a few students to explore on their own some ways to measure angles that would offer consistent results.

As was now customary, all their work (diagrams and written explanations) was added to the "map of findings" posted on the classroom wall.

Synthesizing/Communicating the Results of the Inquiry

At this point Judi was looking for an opportunity to begin wrapping up the exploration of the taxi-surface in order to move on to examining a new surface. She therefore decided to give the students a copy of Kort's (1989) paper in its entirety (recall that up to that point they had been given only selected sections of this paper) so they could look at the paper as a whole and begin to get a sense of the approach the author used to explore taxigeometry and how she communicated the results of this exploration. (*This time, the reading of Kort's paper was intended to play the role of getting a 'model' for how to synthesize/apply/ communicate results from the inquiry.*) As Judi struggled to define a strategy for how this text could be read most productively, the students suggested, "Let us do whatever we want. If we want to do a sketch, if we want to do a map, if we want to do cards, if we want to do a paper— whatever!" The teacher agreed to this plan after some discussion, which produced more ideas about how to respond to this paper, such as reacting to the paper as a whole, or to just parts of it, or using it as a springboard to pursue an "old" idea they were interested in.

The students took full advantage of the freedom granted them and produced a variety of texts and models that they then presented to the rest of the class. One student chose to actually build a geoboard (referred to once in the reading) because, as he noted when he showed it to the rest of the class, "I need to touch things—I don't like this moving it around on a grid paper. I need to touch it—I need to really see it." Another student had pursued an idea about taxi-triangles whose sides can cross over each other. A pair of students created what they called a "taxi-globe" by drawing a taxi-circle and then imagining that it had been spun around the vertical axis of symmetry to generate a three-dimensional figure; they showed their model to the rest of the class while explaining some of the implications of this surface.

In all these situations the students made consistent use of their diagrams and models to support their presentations. (*The reading of these nonverbal texts created by the presenters, in combination with other forms of communication, functioned as a critical component of presenting results from the inquiry.*) And, on all these occasions, the audience also participated actively in these reading events, and their questions to the presenters suggested that they used the texts to make sense of and critically interpret the ideas put forth (*an example, instead, of using reading— on the part of the audience—to react to the presentation of results from the inquiry*).

A complementary opportunity to synthesize and apply what they had learned in their exploration of taxigeometry was created by the students themselves when they suggested a class visit to the city center to view an architectural exhibit of blueprints and scale models that could inspire the design of architectural plans for their own city, "Gridland." (*In this case, the "reading" of the plans and designs available at the exhibit served the function of getting 'models' for how to synthesize/ communicate results that were very different from those a written paper might provide.*) A few students indeed took inspiration from what they saw at this exhibit and created architectural plans for their own "taxi-buildings," which they presented to the class.

John Sheedy's mathematical story, "Moving Around the City" (Borasi, Sheedy, & Siegel, 1990), implicitly served as yet another model (much as the teacher had hoped), as one student independently decided to write his own "story" about a city and read it to his classmates (*another example of using reading to get a model for how to synthesize/communicate results, followed by a use of reading to present results from the inquiry*).

Taking Stock and Looking Ahead

In an attempt to bring closure to the first inquiry and identify ideas and approaches that might inform future inquiries, the final phase of the "Taxigeometry" Inquiry Cycle focused on pulling together and reflecting on all of the experiences to date. Judi orchestrated several activities to achieve these goals.

The first of these involved the introduction of Brown and Walter's (1990) "What-if-not" problem-posing strategy in order to demonstrate an alternative and more systematic approach to exploring problems than the one students had spontaneously used during their taxigeometry inquiry. This was accomplished first of all by assigning the reading of an article (Walter & Brown, 1969) describing this process (*an example of using reading to gather tools/strategies/resources for future inquiries*). Along with this article, the students were also given a paper that showed how this approach could be applied to a taxigeometry topic (*an example, instead, of using reading to get a 'model' for something that could be used in future inquiries*).

To invite students' reflections on the process experienced in their exploration of taxigeometry, the teacher then had the students read the article "The Power of Stories in Learning Mathematics" (Borasi, Sheedy, & Siegel, 1990), a professional article that had been written by three members of the RLM Project and published in a national language arts journal. As she did with other texts students had previously read, Judi divided the article into several sections and had them read each section in a different way. Before students read the first section of the article, which consisted of a brief introduction followed by the story students had read earlier ("Moving Around the City" by J. Sheedy [Borasi, Sheedy, & Siegel, 1990]), the teacher wrote three questions on newsprint (What has reading this story done for us? What could it still do? What might it have done?) and asked the students to write their responses to these questions so they could discuss them at the next class meeting. This first reading was planned to encourage students to identify and articulate the power of stories from their own experiences *before* they read what the authors thought (*an example of using reading to elicit reflections on what took place in the inquiry; note the role played here by rereading a text the class had encountered earlier*).

In the next class, Judi continued the reflection process by asking students to read aloud their responses to the questions she had listed while she recorded these ideas on the newsprint taped to the front blackboard, asking for elaboration and reactions from the class as a whole as she did so. This process produced the list reported in Figure 6.6. In contrast, the second section of the article was read in class using a whole-class Say Something strategy so that the students could hear one another's spontaneous thoughts about the relationship between their list of the benefits of reading stories in a mathematics class and the authors'. (*Both the reading of the students' written responses and the reading of the second part of the article with Say Something represent differ-*

Figure 6.6. Reflections on reading "Moving Around the City."

What did reading this story do for us?

- Helped me understand the geometry better—had to try to work out pictures (shape) self first and then got answer and could analyze my approach.
- Made me think about how a city is planned and how it could be planned out mathematically (logically, systematically) instead of for other reasons.
- Eventually helped me *accept* another type of geometry—cuz real applications first, then it was math and I could go back to the story and to understand the math.
- Story as an intro made it easier to understand—sets up to see/accept something different.
- Could identify with character's confusion and wanted to clear it up.
- Put self in character's place and had to figure it out—we then had a vested interest (no pictures).
- Made sense to some but not all—it gave the confused hope.

What could it still do?

- Help us if we *really* moved; give us a mathematical technique for finding our way around.

What might it have done?

- Helped to see math/geometry from a different perspective and *thru* different eyes.
- Might have led us somewhere else if we came up with different ideas.
- Might have got us to ask questions about *layouts* of other places—amusement parks, etc.

---

ent examples of reading to share and build upon individual reflections on the inquiry).

The reading of the third and final section of this article was designed to serve yet two additional functions. This section consisted of the author's thoughts about the benefits of writing a mathematical story as well as a new story ("Moving Outside the City" by R. Borasi [Borasi, Sheedy, & Siegel, 1990]) that extended the first by considering problems that might arise if the surface were a sphere rather than a "flat" grid. Students were asked to read this section of the article for homework and come prepared to talk about it at the next class meeting. The discussion that ensued was particularly lively because the class had decided to work with spherical surfaces in their next inquiry; as a result, they read the story in the same spirit they read the one that had inspired their exploration of taxigeometry, namely, by drawing their own texts and using a globe as a resource in order to make sense of the problems described in the story (*as such, the reading of this section of the article represents a combination of using reading to look ahead to new inquiries and to share and build upon ideas for new inquiries*).

The final series of activities in the unit was designed to elicit students' reflections on the *entire* experience by recalling and synthesizing both the process and the content of their learning and, in doing so, prepare for evaluations of individual students as well as set the stage for new inquiries.

With the directions to begin thinking about these issues for homework, the whole class took a "Walk Down Memory Lane"—a process the students were all familiar with, because it had been used systematically in the preceding "Math Connections" course as well as in most courses Judi taught. Reading and referring to the "trail" the students had created over the course of the inquiry by posting texts representing their "findings" on the classroom walls added greatly to this process (*this is another and quite different example of using reading to elicit reflections on what took place in the inquiry from the one involving rereading Sheedy's story [Borasi, Sheedy & Siegel, 1990]*).

This discussion was followed by the creation of a "What have I learned?" list—another frequently used practice in Judi's classes (as illustrated in Chapter 5). As students shared, discussed, and elaborated upon the students' individual lists of what they had learned from the unit they had prepared for homework, the teacher recorded each item on newsprint so as to create a collective "What did I learn?" list reproduced in Figure 6.7. (*The reading of students' lists and newsprint that occurred in this event represents an example of using reading to identify, discuss, and appreciate the significance of what was done/learned through the*

Figure 6.7. "What did I learn?" list.

1. We could change the rules in math and explore the results
2. [By] changing 1 Euclidean rule we developed an entirely new geometry system
3. Generating our own ideas and interpretations of something & trying them & making sense for ourselves
4. Definitions—difference between definition and characteristics, what is the appropriate definition for this context [There is a picture of a double arrow here.]
5. Definition of a figure could result in a different "look" in a different space
6. Be able to remove selves from familiar (math stigmas) & accept new findings

inquiry as well as to share and build upon individual reflections on the inquiry.)

Finally, because the end of the "Taxigeometry" Inquiry Cycle co-incided with the end of a marking period, the teacher and the students engaged in the school-wide evaluation process previously described in Chapter 5 in the context of the "Math Connections B" course. First, the teacher prepared a letter for parents describing what the class had done during the unit, to which each student added what she or he had personally gained from the experience. Then Judi and the students jointly decided what would be evaluated, why, and how.

In individual evaluation conferences, teacher and student discussed the student's effort and work during the marking period, identified areas she or he needed to work on in the future, came to agreement about what the evaluation form should say, and composed the narrative section of the evaluation form together. This discussion was informed by considering the written work the student had produced during the inquiry cycle and by referring to preliminary notes made by the teacher in preparing for this discussion of the students' participation and per-formance during this part of the course. (*The use made of students' work and teacher's notes in this case represents an example of using reading to evaluate students' participation, performance, and learning throughout the inquiry.*)

Narrative 6: The "Census" Inquiry Cycle— Learning Statistical Concepts and Techniques in the Context of Real-Life Mathematics

Lisa was getting ready to begin a unit on statistics in her pre-alge-bra class (see Chapter 3 for a description of this instructional setting) just around the time the 1990 U.S. National Census was going to be taken. Every household in the United States would receive a census form to be completed and returned to the Census Bureau, and the media was full of information and debates about this important event. Lisa thought this topic could offer her students a great opportunity to see how statistics was used in real-life situations and to engage in genuine mathematical inquiry while at the same time learning the rudiments of statistics in a meaningful context. With these goals in mind, she suggested that, while the U.S. Census was being taken, the class could themselves design and take a census of their school. Her students thus participated in a variety of activities involved in conducting a school census—defining the questions to ask their classmates, deciding how to organize and analyze the data thus collected, learning some statistical techniques in order to do so, and, finally, presenting their results to the rest of the school. These presentations, rather than reflections on the experience as a whole (as in the "Taxigeometry" Inquiry Cycle), represented the culmination of this unit.

Setting the Stage and Focusing the Inquiry

To provide models and inspiration for the students' own school census, the teacher began the unit by spending several lessons discussing some reading materials she had collected about the U.S. Census (*an example of reading to generate interest, background knowledge and plant seeds for the inquiry as well as spark ideas for a specific inquiry*). These texts included brief essays about the history of the U.S. Census, tables and other diagrams reporting some interesting results from past censuses, examples of census forms, and newspaper articles on the U.S. Census contributed by the students themselves.

Prior to these readings, the students had completed a questionnaire on the U.S. Census intended to help them see uses and implications of taking a national census they had probably never considered (*an example of using reading to elicit and/or challenge students' initial conceptions and knowledge of the topic to be explored*). Students were asked to indicate whether statements such as the following were true: The Constitution requires that a census be taken in the United States every 10 years; the results of a census help guide thousands of decisions that affect everyone; in the 1980 census, there was an undercount of the nation's population. The questionnaire also asked students to correctly complete statements such as these: The population of the United States in 1790 was about (a) 63 million, (b) 400,000, (c) 4 million, (d) 227 million; the state with the largest population in 1980 was (a) Alaska, (b) California, (c) Delaware, (d) New York. In order to make sense of students' responses to this questionnaire, the teacher also suggested they tally these responses—thus capitalizing on this reading experience to introduce the students to this useful statistical tool (*an example of using reading to create the need for and introduce a tool/strategy/resource useful to the inquiry*).

Carrying Out the Inquiry

Lisa felt it was crucial that the students take full responsibility for developing and analyzing their school census, including choosing and formulating the questions to be asked. She therefore asked each student to write down 10 questions that she or he would be interested in asking schoolmates while the previous activities were taking place (see Figure 6.8 for a sample of these student-generated questions).

Lisa then duplicated all the sets of questions thus generated and asked the students, in pairs, to categorize them; these categories and their related questions were then recorded on the board and closely examined by the whole class so as to reach consensus on the 10 ques-

Figure 6.8. Samples of student-generated questions for the school census questionnaire.

Sample 1:
1. How many brothers and sisters do you have?
2. How many radios do you have in your house?
3. How many pets do you have?
4. What is your favorite holiday? Why?
5. Do you like school? Why?
6. Who do you admire the most? Why?
7. What is your favorite t.v. show?
8. What is your favorite color?
9. What is your favorite subject?
10. What type of music do you like?

Sample 2:
1. Including yourself how many children are in your family?
2. Are there more girls or boys?
3. Do you live in a one- or two-parent home?
4. How many pets do you have?
5. What type of music do you like?
6. What radio station do you listen to?
7. Do you have a VCR? A microwave?
8. What is your favorite t.v. show?
9. What is your favorite movie?
10. What is your favorite song?

tions to be included in their school census questionnaire (*an example of reading student-generated texts so as to generate specific questions that would frame their inquiry*). To create a questionnaire that would function successfully as the data-gathering instrument for their school census, the students then collaborated on rewriting each of these questions and their response formats, reading them for editing (*an example of using reading in the process of gathering data to answer specific questions*). Throughout this process, they often referred to the U.S. Census forms to see how questions were phrased and answers structured in questionnaires of this kind (*to get a 'model' to carry out an aspect of the inquiry— namely, the creation of their school census form*).

The school census form the class thus created (reproduced in Figure 6.9) was distributed and completed by 491 out of the 557 students in the school during their homeroom period.

Figure 6.9. The final school census questionnaire.

CIRCLE THE CORRECT RESPONSE

1. Are you a
    MALE / FEMALE

2. How many people live in your household?
    1 2 3 4 5 6 7 8 9 10

3. Are your parents divorced?
    YES / NO

4. Does your family own a computer?
    YES / NO

5. How many people in your family watch "The Simpsons"?
    0 1 2 3 4 5 6 7 8 9 10

6. Estimate your school average
    (A) BELOW 60   (B) 60–70   (C) 70–80   (D) 80–90   (E) 90–100

7. How do you get to school?
    WALK   BUS   DRIVEN   OTHER

8. Do you participate in any after-school activities?
    YES / NO   LIST 3 _____, _____, _____

9. Do you participate in any after-school sports?
    YES / NO   LIST 3 _____, _____, _____

10. Do you presently have a
    GIRLFRIEND / BOYFRIEND

To directly involve all of her students in the analysis of these data, Lisa designated each student as the "enumerator" for a given homeroom. The tabulation of the school census questionnaire was carried out in class. For each question, each enumerator first read through the packet of completed census forms from his or her assigned homeroom to identify the responses given to this question and "tallied" these responses (*an example of reading to analyze/make sense/use the data collected*). The results of these tallies were then read aloud and recorded by the teacher on the board in a table form, so as to create school-wide statistics (*a use of reading to share and build upon individual contributions to the ongoing inquiry*).

Often, this process was not straightforward and led to the introduction of new statistical concepts, techniques, or both, so as to create meaningful summaries and representations of the data. For example, responses to the question "How many people live in your household?" (1, 2, . . . , 10) were not easy to tabulate, because of the range of possible answers. This led to a lesson on frequency and histograms followed by the in-class reading and discussion of a chapter from *How to Lie with Statistics* (Huff, 1954) introducing the statistical concepts of mean, median, and mode in a discursive way, weaving together technical explanations with significant examples from everyday life (*a prototypical example of using reading to gather tools/strategies/resources to carry out the inquiry*).

In another case, newspaper articles discussing the problem of "counting the homeless" as part of the national census raised for some students the question of how representative their school census data were—considering that a number of students in the school had not completed the questionnaire (*yet a different example of how reading could contribute to generate specific questions/conjectures at a later stage of carrying out the inquiry*). This concern, in turn, was addressed through the in-class reading and discussion of another excerpt from *How to Lie with Statistics* (Huff, 1954), which dealt with the problem of sampling (*another example of reading to gather tools/strategies/resources to carry out the inquiry*).

Synthesizing/Communicating Results from the Inquiry

Another very important aspect of the unit was the expectation that, in the end, each student would be responsible for reporting results from the census back to the students in his or her assigned homeroom. To provide some structure for this culminating activity, Lisa required each enumerator to prepare and then present a poster summarizing the most interesting results of the census taken in his or her assigned homeroom.

In order to prepare this poster the students had to make a number of important decisions (e.g., what questions to focus on, what statistics to use) as well as select relevant information from the preliminary tallies and summary tables created when tabulating the questionnaire responses (*an example of reading—and transforming—preliminary written records in order to produce a written report on results from the inquiry*). They also had to decide how to organize and represent this information in the most effective way by using statistical graphs and/or other mathematical tools. In this process, students often referred to a poster summarizing school-wide results that the teacher had prepared and presented so as to provide a model for the students' own work (*an example of reading to get a 'model' for how to synthesize/communicate results*).

As they worked on their posters, students also continuously reviewed their work so as to edit it (*yet a different use of reading to produce a written report on results from the inquiry*). Several students also spontaneously helped each other at this stage by looking at each other's posters and identifying errors, suggesting improvements, and so on (*an example of using reading to provide feedback on drafts of written reports on the inquiry*).

The variety of posters students produced is evidence of how they were able to take advantage of the open-ended nature of this task and demonstrate their understanding of both the statistical techniques they had learned and the information revealed by the school census.

As the enumerators gave their presentations to the students in their assigned homerooms, they often referred to their individual posters for illustrations or specific results (*a use of reading in support of presenting results from the inquiry*). At the same time, referring to the poster provided the audience with a way to follow the presentation and often invited further questions for the presenters (*an example of reading to react to the presentation of results from the inquiry*).

Functions of Reading Across and Throughout Inquiry Cycles

The previous narratives introduced 29 of the 30 different categories of reading functions that occurred within the three inquiry cycles (for more details on the frequency and distribution of these reading functions across the three instructional experiences, see Siegel, Borasi, & Fonzi, 1998). Because the narratives we used to arrive at these functions had been divided into four chronological phases of the inquiry cycle, it was not surprising that each reading function seemed related to the specific "chronological phase" of the inquiry cycle in which it occurred (i.e., setting the stage and focusing the inquiry, carrying out the inquiry, synthesizing/communicating results from the inquiry, or taking stock and looking ahead). A more unexpected finding was that some of the "embedded" components of the inquiry cycle we had identified (i.e., gathering tools/strategies/resources, getting a model, and collaborating with other inquirers) were also associated with specific reading functions. As a result, we came to conceptualize the reading functions as falling along two dimensions: "chronological" categories associated with specific phases of an inquiry cycle and "embedded" components of inquiry that cut across the chronological phases. We have tried to capture this relationship between reading functions and chronological phases/embedded components of an inquiry cycle in Figure 6.10.

The seven larger groups of functions thus identified (i.e., the four classes of functions associated *only* with a chronological phase of the inquiry, and the three created by considering the reading functions specific to one of the embedded components) seemed particularly significant to our analysis in that they helped identify "clusters" of reading functions that had similar characteristics along with some unique features. Therefore, in what follows we have chosen to organize our discussion of reading functions around these seven clusters in order to better define and explain the significance of each element of a "math inquiry cycle." Each reading function is discussed in terms of the specific ways the particular function was achieved through reading; patterns within and across functions are highlighted by looking at the kind of texts that were read, the manner in which they were read, and the purpose for reading them.

Functions of Reading in "Setting the Stage and Focusing the Inquiry"

The reading experiences that occurred during this initial phase of the inquiry cycle served several complementary functions, which make explicit the kind of instructional experiences teachers may want to organize in order to stimulate and support the launch of students' inquiries. The reading experiences we placed in the first category, *elicit and/or challenge students' initial conceptions and knowledge of the topic to be explored*, involved reading and responding to questionnaires and surveys. The key feature of these texts was the use of thought-provoking

Figure 6.10. Summary of reading functions in relation to chronological phases and embedded components of a "math inquiry cycle."

Embedded Components	Chronological Phases of Inquiry			
	Setting the Stage & Focusing the Inquiry	Carrying Out the Inquiry	Synthesizing and Communicating Results	Taking Stock and Looking Ahead
	Reading to...	Reading to...	Reading to...	Reading to...
	elicit and/or challenge students' initial conceptions and knowledge of the topic to be explored	generate specific questions/conjectures	produce a written report on results from the inquiry	elicit reflections on what took place during the inquiry
	generate interest, gain background knowledge, and plant seeds for the inquiry	gather/generate data to address specific questions/conjectures	present results from the inquiry	identify, discuss, and appreciate the significance of what was done/learned through the inquiry
	become aware of affective issues that could arise during the inquiry	analyze/make sense/use the data collected to answer questions/test conjectures		evaluate individual students' participation, performance, and learning throughout the inquiry
	make things problematic to raise questions worth exploring	stimulate deeper inquiry		look ahead to new inquiries
	spark ideas for a specific inquiry	verify and/or validate the process/results of one's inquiry in light of an outside source		
	make decisions about the focus, scope, and organization of the inquiry			

Gathering Tools/ Strategies/ Resources	create the need for and introduce tools/strategies/resources useful to the inquiry	gather tools/strategies/ resources necessary to carry out the inquiry		gather tools/strategies/resources for future inquiries
Getting a Model	get an image of the kind of inquiry to be undertaken	get a model to help carry out some aspects of the inquiry	get a model for how to synthesize/ apply/communicate results	get a model for something that could be used in future inquiries
Collaboration with Other Inquirers	share ideas to generate a wide range of perspectives/possibilities	share and build upon individual contributions to the ongoing inquiry	provide feedback on drafts of written reports on the inquiry react to the presentation of results from the inquiry	share and build upon individual reflections on the inquiry share and build upon ideas for new inquiries

questions as a springboard for eliciting students' conceptions about the inquiry domain, which in turn allowed teachers to learn more about the knowledge and beliefs students brought to the inquiry cycle. Unlike the other categories in this phase of inquiry, reading may seem at first to play a minor part because it is the students' written responses that provide the desired information. However, in the case of questionnaires like those used in the "Taxigeometry" and "Census" cycles, reading the questions was what stimulated students' thinking and reflections about the topic to be explored, thus planting seeds for students' inquiry by building on and challenging students' knowledge and beliefs.

The next two categories highlight another important feature of the initial phase of an inquiry cycle—preparing students both cognitively and affectively to undertake a specific inquiry. The reading experiences that were coded as *generate interest, gain background knowledge, and plant seeds for the inquiry* tended to serve all three of the functions named in the title simultaneously. At this early exploratory phase of the inquiry cycle, teachers used brief essays, articles, and newspaper items to build students' interest and background knowledge about the domain being explored, all in an effort to spark curiosity about the domain. Equally important at this point in the inquiry is the reading function we called *become aware of affective issues that could arise during the inquiry*. Feelings are an often ignored yet much documented aspect of mathematics learning (e.g., Borasi, 1990; Buerk, 1981), and reading can be a way for students to confront these feelings. In cases such as these, students read a text to understand what was written and at the same time to have a "lived through experience" (Rosenblatt, 1938, 1978), that is, to read as if one were experiencing for oneself the events, feelings, and thoughts represented in a text. Although this kind of reading is usually associated only with reading literature, it provides an apt characterization of the way reading helped students gain awareness and hence prepare for the affective issues that might arise during the inquiry.

The next category, *make things problematic to raise questions worth exploring*, makes explicit the problematizing function that, as the works of Peirce (1877/1982) and Dewey (1933) suggest, lies at the heart of doing inquiry in that it generates doubt and gives rise to the feeling that there is a problem needing resolution. We believe this function is especially important when initiating inquiry in the context of school mathematics, because students regard so much of mathematics as fixed and immutable that they may not be able to come up with a question worth pursuing unless their views of the domain are problematized or challenged in a way that sets problem posing in motion.

As students get closer to identifying a problem or question to frame their inquiry, there is a shift in the function reading serves. The category *spark ideas for a specific inquiry* reflects this shift. Unlike earlier categories in "setting the stage and focusing the inquiry" in which reading served to open up a domain of interest, the function of reading in this category is to begin closing in on a specific inquiry students might undertake. As a result, it is likely that the texts read for this purpose would be directly related to the topic of that inquiry (e.g., the shift from reading about alternative geometries in general to reading about taxigeometry in particular).

Finally, as the "Taxigeometry" cycle shows, students may get ideas for and make decisions about a specific inquiry simultaneously and spontaneously. Reading (and writing), however, can support *making decisions about the focus, scope, and/or organization of the inquiry* in important ways, especially in inquiry cycles where these decisions are made quite explicitly (as illustrated earlier by the "Racing" project that took place in the context of the "Math Connections B" course). In particular, the practice of recording on newsprint potential topics, questions, alternative approaches, or all three, for carrying out the inquiry can aid the class in identifying various possibilities. Making these ideas public has the added advantage of opening them up to discussion so that the class may eventually reach an informed and democratic consensus about the focus of the inquiry to be undertaken, or a plan of action.

The categories discussed so far suggest that reading can serve multiple functions at this initial phase of an inquiry cycle, all of which enable learners to open a particular area of knowledge to potential inquiry while simultaneously opening their minds to the possibilities that emerge. A close look at the reading activities teachers organized to achieve these functions indicates that the texts read in this phase of inquiry were primarily essays, stories, and brief informational articles that represent mathematics in a manner that goes beyond the technical view so prevalent in school mathematics. Despite the temptation to think of these texts as the main actors in these reading activities, they remain potentials unless teachers invite students to read in a generative mode, which often involves the production of student-, teacher-, and class-generated texts. Orchestrating these reading activities—including the choice of texts, strategies for reading them, and the class discussions that arise from sharing students' responses and interpretations of these texts—is what brings this phase of inquiry to life and what makes the teacher's role in it so significant.

Functions of Reading in "Carrying Out the Inquiry"

If during the initial phase of the inquiry cycle reading serves as a way to open up and problematize a particular domain so as to engage students' interest and support their efforts to find a problem or question rich enough to pursue, the reading students do as they carry out the inquiry is more focused and problem-driven. The first three categories in this phase of the inquiry—*generating specific questions or conjectures, gathering the relevant data*, and *analyzing those data to answer the question or conjecture posed*—highlight the "technical" reading that is characteristic of this phase of math inquiry cycles. In both the "Taxigeometry" and the "Analog & Analytic" cycles, reading was central to carrying out the inquiry because it was the reading of student-generated diagrams, along with the reading of definitions or area formulas for particular figures, that provided the starting point for making and testing conjectures. In the "Census" cycle, reading was also a crucial element in the process of creating the census questionnaire and analyzing the data collected by means of this tool. The nature of this reading was different from that in the other two inquiry cycles, however, as it involved editing questions, extracting information from forms and tables, and transforming this information in order to make it more meaningful through the use of statistical techniques. Despite these differences, the reading students do at this point in the inquiry cycle looks more like the kind of reading that educators have traditionally associated with reading mathematics (e.g., Shuard & Rothery, 1984), as it involves reading tables of data, graphs, and figures, and transforming them using a variety of mathematical concepts and techniques. What marks these reading experiences off from those observed in traditional mathematics classrooms, however, is the purposefulness of the reading. Rather than reading data, graphs, and figures to complete assigned exercises, in this phase of the inquiry students read to resolve problems they have had a role in identifying; thus the reading has a purpose students may be more invested in.

The two other categories we identified within the "carrying out the inquiry" phase involve texts and strategies for reading them that are more similar to those found in "setting the stage and focusing the inquiry." The first, *stimulate deeper inquiry*, usually occurs once the students' inquiry is under way, because the reading experiences coded as falling into this category were a way for the teacher to push students to think about their inquiry more deeply, or perhaps somewhat differently, than they had been doing up to that point. The idea that one can hold up the work of a so-called authority on a topic as a mirror for considering one's own efforts is at the heart of reading to *verify and/or validate the process/results of one's inquiry in light of an outside source*. As described in the "Taxigeometry" cycle narrative, sections of a graduate student's paper were used in just this way. This experience offered students an opportunity that is rare in secondary mathematics instruction, namely, to use mathematical work produced by an outside source as a reference point for their own work; it is more common for students to be expected to treat such work as an authoritative, rather than as a provisional, account of mathematical thinking. Therefore, in addition to giving students a chance to see how another inquirer approached a similar problem, reading, writing, and talking about this text helped the students realize that what they had done intuitively could be formalized and "counted" as "real" mathematical work!

These last two reading functions show how reading can serve as both a further stimulus and a mirror for students' inquiries. As was the case for the reading functions encountered in "setting the stage and focusing the inquiry," these reading activities were carefully orchestrated by the teachers and represented their attempts to help students learn as much as they could from the inquiry by considering an idea, point of view, or approach they might not have thought of on their own.

Functions of Reading in "Synthesizing/Communicating the Results of the Inquiry"

Although students have many opportunities to share their thinking with others throughout the inquiry (a point we explore in more depth when discussing the function of "collaborating with other inquirers"), this activity becomes formalized as the audience for that sharing shifts from "insiders" to "outsiders." Reading has two main functions in this phase of the inquiry cycle. The first relates to the reading students do to *produce a written report on results from the inquiry*, whereas the second is associated with the reading students do to *present results from the inquiry*.

In the inquiry cycles we have analyzed, students engaged in two kinds of reading when *producing a written report of results from the inquiry*. The first kind of reading consisted of reading preliminary results, tables, and the like, and synthesizing/transforming those texts in ways that would allow an outside audience to understand the results of the inquiry (as illustrated by the posters each student created at the end of the "Census" cycle). Although reading to transform preliminary data or texts and in this way construct a report of the results of an inquiry is not unique to mathematical inquiries, transforming data using mathematical procedures (such as the statistical techniques used in the "Census" cycle) is distinctly mathematical in nature.

In addition to reading and transforming other texts, students also engaged in another kind of reading while writing up the results of the inquiry, namely, the reading that writers typically do in the course of composing, revising, and editing their texts. This reading occurs throughout the entire process of preparing a report on the inquiry and includes reading to generate and fine-tune meanings as well as reading to edit for conventions of grammar, spelling, and genre. This second kind of reading to *produce a written report on the results of the inquiry* is ongoing, strategic, and contributes to the production and not just the presentation of the results, because it helps the inquirer shape meanings in particular ways. Although the writing of such reports did not receive much attention in the three inquiry cycles examined here, drawing students' attention to this use of reading and writing may be yet another way for teachers to demystify mathematical knowing for learners.

Students' presentations of results from their investigation often served as the focal event of this phase of the inquiry cycle, and in these events reading functioned as a way to make ideas public. Although there were times when students' presentations consisted of reading their text aloud, more often they used the supporting verbal and/or nonverbal texts they had produced as a "prop" in their presentations, pointing to it, reading selected parts, and holding it up for others to see and interpret— what we defined in the previous chapter as "text-supported" presentations. Consequently, those in the audience were expected to be active meaning-makers as well and to collaborate with the presenter(s) to understand, interpret, and challenge the results; the participation of the audience in these events was so pervasive that it warranted a separate category under the heading *collaborating with other inquirers*, to be discussed in a later section. Making public the results from students' inquiries in the manner described also gave the classroom community an opportunity to acknowledge and place value on the students' learning and, in doing so, celebrate their experiences as mathematical inquirers.

Functions of Reading in "Taking Stock and Looking Ahead"

Although reflection was not emphasized in two of the math inquiry cycles we documented (for various reasons, some of them logistical), it became the focal point of instruction as the "Taxigeometry" cycle came to a close. As was the case in "setting the stage and focusing the inquiry," reading served a variety of functions in this phase of the inquiry cycle, each of which enabled students to take stock of their inquiry experience and look ahead to new inquiries.

The first function reading served in this phase of the inquiry can be characterized as *elicit reflections on what took place in the inquiry*. As illustrated in the "Taxigeometry" cycle, *rereading* a text encountered earlier in the unit can provide a powerful way to set the stage for reflective thinking by evoking in students their memories of reading that text and the work developed around it; this is especially so when this rereading is accompanied by some reflective questions designed to elicit students' reflections on that experience and its value to them as learners, inquirers, and mathematicians. Rereading contributed to the same function in a different instructional activity, "Walk Down Memory Lane," where students were asked to remember and name the events that occurred over the course of the inquiry cycle. In this case, reading the diagrams that had been posted on the classroom walls throughout the inquiry cycle was pivotal in supporting students' efforts to remember and reflect on learning.

However essential it may be for students to name their experience, naming does not by itself ensure that students will draw conclusions about their experience and use it to inform their future inquiries. Hence the functions we called *identifying, discussing, and appreciating the significance of what was done/learned through the inquiry* and *evaluating individual students' participation, performance, and learning throughout the inquiry* are a necessary complement to the one discussed so far. Both the creation of the "What did I learn?" list and the evaluation conferences that resulted in completing the school evaluation forms illustrate the important role reading can play in achieving these functions. For example, as the "What did I learn?" list came into being, students could read their own statements to reinforce their thinking and read their peers' statements to spark new ideas. During the individual evaluation conference, reading allowed both the teacher and the student to reflect on what the student had done and construct an interpretation of that experience in reference to the students' artifacts, the teacher's notes, and the criteria listed on the official evaluation document. In this way, the text became a site for the negotiation of meanings, and the collaborative reading, writing, and talking that characterized these events provided opportunities for students and teachers to reflect on and celebrate students' learning.

Reading the final section of the article "The Power of Stories in Learning Mathematics" (Borasi, Sheedy, & Siegel, 1990) served an entirely different function in the "Taxigeometry" cycle and was therefore coded as a new category, *looking ahead to new inquiries*. The function reading played here is very similar to those described earlier in "setting the stage and focusing the inquiry," as the text was used as inspiration for a new inquiry. This is not an unexpected finding, because inquiry is usually thought of as regenerative; the endpoint of one inquiry provides the starting point for another.

Functions of Reading in "Gathering Tools/Strategies/Resources"

Although strategy instruction comes at the end of the inquiry cycle as Burke and Harste (1992) describe it, the analysis of all three math inquiry cycles suggested that "gathering tools/strategies/resources" was a recurrent activity. Therefore, unlike the four clusters of reading functions discussed so far, the reading functions described in this section did not take place at a particular point in the inquiry but rather occurred *throughout* the inquiry cycle. We observed, however, that the kind of reading associated with an embedded component remained constant across the specific functions that made up each component, though for a purpose that shifted in relation to the particular phase of the cycle within which the reading occurred.

Specifically, whenever students read a text so as to learn or become aware of a tool, strategy, or resource useful for their inquiries (whether it was the one they were planning—in "setting the stage," the one they were currently engaged in—when "carrying out the inquiry," or one they might pursue at some future date—as they finally "looked ahead"), they focused on understanding the specific tool, strategy, or resource offered in the text. For this reason, we suggest that the reading done to gather tools/strategies/resources primarily involves strategic comprehending, which may often be accompanied by judicious skimming in order to locate the most appropriate portion of the text. At the same time, interesting differences can be noted as students read to "gather tools/strategies/resources" during different phases of their inquiry.

At the beginning of the inquiry cycle, when the focus of the inquiry has not yet been determined, a specific tool may be introduced only because of its *potential* usefulness to the upcoming inquiry. To make the experience genuine and not reduce the inquiry to a traditional application experience, it was very important at this point that the reading experience orchestrated by the teacher not only enable students to gather such a tool but also create the *need* for it—hence the characterization of the reading function as reading to *create the need for and introduce tools/strategies/resources useful to the inquiry*. When students are carrying out the inquiry, the activity of gathering tools/strategies/resources is different, because the students now know they need certain supports to move forward in their inquiries, and therefore they approach the reading in a more focused and strategic way. Finally, in the last phase of inquiry when the class takes stock of their inquiry experience and looks ahead to new inquiries, reading can function as a way to *gather tools/strategies/resources for future inquiries*. This phase may be the point in the inquiry where specific techniques and strategies can be explicitly taught in response to needs that have become evident as a result of explicit reflection on the students' inquiry experiences (what Burke and Harste [1992] refer to as "strategy instruction")—as illustrated, in part, by the introduction of the "What-if-not" strategy for problem posing in the "Taxigeometry" cycle.

It is especially interesting to note that we do not have examples of gathering tools with respect to synthesizing/communicating results in the three inquiry experiences we examined. This does not mean that reading could not serve this function in other inquiry cycles; rather, it serves to remind us that, because the categories of reading functions generated by this study were grounded *entirely* in data from the three-inquiry experience, the set of categories we identified could be expanded and refined as additional experiences are considered. At the same time, the absence of examples of reading to gather tools at this stage of the inquiry can be taken as an indication that, in the context of mathematics instruction, less attention is paid to producing written reports on the inquiry than might be the case in a social studies or English class.

Functions of Reading in "Getting a 'Model'"

Reading to "get a 'model'" was quite different from reading that was done to achieve the functions associated with the chronological phases of the inquiry cycle and even "gathering tools/strategies/resources." Rather than focusing on the content per se, the explicit and sometimes implicit message to students was to read the text with an eye toward the "format" of the text in order to learn how to do something the author did (e.g., formulate questions for a census questionnaire; conduct a more systematic inquiry of issues within taxigeometry; synthesize and communicate a report of one's investigation; or use a systematic approach to problem posing). Given this orientation to the text, students did not always read the text in its entirety, nor did they necessarily read it only once; this suggests that the reading done to achieve this function was selective and strategic in order to achieve a very specific purpose.

Once again, despite this common way of reading, students read texts "to get a 'model'" for different purposes at various points in the inquiry. Texts were read to *get an image of the kind of inquiry to be undertaken* early in the cycle; to *see how some approaches or tools might help conduct their inquiry* when carrying out the inquiry; to *gather inspiration and/or a concrete image for specific formats that could be used to communicate their results to others* when preparing to synthesize and report on the inquiry; and, finally, to *get an image of inquiries and/or specific approaches that might be useful in future inquiries* in taking stock and looking ahead.

Functions of Reading in "Collaborating with Other Inquirers"

Collaboration was so pervasive in the three inquiry cycles we analyzed as to be almost invisible. Reading supported this collaboration throughout the inquiry in many ways, most notably by providing students with vehicles and opportunities to make their thinking public. As was the case with the "embedded components" discussed previously, the functions reading served in this cluster changed as the inquiry unfolded.

In "setting the stage and focusing the inquiry," collaborating with other inquirers was done in order to *share ideas and generate a wide range of perspectives and possibilities*. For example, in both the "Taxigeometry" and "Analog & Analytic" cycles, students shared their ideas with one another in small and large groups by reading and talking their way through various essays as well as by reading aloud journal entries they had written in response to these essays. By making public their thinking in this way, the students and teacher were able to consider these ideas further and, in so doing, begin to formulate and gradually shape their inquiries.

The focus of this sharing shifted as the students started to "carry out the inquiry." In this phase of the cycle, students mostly shared texts *they* had generated in order to *share and build upon individual contributions to the ongoing inquiry*. A special feature of these reading activities was the goal-oriented nature of the collaboration; students did not just read and discuss one another's diagrams or census data but often acted upon these texts, identifying patterns, suggesting other approaches, and challenging interpretations, all in an attempt to address the particular questions and conjectures at hand. These interactions not only moved the inquiry forward but helped build consensus among the inquirers. In this way, students had an opportunity to experience inquiry as a social practice involving the negotiation of meanings among members of a community.

Collaboration among inquirers further changed and took several new forms in "synthesizing/communicating results from the inquiry." First of all, in some cases students read each other's work *to provide feedback on drafts of written reports on the inquiry*—as illustrated in the "Census" cycle when students were creating their final posters. In other situations, students read to *react to the presentation of results from the inquiry*. Reading the diagrams and posters presenters often used as visual supports enabled students in the audience to take an active part in the presentations and increased the likelihood that students would raise questions that would both clarify the ideas presented and suggest new problems and questions to explore.

Finally, collaboration with other inquirers occurred in the "Taxi-geometry" cycle as students "took stock of their experience and looked ahead to new inquiries." Reading aloud individual responses to reflective prompts of various kinds enabled the whole class to *share and build upon individual students' reflections on the inquiry*. This kind of sharing not only invites students to give voice to their perspectives on an inquiry experience but allows them to consolidate and elaborate those ideas in light of multiple points of view—especially when students' responses are recorded on newsprint. In addition, reading functioned as a mode of collaboration in order to *share and build upon ideas for a new inquiry*—once again in a manner similar to that described in "setting the stage and focusing the inquiry."

The reading functions identified within this last cluster of embedded components are significant not only because of the contribution collaboration makes to students' inquiries but also because of the potential impact these experiences may have on students' conceptions of knowing and doing mathematics. The opportunity to experience firsthand the social construction of mathematical knowledge may be important in helping students reconsider what mathematics is all about.

Summary and Conclusions

The findings presented in this chapter lend support to our initial hypothesis that reading can contribute in significant ways to students' engagement in mathematical inquiries. At the same time, this study has helped us gain a better understanding of "math inquiry cycles," because the reading functions we identified are closely related to the chronological phases and embedded components and therefore allowed us to further clarify the characteristics of these elements. Just noting the names of the six reading functions associated with "setting the stage and focusing the inquiry," for example, can offer insight into this phase of the inquiry (see Figure 6.10). Furthermore, once we noticed the relationship between the names of the functions and the phase/component of the inquiry cycle, it became evident that the functions thus identified are general enough to be accomplished also by using activities *other than reading*. This by itself may be a useful finding in that the identification and naming of these functions may encourage mathematics teachers and mathematics education researchers to develop and study other instructional experiences that could serve similar roles in "math inquiry cycles." In the context of the three inquiry cycles we analyzed, however, reading was not a "frill" or an "enrichment activity," something students did to *supplement* their engagement in mathematical inquiries. Rather, reading was what brought the inquiry cycle to life; as a result, we came to think of reading as so integrated into the inquiry cycle as to be a way of doing inquiry.

When we looked closely at the ways that reading achieved the functions associated with these seven key elements of an inquiry cycle, we noticed another interesting pattern. What was especially intriguing was the way that each cluster of reading functions seemed to be achieved through a different kind of reading, which represented different lines of research in the field of reading and language education—briefly outlined in the review of the literature presented in Chapter 2. For example, reader response theories such as Rosenblatt's (1938, 1978) transactional theory of reading provide an apt description of the reading experiences identified in "setting the stage and focusing the inquiry," because the focus of these reading experiences was on making connections to and reflecting on personal experiences that came to mind as students read various texts in order to generate questions and directions for their inquiries. Rather than an activity undertaken primarily to understand the author's message, the reading had a more generative quality that was appropriate given the goal of this phase of the inquiry cycle. Not surprisingly, this was the point in the inquiry when we observed more examples of "reading rich math texts generatively"—the kind of reading specifically explored in Chapter 4—although other kinds of reading took place as well (such as reading and responding to questions in a questionnaire, or reading newspaper articles as a possible source of inspiration for the students' own inquiries but without using transactional reading strategies). The reading students did while "carrying out the inquiry," in contrast, was more technical and strategic, because they needed to understand the texts they read in order to move their inquiries forward. As noted earlier, this is the kind of reading usually associated with reading mathematics and has been studied primarily by cognitive psychologists and mathematics educators interested in the reading of technical mathematics texts. Our findings also suggest that students read very differently when "synthesizing/communicating results from the inquiry," as they did most of this reading in the course of preparing and presenting reports of their inquiries. This kind of reading has been studied by researchers interested in the connections between reading and writing, especially the role reading plays in composing texts. And during "taking stock and looking ahead," reading once again involved the kind of reading associated with reader-response theories, owing to the attention these theories pay to the reader's experience while reading and to a generative reading of texts.

We observed similar patterns with the "embedded" components of the inquiry cycle, although in these cases the common element tended to be the use of specific reading practices identified in Chapter 5 (as summarized in Figure 5.5). For example, in "gathering tools" the reader's goal was understanding the text in light of the particular situation in which it was going to be used, and thus this reading usually involved the practice of "reading with a focus on extracting specific information," often preceded by "skimming the text to make a decision" as to whether it might contain the desired information. In the case of "getting a 'model,'" the reader needed to focus her or his attention on the form of the text rather than on the message per se and thus engaged in the practice of "reading to get an example." The reading that was done to "collaborate with other inquirers," on the other hand, was quite different from the reading associated with the other two "embedded" components, because it usually involved oral reading either to "make ideas public" and thus initiate a dialogue, or to generate a shared text from texts representing individual thoughts.

The finding that clusters of reading functions and particular theories or reading practices were connected suggests the need for educators interested in the problem of reading mathematics to broaden the definition of reading in a mathematics class if they wish to fully capitalize on its potential to support students' inquiries. The connections we have noted indicate that reading mathematics in the context of math inquiry cycles is so complex as to require *multiple* theories and interpretive lenses rather than the few that have dominated research and practice on reading mathematics thus far.

CHAPTER 7

Conclusion

If the starting point for our research on integrating reading in mathematics instruction was a reframing of the problem of reading mathematics from an obstacle to a resource for learning mathematics, its conclusion is the awareness that educators will need to draw on *multiple* theories and perspectives to recognize what reading can offer mathematics teachers and students. As we began the RLM Project, we were guided by a conception of reading mathematics grounded in a transactional theory of reading and goals for school mathematics that challenged many long-standing curricular priorities and teaching practices. Yet, as a result of our collaboration with teachers who approached knowing and learning mathematics as inquiry and who paid explicit attention to reading as a result of their participation in the RLM Project, we began to see that even this "new integration" of reading and mathematics was too limited, as it could not account for the varied ways that reading was woven into Judi's and Lisa's classrooms. Only when we looked beyond transactional reading theory to social practice and functional perspectives on reading did we see just how integral reading could be to inquiry-oriented mathematics classrooms. In this chapter, we bring together the findings of the three studies described in Chapters 4, 5, and 6 to summarize our expanded view of integrating reading in inquiry-oriented mathematics classrooms, outline key implications for the practice of mathematics education, and identify directions for future research.

An Expanded View of Integrating Reading
in Inquiry-Oriented Mathematics Classrooms

In Chapters 4, 5, and 6, we presented in-depth discussions of what each perspective on reading can contribute to inquiry-oriented mathematics classrooms. There we examined specific findings about the instructional value of "reading rich math texts generatively," how social practices involving reading became a way to be a mathematician in

Judi Fonzi's classroom, and the functions reading can have in "math inquiry cycles." As a complement to these analyses, here we cut across the three studies and show how the findings that resulted suggest an expanded understanding of *why*, *what*, and *how* students can read in mathematics classrooms that are inquiry-oriented.

Why Students Might Read in Mathematics Classrooms

First of all, we can identify three complementary purposes that reading can have in inquiry-oriented mathematics instruction: (a) reading as a means of learning from text; (b) reading as a means of supporting and enhancing students' mathematical inquiries; and (c) reading as a means of negotiating a learning community. Although it is somewhat artificial to list these purposes separately, because they were often combined in the reading events we documented, we think it may be helpful to discuss each one in turn, as these three purposes greatly expand the traditional reasons for reading in mathematics classrooms as well as our original ideas about *why* math teachers should consider integrating reading experiences in their everyday practices.

1. *Reading as a means of learning from text*
Learning from text is probably the most "obvious" reason students read in any subject area, and we continue to regard it as a worthwhile reason for students to read in a mathematics classroom, if we keep in mind the challenges we initially raised about the two most common beliefs about "learning from text" in mathematics classrooms (i.e., the expectation that the goals of such reading are limited to gathering information or skills from technical texts and the belief that such learning is achieved simply by "mining" the text). As the instructional experiences reported throughout the book have shown, there is more to "learning from text" than extracting facts and techniques from math textbooks. Students in inquiry-oriented mathematics classrooms can read not only to learn new technical information and skills from math textbooks but also to gain a better understanding of "big math ideas" (as when they read about the application of an important mathematical concept), to develop an appreciation for the nature of mathematics (as when they read about the history of mathematics or ethical issues related to the use of mathematical results), and to gain an understanding of some valuable mathematical processes (as when they identify specific problem-solving strategies from an account of how certain mathematical results were achieved). In addition, students can read texts to learn how to do something the text does, thus treating the text

as a model, to gather background information about a topic they wish to explore further, or even to validate and elaborate upon results they themselves have achieved.

Accomplishing these goals through reading often requires that students construct meanings by acting on and acting out texts, and this, in turn, means that one cannot separate reading the text from talking, writing, drawing, and engaging in mathematical activities that enact the text. Thus, in inquiry-oriented mathematics classrooms, learning from text involves generating meanings and exploring ideas represented in texts and may occur in the context of math inquiry cycles or as part of a unit of study. Whatever the context of its use instructionally, it is important to keep in mind that this interpretation of learning from text as publicly negotiating meanings also becomes a social practice in an inquiry-oriented mathematics classroom and thus part of what it means to be a mathematician in that setting.

2. Reading as a means of supporting and enhancing students' mathematical inquiries

However important, learning from texts is only *one* of the many purposes for reading when students engage in mathematical inquiries, one that will usually occur as they are trying to "gather tools/ resources" or "gather models" at various stages of their inquiry. In addition, reading can spark students' interest in a topic or problem, suggest ideas and directions for inquiry, articulate tasks and decisions that need to be accomplished, help students review and revise their tentative conjectures, support students' presentations of their results, invite students' reflections on their work, and facilitate communication within the community of inquirers (see Figure 6.10 for a more comprehensive list of these complementary functions of reading and how they may play out in different phases of a math inquiry cycle). Our experiences suggest that all these functions of reading can play critical roles in a mathematics classroom that aims at supporting student inquiry, even if some of them may be accomplished through more strategic ways of reading rather than through the generative approach we invite students to employ when "learning from text." The sense in which reading can be seen as a way to support students' mathematical inquiries is further expanded when one considers how some reading practices—such as the reading involved in making ideas public and generating something new—were so much a part of Judi Fonzi's inquiry-oriented classroom that in that setting it became impossible to separate engaging in reading from engaging in mathematical inquiries.

3. *Reading as a means of negotiating a learning community*

Even outside of a specific "math inquiry cycle," reading can contribute in important ways to the practice of inquiry and the creation of a learning community by providing concrete ways to participate in such a community and to negotiate with students the norms, values, and practices that constitute classroom life in an inquiry-oriented mathematics classroom. In the two classrooms featured in this book, the teachers valued the idea of knowledge as complex and ever open to revision—that is, knowing as inquiry—and this value led them to negotiate norms for social relations, classroom discourse, and classroom practice that were quite different from those usually observed in secondary mathematics classrooms. Indeed, it is hard to imagine, for example, how confusions, anomalies, and contradictions that motivated and resulted from students' inquiries could be taken up unless negotiation itself was a norm for classroom life. Moreover, because negotiating meaning was a public rather than a private practice, reading practices could provide students with a way to participate in this learning community. As our analysis of Judi Fonzi's classroom showed, being a mathematician in this classroom meant using transactional strategies to collectively make sense of a text read, reading aloud individual journal entries to construct a class list of ideas for inquiry, and reading and discussing the hypotheses or results that had been recorded on newsprint in the course of a class inquiry. These findings suggest that using certain reading practices in a mathematics classroom can not only support students' inquiries and learning but also enable students to participate in and come to value a community in which exploration, negotiation, and collaboration are norms.

What Students Might Read in Mathematics Classrooms

The three complementary purposes for reading outlined above call, in turn, for the use of a much wider variety of texts, and ways of reading them, than is usually encountered in mathematics classrooms. Although we suggest that teachers' decisions about *what* to read and *how* to do so will always be informed by their specific *purpose* for such a reading experience, we think it is worthwhile to articulate the variety of *choices* that are available for teachers to consider—because our research has identified a much wider range than is usually observed in secondary mathematics instruction and wider still than the kinds of texts and reading strategies we proposed when we began the RLM Project.

One of the reasons we originally undertook this study was our realization that mathematics students could benefit from reading many things other than simply worksheets or sections of their mathematics textbook. Our initial expectation was that what we called "rich math texts" (e.g., essays, articles, stories, and even cartoons addressing math-related topics) could provide a wealth of learning opportunities for students. Although this hypothesis found support in several instructional episodes (as illustrated in the narratives reported in Chapters 4 and 6), we soon realized that there were other kinds of texts that could play an important role in inquiry-oriented mathematics classrooms (as illustrated by the extensive list of texts used in the "Math Connections B" course reported in Figure 5.6). Among the texts we identified were journal entries, questionnaires, a teacher-developed plan for inquiry, statements recorded on newsprint, posters, final reports, drawn figures, and even tables of data such as a bus schedule.

That many of these texts were produced by the teacher and by students to be read and discussed as part of ordinary classroom practice is especially significant, as it suggests the value placed on text as a starting point for communication, negotiation, and collaboration within a learning community. In addition, the spontaneous use made of diagrams, posters, and even videos (e.g., "The Theorem of Pythagoras" [Project Mathematics! 1989]) in several of the instructional experiences we examined suggests the value of further expanding the traditional interpretation of text as "printed matter" to include a variety of multimedia texts—an interpretation that seems especially important in light of the students' increased access to such texts on CD-ROMs and through the Internet.

Finally, our analysis of how these texts were used in inquiry-oriented mathematics classrooms made it evident that however "rich" the math-related stories and essays we initially focused on may seem, the "richness" of a text depends more on the uses made of it in the classroom than on any intrinsic characteristics of the text itself. Indeed, it was interesting to note that most of the texts eventually used in Judi's and Lisa's classrooms were probably never intended for an audience of math students!

How Students Might Read in Mathematics Classrooms

The insight that the "richness" of any particular text is dependent on its use brings us back to the importance of also expanding the interpretation of *how* texts can be read in a mathematics classroom. As we began our research, one of our main goals was to enlarge the repertoire of *reading strategies* available to mathematics teachers by adapting some of the transactional reading strategies proposed in the reading literature. Our first study (as reported in Chapter 4) achieved this goal by developing several variations around the Say Something, Cloning an Author, and Sketch-to-Stretch strategies while also identifying yet another strategy—which we called Enacting the Text—that is consistent with a transactional perspective on reading yet was derived from the teachers' spontaneous practices rather than the reading literature. Our classroom data suggest the value of using any combination of these strategies to enhance mathematics students' ability to "make sense" of complex, math-related texts and to use these texts as springboards for further mathematical explorations and classroom discussions—thus increasing the potential of these texts to support students' mathematical learning.

Our later studies, which made us more aware of purposes for reading other than "learning from text," also demonstrated that in some cases—for example, when students read their work aloud, read statements recorded on newsprint, or read directions for an assignment—focusing on how to read such texts or on useful reading strategies made little sense. In such cases, reading these texts was straightforward and the significance of these reading practices depended, instead, on the extent to which they helped accomplish the learning experience in which they were embedded. Thus our sense of *how* students might read in a mathematics class expanded considerably, because our original interpretations of "reading" and "text" could not account for all the ways reading was incorporated into mathematics classrooms in which learning mathematics emphasized exploring and negotiating meanings together.

Implications for Mathematics Education

We hope that the expanded interpretation of reading in inquiry-oriented mathematics classrooms summarized in the previous section will encourage mathematics teachers to reverse the current trend of minimizing the use of reading in mathematics instruction. Teachers' attempts to avoid putting an additional obstacle in the way of their students' mathematics learning by reducing the amount of reading they encounter in mathematics instruction may, instead, be replaced by an effort to look for opportunities to tap the potential reading offers students in learning mathematics. We expect this will involve the following considerations:

- The design of meaningful instructional experiences that integrate reading with writing, talking, and mathematical activities so as to provide mathematics students with richer opportunities for learning.
- The development and negotiation with students of reading practices that become part of a class's everyday life and thus serve to build and sustain a learning community that values collaboration and negotiation of meaning.

We believe that the categories of reading practices and functions generated by our research and summarized in Figures 5.5 and 6.10, as well as the ways of reading texts generatively articulated in Chapter 4 and the variety of texts used in some of the experiences we documented (as identified in Figure 5.6), may be helpful to teachers interested in incorporating reading for some of the purposes we have described. These lists can provide mathematics teachers with concrete ideas about reading experiences beneficial for their students. Even if planning such experiences still requires many decisions about what and how to read as well as how this reading can be integrated into other components of the instructional experience in order to accomplish the instructional purposes the teacher has in mind, the categories and lists of texts developed as a result of our research may expand teachers' instructional repertoires.

At the same time, it is important to keep in mind some limitations of these "lists." First, we never intended our categories to provide a comprehensive set of either reading practices or reading functions; they were generated as a result of a data-based categorization. What we consider more important is that teachers can use our lists as a resource for planning while at the same time taking up the questions we were forced to confront throughout this project—what counts as "reading" in a mathematics class and how to define "mathematics," "teaching," and "learning."

Although we hope that the successful instructional experiences reported in this book will encourage teachers to use reading in similar ways in their mathematics classrooms, we think they may need to keep in mind some of the conditions that made it possible for Judi Fonzi and Lisa Grasso Sanvidge to integrate reading so fully into their teaching. As described in Chapter 3, both teachers shared the inquiry perspective on mathematics instruction outlined in Chapter 2, and this perspective infused all of their teaching, including values, goals, and practices, thus enabling them to more readily see what reading experiences could offer their students. Moreover, both teachers had participated in extensive professional development that helped them expand their views of reading and offered ongoing support when they began to incorporate reading in their own classes. The awareness of factors such as the influence of teachers' beliefs on their instructional practices and the need for professional development experiences that support instructional changes have important implications for both the reform of school mathematics and the education of teachers.

First, reading experiences such as those described in this book cannot be simply "added on" to what is occurring in traditional mathematics classrooms without rethinking the goals and values informing those classrooms. In order to be truly effective, such reading experiences need to go hand in hand with larger reform efforts. As our own research in two more "traditional" instructional settings suggests (Siegel, Borasi, Fonzi, & Smith, 1996; Borasi, Siegel, Fonzi, & Smith, 1998), merely introducing isolated reading experiences has more limited effects and benefits than those observed in the classes portrayed in this book. Hence teachers and administrators may want to consider using the integration of reading in mathematics instruction we propose as a vehicle for moving toward the new goals, teaching practices, and classroom environments promoted by the most recent calls for school mathematics reform (e.g., NCTM, 1989, 1991).

Second, because most mathematics teachers have not examined their own views of reading, they may find it difficult to immediately see the value of reading in their classrooms. Hence, before teachers can expand their repertoire of math-related reading activities and make use of the research findings reported in this book, they may need to reflect on their own beliefs about reading and consider what may be gained from thinking about reading in the context of mathematics instruction in the ways we have outlined.

These were issues we considered carefully when we designed the RLM Project, and although we did not make the professional development component of the project a focus of our research, our own experiences as teacher educators—both within the context of the RLM Project and in other settings—as well as the recent literature on mathematics teacher education (e.g., Borasi, Fonzi, Smith, & Rose, in press; Schifter & Fosnot, 1993) lead us to suggest using the following combination of professional development experiences to support teachers interested in taking up the challenge of integrating reading in mathematics instruction:

- Engaging teachers in "experiences as learners" in which they themselves engage in reading events involving a variety of texts, reading strategies, and purposes and then reflect on these experiences, with the goal of becoming aware of the advantages and drawbacks of these alternative ways of reading for mathematics instruction (as illustrated by the experiences developed in the RLM seminar, described in Chapter 3).

- Providing teachers with narrative descriptions of classroom experiences that illustrate how reading can be integral to mathematics instruction, supplemented by analyses of these experiences, so as to help teachers develop images of how these experiences can play out in a classroom and how students may respond to them—a role that can be played by the various narratives presented throughout this book.

- Engaging teachers in "supported experiences as teachers," in which they begin to incorporate reading experiences in their classroom with the support of teacher educators and/or a peer group—as was done during the collaborative action research component of our RLM Project, wherein each classroom teacher met regularly with a team to plan units collaboratively and discuss the results of these experiences and team members made classroom visits and offered support.

- Encouraging teacher inquiry and research on the uses of reading that develop in their mathematics classrooms, so that they can continue to explore questions about what students gain from these experiences and what "counts" as reading in mathematics instruction—and, in doing so, enhance their own classroom practice as well as the professional conversation about the contribution reading may make to mathematics instruction.

Directions for Future Research

Taken as a whole, the research reported in this book offers a new way of thinking about integrating reading in inquiry-oriented mathematics classrooms and shows how this expanded view may help teachers and students achieve many of the goals of school mathematics reform. At the same time, the nature of our research and results remains *exploratory*, as it was based on the in-depth study of two specific classrooms. Future studies developed in a variety of instructional settings could further support and elaborate on our research findings by (a) identifying an even broader set of texts, reading strategies, practices, and functions relevant to mathematics instruction; (b) documenting the effects of specific reading experiences or sets of practices on students' mathematical learning and on the classroom environment, and (c) identifying the factors that may enhance or diminish the potential of such reading experiences.

It would also be interesting to explore the implications that our expanded view of reading in mathematics has for other "reformed" mathematics classrooms, given that an inquiry orientation is only one of the ways to engage in the reform of school mathematics consistent with the NCTM Standards (NCTM, 1989, 1991). We would be especially interested in examining the nature of the reading practices and functions observed in classrooms that use some of the innovative NSF-funded curriculum series such as *Connected Mathematics* (Lappan, Fey, Fitzgerald, Friel, & Phillips, 1998) and *Investigations in Numbers, Data, and Space* (TERC, 1998), once these teachers had opportunities to participate in professional development experiences such as those described earlier.

Some of the insights that emerged from our study also suggest questions that may be worth pursuing further in order to more fully understand how reading could contribute to mathematics instruction. First, the recognition that all math-related texts are potentially "rich" invites research on whether and how the transactional reading strategies discussed in Chapter 4 can help students read "technical" mathematical texts more effectively and generatively. Similarly, our "discovery" of the Enacting the Text strategy, which emerged from the spontaneous practices of the mathematics teachers with whom we collaborated, suggests that another source of strategies for reading "technical" mathematical texts could come from studying how professional mathematicians and mathematics teachers approach the reading of such texts. Second, the finding reported in Chapter 6 that different theories of reading may be needed to explain the complementary functions of reading in "math inquiry cycles" may make it worthwhile to return to the literature on teaching reading and writing for strategies other than the transactional ones we considered. For example, it might be productive to investigate what uses and adaptations of reading/writing strategies developed to support the composing process could be helpful to students when generating and revising math-related texts, strategies we realized were missing when students constructed texts to communicate the results of their inquiries to outside audiences (see Figure 6.10). Finally, we believe that our findings about what reading contributes to mathematics instruction could be further enhanced and complemented by future research focusing on "literacy events" in mathematics classrooms rather than on reading or writing or talking alone. Consistent with the conceptual shift already under way within the field of reading education, our research has shown that reading, writing, and talking do not work separately in practice, and if we want to understand how they work together, we need to conceptualize and study them as interrelated.

Although our discussion thus far has focused on reading in the context of school mathematics, some of the results of our study also have implications for research and practice on reading in content areas other than mathematics. First, we believe that researchers studying reading in content-area classrooms may benefit from broadening their analytic lens beyond a focus on strategies for learning from text and make what is commonly thought of as "instrumental" reading a phenomenon of interest. As the study presented in Chapter 5 shows, so-called instrumental reading practices play an important part in the construction of classroom meanings and identities and are "instrumental" to classroom experiences in a much deeper sense than is usually understood. Our research therefore suggests that it may be productive to take up the question of instrumental reading in content-area classrooms and pursue it from a social-practice perspective on reading, as this perspective would make visible the ways that text-related interactions contribute to the construction of a particular instructional ideology. Moreover, we think our findings point to the value of adopting multiple perspectives on reading—such as transactional, social-practice, and functional—when studying reading and learning in content-area classrooms. Future studies of reading in content-area classrooms may adopt theoretical perspectives on reading we did not consider, and in such cases the research is likely to go beyond the findings we have presented and further expand educators' understanding of the nature and role of reading in content-area classrooms.

Another important result of our research is the insight we gained about the instructional ideology at work in Judi's and Lisa's classrooms, an ideology we have characterized as "inquiry-oriented." More specifically, the instructional experiences developed in these classrooms showed us that there were two critical and interconnected dimensions of instruction that enabled students to experience mathematics learning as inquiry: (a) learning experiences—such as "math inquiry cycles"—that could foster a sense of exploration; and (b) a set of social norms and values with students that could orient them to inquiry regardless of whether they were participating in an inquiry cycle or solving a conventional textbook problem. Whereas the research reported in this book identified the many roles that *reading* can play in designing experiences and negotiating norms and values that foster inquiry, future research could explore how *avenues other than reading* can also play these roles.

Concluding Thoughts

Despite the *exploratory* nature of our study of reading in inquiry-oriented mathematics classes, the richness of the findings and the new questions they have generated indicate the wealth of possibilities that open once the problem of reading mathematics is approached through interdisciplinary research that brings together current developments within the fields of reading and mathematics education. Throughout this book, we portray reading as an extremely varied and complex activity that contributed to mathematics instruction in several complementary ways in the classrooms studied. Becoming aware of this complexity, however, required us to expand our view of reading: first, by looking at reading not as the straightforward extraction of information from a text but rather as a meaning-making activity (as consistent with a transactional perspective on reading); second, by rethinking what "counts" as reading in a mathematics classroom (as a social-practice perspective on reading suggests); and, third, by examining the functions that the reading events thus identified played in specific inquiry cycles (as suggested by a functional perspective on reading). At the same time, we can only appreciate the contributions this expanded view of reading might make to mathematics instruction if the goals for school mathematics were reconceived so as to align with proposals in the mathematics reform literature, and if we broadened our interpretation of knowing and learning mathematics by building an inquiry framework from the work of scholars from many fields who have pursued the question of what counts as knowing and learning mathematics.

Our study also confirms the value of collaborative action research that is informed by theory but open to continuous revision in light of documentation of classroom experiences as well as ongoing conversations with collaborating teachers. Indeed, not only did we refine and elaborate our initial ideas about expanding the set of reading experiences relevant to mathematics instruction as a result of our classroom collaborations, we also went beyond those perspectives to new insights about just how integral reading could be to mathematics instruction while generating new questions about teaching and learning in inquiry-oriented mathematics classrooms.

As a result, we hope the research findings and narratives of classroom experiences presented in this book will not only inspire new uses of reading in mathematics classroom but also begin new conversations among reading and mathematics educators and invite other mathematics and reading educators and teachers to cross the boundaries and engage in interdisciplinary research on reading mathematics.

Appendix: Research Questions and Data Analysis Procedures

The centerpiece of this book is a presentation of the findings of research carried out in the context of the RLM Project and two follow-up studies. Although we produced these findings through systematic research, we chose to present them in a way that would address an audience of not only researchers but also teachers, teacher educators, and others engaged in professional development and educational reform activities for whom our work might have relevance. As a result, we did not include information on the specific research questions or data analysis procedures used to generate the findings presented in Chapters 4, 5, and 6. The purpose of this Appendix, therefore, is to fill this gap by reporting our methodological procedures for each study.

The analysis of the classroom data generated by the RLM Project and the follow-up studies was a multistep process and varied somewhat depending on the specific research questions that guided each of the three studies we undertook. In each case, however, the first step consisted of constructing written narratives from the field notes, mechanical recordings, and artifacts available. Narratives for all the experiences developed in the collaborative classroom research phase of the RLM Project as well as the "Census" and "Taxigeometry" experiences were prepared, and these narratives constitute the database for the project. It is important to clarify that these narratives are not verbatim transcripts, although whenever possible and appropriate they include a significant amount of transcribed classroom discourse as well as descriptions that attempt to capture the substance, tone, and meaning of ongoing classroom interactions. In light of the recent scholarship on ethnographic writing (Clifford, 1983; Clifford & Marcus, 1986; Tyler, 1985; van Maanen, 1988), it should be noted that these narratives adhered to traditional rhetorical practices in ethnographic writing in that they were written as realistic accounts that offered a single point of view; in other words, we did not attempt to construct multivoiced narratives that represented the social worlds and literacies of the students, although that would be an important focus for future research. Even the production of realist narratives is not straightforward and represents the intentions and biases of the researcher "flattened" through writing. Still, they allowed us to reduce the data in a way that permitted further analysis and sense-making.

The next step—which involved selecting an appropriate subset of the classroom experiences for more in-depth study, developing appropriate units of analysis, and developing specific data analysis procedures—was instead unique to each of the three studies we conducted; they therefore need to be described separately and in relation to the particular research questions and theoretical perspectives assumed in each case.

Research Questions and Data Analysis Procedures for the Study Reported in Chapter 4

In our first look at the classroom data, we tried to answer the original research question that had motivated the RLM Project: "How can mathematics instruction take advantage of transactional models of reading so as to foster critical thinking, defined as an attitude of inquiry, and a deeper understanding of mathematics?" (Borasi & Siegel, 1988). For this reason, we chose to focus only on those RLM units developed and fully documented within the context of the RLM Project as originally planned—that is, the geometry unit developed in the rural/suburban middle school, a probability unit developed in the suburban high school, a logic unit and a probability unit developed in the urban high school, and the "Math Connections B" course developed in the public alternative high school.

We began by attempting to identify a unit of analysis that would be rich enough to allow us to understand the generative reading experiences without stripping away meaning and, at the same time, manageable enough to allow us to analyze patterns in the classroom narratives regarding the specific uses made of reading. This was not an easy task! After considerable debate and exploration of a number of alternatives, we settled on a unit of analysis that we called an *RLM Episode* and defined it as "the set of learning experiences developed around the generative reading of a rich math text." The four researchers who participated in the data analysis (Raffaella Borasi, Marjorie Siegel, Judith Fonzi, and Constance Smith) then engaged in a first analysis of the classroom narratives in order to identify all the RLM Episodes that occurred in the five instructional units. More specifically, for each unit, one of these researchers (who had participated in the research team that designed the unit) examined the data collected on that unit and, using the above definition, identified all RLM Episodes that occurred in it, including borderline cases. The list thus generated was then discussed and final choices were made by consensus of all four researchers (a group that always included at least one person who had not been part of the research team that designed the unit).

This process was neither straightforward nor unproblematic, but eventually it helped us refine our initial definition of an RLM Episode, because we encountered a number of interesting events involving productive uses of reading by the students that did not fit our original ideas and expectations. For example, at the beginning of the "Math Connections B" course, students watched a video in class while recording ideas on index cards (a variation of the Cloning an Author reading strategy [Harste & Short, 1988]); we decided that although this instructional episode clearly involved a transactional reading strategy, it should not be counted as an RLM Episode because it did not involve a written text. Another example of an episode that we decided not to "count" as an RLM Episode was an instructional event in which the teacher in the "Math Connections B" course held up a children's book and read a few pages from it to illustrate a possible math connection; although this episode undoubtedly involved a "rich" text, it was not read using a transactional strategy, which we decided needed to be an essential part of our definition of an RLM Episode. In contrast, the group was unanimous in deciding that translating into words a "fictitious Greek manuscript" representing various diagrams (without verbal explanations) from which area formulas could be derived should be considered an RLM Episode, as we agreed that a text without words could still be considered a rich text and that the way students worked with the text was a good example of "transmediation" (Siegel, 1984) in that it involved the transformation of the original text using a different symbol system (i.e., from diagrams to words). In sum, these discussions helped us further clarify our interpretation of "reading rich math texts generatively" and at the same time made us aware that this was only *one* of several possible ways to conceptualize the role of reading in mathematics instruction—a point we explored in depth in our second study.

At the conclusion of this process, we had identified a set of 18 RLM Episodes that occurred in the context of the 5 RLM units—5 in the geometry unit, 3 in the probability unit taught in the suburban class, 1 in the logic unit and 1 in the probability unit taught in the urban class, and 8 in the "Math Connections B" course (see Siegel, Borasi, Fonzi, & Smith, 1996, for a brief narrative description of each of these RLM Episodes).

For each of the RLM Episodes thus identified, all the available data were compiled and a detailed narrative of the event prepared whenever one was not already available. These data were then examined in order to identify each instance when reading occurred and, for each of these cases, *what* the students read, *how* they read it, and *why* they read it were recorded in the form of a table (for an example of these tables, see Figures A.1 and A.2, created for the two vignettes reported in Chapter 4). Once again, this analysis was conducted by a researcher who had participated in the experience, and the results were reviewed by another researcher, with disagreements resolved by consensus after discussion.

On the basis of this preliminary analysis, all four researchers then reviewed the entire set of RLM Episodes in order to select a small subset that would well represent this corpus; at this point in the analysis, our goal was to create thick descriptions that would show what "reading rich math texts generatively" looked like in practice and allow us to generate some initial categories related to how reading experiences could be incorporated into mathematics curricula, how students used these reading experiences, and what students gained by doing so. The two episodes reported in Chapter 4 were chosen because we agreed that, taken together, they fully illustrated the potential of reading rich texts generatively, explicitly addressed the range of learning goals we were interested in supporting, involved variations of the four major transactional strategies we identified, and represented the first time these particular strategies were introduced to that group of students.

The complete set of data available for these two RLM Episodes (including field notes from classroom observations and planning meetings) was examined further by all four researchers to generate categories related to three more specific research questions that had been suggested by our preliminary analysis of the data: (a) What, why, and how did students read in these experiences? (b) How did the classroom teacher orchestrate such reading experiences? and (c) What did the students gain from these experiences? The researchers also examined the data to gain further insights about "reading rich math texts generatively" more generally. The results of these independent analyses were discussed by the whole group and revised, elaborated, and consolidated as a result of this discussion. It is important to note that the vignettes reported in Chapter 4 were created only *after* this analysis was completed, in an effort to highlight the findings of our analysis and include all the data necessary to substantiate these findings while still reducing the original complete narrative to a more readable length. These considerations also led us to include only a portion of the original RLM Episode in the "Math & War" vignette.

Figure A.1. What, why, and how students read in the "Mathematics and War" vignette.

What was read	Why it was read	How it was read
"Underneath the Fig Leaf," paragraph introducing a series of brief essays on various connections between mathematics and life.	To demonstrate the "say something" strategy before trying it in pairs; To introduce the two articles students would choose and read in pairs; To help students appreciate the fact that professional mathematicians see mathematics as connected to many aspects of life.	Class read the paragraph silently and then "said something" out loud; these comments were written on newsprint.
Newsprint of student responses, a written record of the introductory "say something" experience.	To help students value the shift in their comments from frustration with the language to understanding the connection between the text and their class.	The researcher/teacher read and discussed the students' comments aloud while students followed along.
Student choice: "Mathematics and War," a short essay on the relationship between mathematics and war. "Mathematics and the Marketplace," a short essay on the relationship between mathematics and economics.	To deepen students' understanding of the applications of mathematics to life by exploring the relationship between mathematics and war; To develop a strategy that could be used for sharing information in the future.	Two groups (Char, Jolea, & Margie; Van & Shellie) read the text silently, stopping at each paragraph to "say something" about what they had just read. Four other pairs of students also used "say something" to read.
Students' sketches	To value and learn from the different themes students explored while reading their articles; To value the uses of sketches to share information.	Students and teachers interpreted the drawings as the artists explained their thinking.
"Powerful statements" recorded by the teacher during the sharing of articles.	To make explicit and value the insights students expressed about the process and content of the experience.	The teacher read statements aloud.
Newsprint of students' reflections about the Say Something and Sketching strategies.	To reinforce students' comments.	Silently, individually (no actual evidence of reading).

Figure A.2. What, why, and how students read in the "Egg Man" vignette.

What was read	Why it was read	How it was read
"Adventures of an Egg Man," a long essay on the construction of a large egg to serve as a monument.	To help students appreciate how real-life situations may involve doing mathematics in a variety of ways; To help students recognize the properties of geometric figures and their significance; To learn a strategy that would support students' engagement with a difficult text.	Students wrote comments or questions on 10 3x5 cards as they read the essay at home.
Teacher's directions for group activity with cards, written on board.	To provide clear directions for group work and a reminder to refer to during group work if needed.	Teacher read directions aloud and commented on them as she did so; students read them silently if they chose.
Index cards written by individual students.	To support and deepen students' understanding of the text.	Students worked in small groups; read cards aloud, sorted similar cards into piles, selected the most important of these for further discussion.
Directions for homework assignment.	To understand the homework assignment.	Students read directions silently and individually.
"Adventures of an Egg Man" and course textbook.	To help students become aware of the names of many shapes within a meaningful context.	Students searched texts selectively to find names of geometric shapes.

Two cards with questions about circles, prepared by students during initial reading experience.	To value students' questions; To use students' questions as the motivation for rereading an important section of the essay.	Teacher read questions from student-generated cards on circles aloud to class.
The section of the "Egg Man" essay on constructing a circle, an ellipse, and an egg.	To help students understand the construction of a circle and ellipse and relate each to the basic property of that figure; To provide a demonstration for how to approach the homework; To answer the student questions that initiated this reading event; To help students understand similarities/differences between circles, ellipses, and eggs.	Students first read relevant section of text individually and silently; the teacher then guided a rereading of it in which a student actually did what was described in the text for circle and ellipse ("enacting the text"), and addressed at the same time the questions that motivated the reading.
List of "most interesting" index cards (as defined by either students or teacher) prepared by teacher.	To help students explore a math question in more depth and thus deepen and go beyond their understanding of the essay; To value the students' ideas and questions about the essay.	Students read through list, chose one question, and tried to answer it for homework.

The other 16 RLM Episodes were then reviewed in light of the categories generated from the in-depth analysis of the two selected RLM Episodes in an effort to find additional support, discrepant cases, or both (Erickson, 1986). In this stage of the analysis, we reviewed the entire set of RLM Episodes, searching for evidence of the occurrence/nonoccurrence of the categories generated from the analysis of the two RLM Episodes. For each RLM Episode, one researcher who had participated in that experience examined the data and recorded not only whether the episode reflected an occurrence of that category or not, but also what reasons and evidence prompted this decision; the results of these analyses were then compiled in the summary tables. A complete report of this analysis can be found elsewhere (Borasi, Siegel, Fonzi, & Smith, 1998; Siegel, Borasi, Fonzi, & Smith, 1996). Because this book focuses on the potential of reading in *inquiry-oriented* mathematics classes, we chose to include in Chapter 4 the two RLM Episodes ("Math & War" and "Egg Man" vignettes) that not only illustrated the potential of our original image of "reading to learn mathematics" but highlighted the ways this potential was tapped in inquiry-oriented mathematics classes.

Research Questions and Data Analysis Procedures for the Study Reported in Chapter 5

The in-depth analysis of the classroom data described earlier and, in particular, the creation of tables recording what, how, and why students read in the RLM Episodes we had developed led us to consider a new research question: "What kinds of reading practices characterize a mathematics classroom in which instruction is organized as inquiry?" (see Siegel & Fonzi, 1995, for a research report of this study). It is important to note that this question was *not* one of the original research questions but rather emerged specifically from the collaborative action research carried out in Judi Fonzi's "Math Connections B" course. This setting was unique because it was the only one in which the reading researcher had been present for the whole semester (occasionally taking an active part in the instruction), the only one in which the teacher was interested in participating actively in the analysis of the data, and the only one in which the *entire* course had been carefully documented (rather than just the experiences we had initially conceived as "reading to learn mathematics" experiences). For these reasons, we chose to limit our analysis of reading practices in an inquiry-oriented mathematics class to Judi's "Math Connections B" course.

This study obviously required a unit of analysis different from the RLM Episodes used earlier, something that would enable us to analyze patterns related to what was read, how it was read, and for what purposes throughout the course. Once again, after an iterative process of defining and redefining such a unit of analysis, we decided on a unit that we called an Instructional Event (IE) and used the overall activity as the basis for deciding when one event ended and the next began. We read through the narrative of the "Math Connections B" course and tried to answer the question, "What's going on here?" rather than looking at the event only in terms of the texts used and the purposes for reading them. Focusing on the instructional activity had a dual purpose: (a) to keep the participants' perspectives on the event in mind (we recognized that there were multiple perspectives but defined the event in terms of the instructional activity that was generally understood to be going on during class time) and (b) to analyze the event as a whole rather than reducing it to its logical, though reconstructed, component parts. We then identified what we called Reading Components (RC) that occurred within Instructional Events, and this became the unit that was coded for text, strategy, and instructional purpose. On the basis of these and other conversations about the coding form itself, we agreed on the following definitions:

- An Instructional Event (IE) was defined by the overall instructional activity the class was engaged in; that is, there was some general sense that X was going on during the event. The amount of time devoted to an Instructional Event ranged from half a class period to several class periods; hence, more than one event might take place in a single class period or one event might extend across several days. For example, Day 4 consisted of one Instructional Event—making posters of math connections from magazines students read. During this event, students worked in pairs to skim through magazines, identify all the references to mathematics they could find as well as examples of how the magazines used mathematics, record their findings on a poster, and present their posters to the entire class. Later in the course, the class spent 2 days (Days 36 and 37) on one Instructional Event, in which students worked in small groups to create a theorem about two figures that had the same area, drawing on a variety of resources (e.g., a teacher-prepared list of formulas for computing the area of familiar figures, textbooks, lined and plain paper, rulers, a previously viewed video).
- A Reading Component (RC) was identified in terms of the text and the purpose and was intended to capture the experience of reading so as to be consistent with a transactional perspective on reading, in which the relation of reader, text, and context is conceptualized as

a live circuit (Rosenblatt, 1978). Instructional Events could have no Reading Component, one Reading Component, or more than one Reading Component embedded in them. In the examples mentioned above, "making posters of math connections" consisted of 2 Reading Components, whereas "working in groups to create a theorem" involved 13 Reading Components. In each case, a separate Reading Component was identified each time either a new text was used or there was a new purpose for reading during the Instructional Event.

- Text was defined as any symbolic representation that had the potential to be interpreted.
- Reading Components were coded with regard to what text was read, how the text was used within the Instructional Event, and why the text was read. Three dimensions of instructional purpose ("why" a text was read) were identified: (a) the broad instructional purpose or scope of the activity; (b) what meaning(s) Judi hoped students would construct for each text; and (c) why the text was read in that particular way.

When this final analytic scheme was applied to the narrative, the course was divided into 5 segments, 42 Instructional Events, and 126 Reading Components (see Siegel & Fonzi, 1995, for a complete list of all 42 Instructional Events and related Reading Components).

The final stage of the analysis involved the categorization and characterization of the 126 Reading Components with regard to how and why each text was read. As the process of grouping and regrouping continued, however, the reading practice came to be characterized more in terms of its use in the ongoing activity, so that the question of how a text was read (e.g., whether a text was read line by line as opposed to selectively or nonlinearly) became less important than why it was read (e.g., reading a text aloud to make public some thinking a student or teacher had done). In other words, we wanted our analysis to capture reading in relation to the ongoing instructional activity, which meant we were guided by Judi's intentions and interpretation of the Instructional Events. We do not claim, therefore, that every student interpreted or used the reading in exactly the same way it is characterized; at the same time, in no case do we characterize a reading practice that was not actually enacted by some of the participants.

As a result of analyzing the Reading Components in this manner, we identified 23 categories, grouped into 5 general categories: (a) reading to make public; (b) reading to comprehend; (c) reading to get an example; (d) reading to generate something new; (e) reading to remember (see Chapter 5).

Research Questions and Data Analysis Procedures for the Study Reported in Chapter 6

The results of the previous study, along with our observations of other inquiry experiences developed by both Judi and Lisa, suggested the value of looking more specifically at the functions reading served in a specific kind of inquiry experience—what we came to call a "math inquiry cycle" (as defined and discussed in Chapter 6). The research question informing this third study was articulated as: "What functions can reading play in inquiry cycles developed in the context of secondary mathematics instruction?" (see Siegel, Borasi, & Fonzi, 1998, for a research report of this study). Once again, it is important to note that addressing this question moved us beyond the RLM Project as initially conceptualized.

As we examined the available classroom data to identify "math inquiry cycles" that could be systematically analyzed, it became evident that such examples could be found only in Judi's and Lisa's classrooms, as these two teachers shared mathematical and pedagogical beliefs consistent with an inquiry perspective on learning mathematics (as articulated in Chapter 2). Although a few other examples of inquiry cycles were identified, we chose to focus our analysis on the "Taxigeometry," "Analog & Analytic," and "Census" units, as they most clearly illustrated "math inquiry cycles" and together presented interesting differences with respect to content, development, instructional context, and teacher's experience, as summarized in Figure A.3.

To identify all the reading experiences students engaged in within each of these three inquiry cycles, we first broke down each cycle using the two complementary units of analysis developed in the previous study—that is, we identified all the Instructional Events (IEs) and Reading Components (RCs) embedded in each of these cycles. We then attempted to code this list of IEs and RCs for each of the three inquiry cycles in terms of the broad categories of an inquiry cycle we had first adapted from Burke and Harste (1992): that is, setting the stage; developing and focusing one's question; identifying appropriate approaches, resources, and tools for exploring the question; carrying out the research; collaborating with other inquirers; reflecting on and expanding the results of one's inquiry; communicating with outside audiences; identifying problems and planning strategy instruction; and offering invitations for new beginnings. As we did so, however, we realized that some of these categories seemed to represent "chronological phases" within the inquiry cycle, whereas others (e.g., identifying appropriate approaches, resources, and tools for exploring the question; collabo-

Figure A.3. Key characteristics of the three math inquiry cycles selected.

Math inquiry cycle	Taxigeometry	Analog & Analytic	Census
Math topic	alternative geometries	analog and analytic thinking	statistics/taking a census
Focus of the inquiry	exploring a new math system	examining the nature of mathematical thinking	engaging in a real-life problem involving math
Stimulus for the inquiry	designed by the teacher with considerable student input	spontaneously developed so as to resolve a controversy	designed essentially by the teacher, based on students' interests
Instructional context	a group of 10th–11th grade students in an alternative urban high school	a group of 9th–11th grade students in an alternative urban high school	8th grade students in a rural/suburban middle school
Teacher's experience	veteran teacher	veteran teacher	first-year teacher

rating with other inquirers) represented important components of an inquiry that were "embedded" throughout the cycle. On the basis of an initial reading of the data, we also decided to combine and rename our earlier modification of Burke and Harste's (1992) categories, resulting in four "chronological" phases of inquiry (setting the stage and focusing the inquiry, carrying out the inquiry, synthesizing/communicating results from the inquiry, taking stock and looking ahead) and three "embedded" components (gathering tools/strategies/resources, getting a "model," collaborating with other inquirers).

The list of IEs and RCs for each of the three inquiry cycles was finally coded with respect to the four "chronological phases" of an inquiry cycle, leaving aside the "embedded" components for the moment, as we could not yet see how they might be connected with the reading functions, if at all. Dividing each cycle into the four "chronological" phases, therefore, allowed us to begin the process of generating and refining categories representing the functions reading played by looking at each IE/RC *in relation to a particular phase of inquiry.*

We then categorized the IEs/RCs from only one of the inquiry cycles ("Census" unit) so that the categories generated from this experience could be later validated, expanded, revised, or all three, using data from the other two inquiry cycles. We examined and characterized each IE and/or RC in this unit in terms of the function it played in the inquiry, trying to find a level of generality that would highlight the specific role it played in the ongoing inquiry without being so specific that the function thus identified could not be easily generalized to other inquiry experiences. For example, an event in which students read and responded to thought-provoking questions in a questionnaire about the U.S. Census was characterized as an example of reading to "elicit and/or challenge initial conceptions and knowledge of the topic to be explored" rather than "reading to respond to questions in questionnaire" or even "reading to get directions for performing a task."

The complexity of the relationship of inquiry and reading in these inquiry cycles often meant that one IE and/or RC served more than one function. For example, because the questionnaire mentioned earlier was also used by the teacher as an opportunity to introduce or review the technique of "tallying responses" that she thought could be useful when the students began to analyze the results of the school census, this event was also an example of how reading functioned to "create the need for and introduce tools/strategies/resources useful to the inquiry." Finally, as we struggled to generate a set of categories that represented the functions reading played in the "Census" unit, we began to see that, in addition to the function of reading associated with the four phases of the inquiry cycle, the "embedded" components were also associated with particular reading functions.

The tentative set of categories generated from this analysis of the "Census" unit was then used to code the IEs and RCs that constituted the "Taxigeometry" and "Analog & Analytic" cycles. This process resulted in further refinement of this initial set of categories, as the need to add several new categories, as well as modify, consolidate, or divide some of the original categories, became apparent. The final result was a set of 30 distinct categories that represented the range of reading functions identified across the three cycles and was then used to code all the IEs and RCs identified in each cycle.

Patterns in the narratives of each inquiry cycle, in which IEs and RCs were coded in terms of the final set of categories, were then examined using several different strategies. First, two tables were created, one summarizing all the reading experiences associated with a particular function across the three inquiry experiences (see Figures A.4 and A.5 for two significant examples) and the other identifying the occurrence of each reading function across the three cycles. We examined the first table for commonalities and differences within and across categories

Figure A.4. Key illustrations of reading functions for "carrying out the inquiry" from the three inquiry cycles.

Reading Functions	"Taxigeometry" Cycle	"Census" Cycle	"Analog & Analytic" Cycle
Generate specific questions/ conjectures	Specific conjectures were continually generated and refined as students looked at the diagrams they had created for figures such as taxi-circles, taxi-triangles, etc., and examined them in light of definitions.	Which questions the school census would focus on was determined through a process involving the reading, categorizing, and selecting of questions generated by individual students. Some methodological questions (e.g., sampling issues) were also raised as a result of reading and analyzing the data collected.	Specific conjectures geared toward the creation of a theorem were continually generated and refined as students looked at the diagrams they had created and examined.
Gather/generate data to address specific questions/conjectures		The students carefully edited the 10 questions they had previously selected for their census questionnaire, referring to the 1990 U.S. Census form as models.	
Analyze/make sense/use the data collected to answer questions/test conjectures	Students critically examined the diagrams for taxicircles, taxi-triangles, etc., they had created in light of specific definitions, so as to evaluate and refine their conjectures about these specific figures and about taxigeometry more generally.	Responses to the school census questionnaire were analyzed by having each student read through the responses given by students in a specific homeroom, and then summarize those responses using appropriate statistics.	Students critically examined the diagrams they had generated in an attempt to prove their tentative theorems using both analog and analytic approaches.

		These "partial results" were recorded in a table, which in turn was used to create school-wide statistics and to answer other questions about students in the school.
		Students read and discussed selected newspaper articles to appreciate how what they were learning could be applied to real-life problems beyond the school census.
Stimulate deeper inquiry	The teacher assigned the reading of sections of a graduate student's paper on aspects of taxigeometry they had only partially or not yet explored (along with some written assignments), to stimulate a deeper exploration of those topics.	The teacher assigned the reading of an article on paper folding (along with a written assignment) to suggest new ways to approach the challenge of using an analog approach to prove their theorems.
Verify and/or validate the process/results of one's inquiry in light of an outside source	The teacher assigned the reading of sections of a graduate student's paper on aspects of taxigeometry they had already explored, as a way to compare and validate their own work.	

Figure A.5. Key illustrations of reading functions for "collaborating with other inquirers" from the three inquiry cycles.

Reading Functions	"Taxigeometry" Cycle	"Census" Cycle	"Analog & Analytic" Cycle
Setting the stage sharing ideas to generate a wider range of perspectives/possibilities	Students shared thoughts they generated from reading the essay and the math story, either as they read the text in class and/or by reading and discussing journal entries written for homework.		Students shared their interpretations of the "Analog and Analytic" essay and the video by reading their journal entries, sketches, and/or cards. Often, these contributions were recorded on newsprint for everyone to read.
Carrying out inquiry sharing and building upon individual contributions to the ongoing inquiry	As students explored specific questions and conjectures about taxigeometry, they shared and critically examined the diagrams and/or definitions they had created with other students. Students also shared the journal responses they wrote after reading the grad student's report on her exploration of taxigeometry.	The questions each student had previously generated were read, categorized, selected, and edited so as to create an agreed-upon school census questionnaire. To analyze the data thus collected, each student became responsible for reading and reporting the responses collected in a specific homeroom to the rest of the class.	As students tried to develop their own theorem in small groups, they shared and critically examined their conjectures and proofs, mostly relying on diagrams they had created. Students also read aloud the journal responses they wrote after reading an article on paper folding.

Synthesizing/ Communicating providing feedback on drafts of written reports on the inquiry	The teacher read aloud her part of the evaluation letter to parents so students could offer feedback, as well as get ideas for writing their own part.	As they prepared a poster summarizing the results of the census for their homeroom, several students looked at each other's posters and provided feedback.	
reacting to the presentation of results from the inquiry	Whenever a student presented the final results of his/her work, the rest of the class participated by asking questions and trying to make sense, often referring to the text (graphic or written) used to support the presentation.	As posters were presented in each homeroom, the audience read the posters and asked the student making the presentation questions about the posters and the oral presentation.	When the students presented their theorems and read their own historical snippets aloud, the rest of the class participated by asking questions and trying to make sense.
Taking stock sharing and building upon individual reflections on the inquiry	Students shared and discussed journal entries written in response to an essay that was read to stimulate their reflections on the experience. The teacher recorded on newsprint individual contributions to a "What did I learn?" list.		
sharing and building upon ideas for new inquiries	Students shared ideas as they read another part of the essay in class, which led them to consider the new topic of spherical geometry.		

and clusters of reading functions and the second table for patterns associated with the occurrence of reading functions across the three inquiry cycles; these observations were discussed among the researchers and the consensus recorded in a theoretical memo. A second narrative was then constructed for each of the three inquiry cycles in order to represent the categories in the context of their use within the cycle (a preliminary version of the narratives reported in Chapter 1 and Chapter 6). Finally, working hypotheses were generated to account for patterns that emerged from this data analysis process.

Reflections on Categories as Analytic Devices

Given that our analyses of reading practices in an inquiry-oriented mathematics class and of reading functions in three math inquiry cycles involved categories generated from the nexus of theory and data rather than categories generated from theory alone, it is important to conclude with some comments on the nature and limitations of the categories we identified in these two studies. First of all, we are well aware that both sets of categories we generated are provisional and open to revision as other inquiry-oriented mathematics classes and math inquiry cycles are considered, as is the case with all category systems that are generated entirely from the analysis of data representing particular experiences. At the same time, these categories accounted for the many uses of reading that occurred in the settings examined and as such can highlight uses of reading that have thus far been overlooked in mathematics instruction. Consequently, we do not regard these sets of categories as the definitive and comprehensive classification of reading practices and reading functions in inquiry-oriented mathematics classes; rather, we offer them as *heuristics* that may help mathematics educators identify and better appreciate possible ways that reading can be used to support student inquiry and, thus, plan richer learning experiences for their students.

References

Abbott, E. (1952). *Flatland*. (6th ed.). New York: Dover.

Adams, M., & Collins, A. (1979). A schema-theoretic view of reading. In R. Freedle (Ed.), *New directions in discourse processing* (Vol. 2). Norwood, NJ: Ablex.

Alvermann, D., & Moore, D. (1991). Secondary school reading. In R. Barr, M. Kamil, P. Mosenthal, & P. D. Pearson (Eds.), *Handbook of reading research* (Vol. 2, pp. 951–983). New York: Longman.

Anderson, R., & Pearson, P. D. (1984). A schema-theoretic view of basic processes in reading comprehension. In P. D. Pearson (Ed.), *Handbook of reading research* (Vol. 1, pp. 255–291). New York: Longman.

Anderson, R., Reynolds, R., Schallert, D., & Goetz, E. (1977). Frameworks for comprehending discourse. *American Educational Research Journal, 14*, 367–382.

Barnes, D. (1976). *From communication to curriculum*. Portsmouth, NH: Heinemann.

Baroody, A., & Ginsburg, H. (1990). Children's learning: A cognitive view. In R. B. Davis, C. A. Maher, & N. Noddings (Eds.), *Constructivist views on the teaching and learning of mathematics* (pp. 51–64). Reston, VA: National Council of Teachers of Mathematics.

Beach, R., & Hynds, S. (1991). Research on response to literature. In B. Barr, M. Kamil, P. Mosenthal, & P. D. Pearson (Eds.), *Handbook of reading research* (Vol. 2, pp. 453–489). White Plains, NY: Longman.

Berthoff, A. (1990). Democratic practice, pragmatic vistas: Louise Rosenblatt and the reader's response. In J. Clifford (Ed.), *The experience of reading* (pp. 77–84). Portsmouth, NH: Boynton/Cook.

Bishop, A. (1988). *Mathematical enculturation*. Dordrecht, The Netherlands: Kluwer Academic.

Bleich, D. (1978). *Subjective criticism*. Baltimore: The Johns Hopkins University Press.

Bloome, D., & Egan-Robertson, A. (1993). The social construction of intertextuality in classroom reading and writing lessons. *Reading Research Quarterly, 28*(4), 305–333.

Bloome, D., & Green, J. (1984). Directions in the sociolinguistic study of reading. In P. D. Pearson (Ed.), *Handbook of reading research* (Vol. 1, pp. 395–421). New York: Longman.

Borasi, R. (1990). The invisible hand operating in mathematics instruction: Students' conceptions and expectations. In T. J. Cooney & R. Hirsch (Eds.), *Teaching and learning mathematics in the 1990s* (pp. 174–182). 1990 Yearbook of the National Council of Teachers of Mathematics. Reston, VA: National Council of Teachers of Mathematics.

Borasi, R. (1992). *Learning mathematics through inquiry.* Portsmouth, NH: Heinemann.

Borasi, R. (1996). *Reconceiving mathematics instruction: A focus on errors.* Norwood, NJ: Ablex.

Borasi, R., & Brown, S. I. (1985). A "novel" approach to texts. *For the Learning of Mathematics, 5*(1), 21–23.

Borasi, R., Fonzi, J., Smith, C., & Rose, B. (in press). Beginning the process of rethinking mathematics instruction: A professional development program. *Journal of Mathematics Teacher Education.*

Borasi, R., Sheedy, J., & Siegel, M. (1990). The power of stories in learning mathematics. *Language Arts, 67*(2), 174–188.

Borasi, R., & Siegel, M. (1988). "Reading to learn mathematics" for critical thinking. Proposal to the National Science Foundation (Award # MDR-8851582).

Borasi, R., & Siegel, M. (1992, August). Reading, writing, and mathematics: Rethinking the "basics" and their relationship. Paper presented at the Seventh International Congress on Mathematics Education, Quebec City, Quebec, Canada.

Borasi, R., & Siegel, M. (1994). Reading, writing, and mathematics: Rethinking the basics and their relationship. In D. Robitaille, D. Wheeler, & C. Kieran (Eds.), *Selected lectures from the 7th International Congress on Mathematical Education* (pp. 35–48). Sainte-Foy, Quebec: Les Presses de L'Université Laval.

Borasi, R., Siegel, M., Fonzi, J., & Smith, C. (1998). Using transactional reading strategies to support sense-making and discussions in mathematics classrooms. *Journal for Research in Mathematics Education, 29*(3), 275–305.

Bransford, J., & Johnson, M. (1972). Contextual prerequisites for understanding: Some investigations of comprehension and recall. *Journal of Verbal Learning and Verbal Behavior, 11*, 717–726.

Bransford, J., & McCarrell, N. (1974). A sketch of a cognitive approach to comprehension. In W. Weimer & D. Palermo (Eds.), *Cognition and the symbolic process.* Hillsdale, NJ: Erlbaum.

Brilliant-Mills, H. (1994). Becoming a mathematician: Building a situated definition of mathematics. *Linguistics and Education, 5*, 301–334.

Brown, S. (1982). On humanistic alternatives in the practice of teacher education. *Journal of Research and Development in Education, 15*(4), 1–14.

Brown, S. (1984). The logic of problem generation: From morality and solving to de-posing and rebellion. *For the Learning of Mathematics, 4*(1), 12–13.

Brown, S., & Walter, M. (1990). *The art of problem posing* (2nd ed.). Hillsdale, NJ: Erlbaum.

Buerk, D. (1981). Changing the conception of mathematics knowledge in intellectually able, math-avoidant women. Unpublished doctoral dissertation, State University of New York at Buffalo.

Buerk, D. (1985). The voices of women making meaning in mathematics. *Journal of Education, 167*(3), 59–70.

Burke, C., & Harste, J. (1992). Teacher as researcher: Classrooms that support teacher and student inquiry. Workshop presented at the Third Annual International Whole Language Umbrella Conference, Niagara Falls, NY.

Campbell, D. (1976). *The whole craft of numbers.* Boston: Houghton Mifflin.

Campbell, D., & Higgins, J. (1984). *Mathematics: People, problems, results.* Belmont, CA: Wadsworth International.

Carr, W., & Kemmis, S. (1986). *Becoming critical: Education, knowledge, and action research.* London: Falmer Press.

Charles, I., & Silver, E. (Eds.). (1988). *The teaching and assessing of mathematical problem solving.* Reston, VA: National Council of Teachers of Mathematics.

Clifford, J. (1983). On ethnographic authority. *Representations, 1*(2), 118–146.

Clifford, J., & Marcus, G. (Eds.) (1986). *Writing culture: The poetics and politics of ethnography.* Berkeley: University of California Press.

Cobb, P. (1994). Where is the mind? Constructivist and sociocultural perspectives on mathematical development. *Educational Researcher, 23*(7), 13–20.

Cobb, P., Wood, T., & Yackel, E. (1990). Classrooms as learning environments for teachers and researchers. In R. Davis, C. Maher, & N. Noddings (Eds.), *Constructivist views on the teaching and learning of mathematics* (pp. 125–146). Reston, VA: National Council of Teachers of Mathematics.

Cohen, S., & Stover, G. (1981). Effects of teaching sixth-grade students to modify format variables of math word problems. *Reading Research Quarterly, 16*(2), 175–200.

Confrey, J. (1991). Learning to listen: A student's understanding of powers of ten. In E. von Glasersfeld (Ed.), *Radical constructivism in mathematics education* (pp. 111–138). Dordrecht, The Netherlands: Kluwer Academic.

Connolly, P., & Vilardi, T. (Eds.). (1989). *Writing to learn mathematics and science.* New York: Teachers College Press.

Curcio, F. (1987). Comprehension of mathematical relationships expressed in graphs. *Journal for Research in Mathematics Education, 18*, 382–393.

Curcio, F., & Artzt, A. (1998). Students communicating in small groups: Making sense of data in graphical form. In H. Steinbring, M. Bartolini Busi, & A. Sierpinska (Eds.), *Language and communication in the mathematics classroom* (pp. 179–190). Reston, VA: National Council of Teachers of Mathematics.

Davis, P., & Hersh, R. (1981). *The mathematical experience.* Boston: Houghton Mifflin.

Davis, R., Maher, C., & Noddings, N. (Eds.). (1990). *Constructivist views on the teaching and learning of mathematics.* Reston, VA: National Council of Teachers of Mathematics.

Dewey, J. (1933). *How we think.* Boston: D. C. Heath.

Earp, N., & Tanner, F. (1980). Mathematics and language. *Arithmetic Teacher, 28*, 32–34.

Eco, U. (1979). *The role of the reader.* Bloomington: Indiana University Press.

Erickson, F. (1986). Qualitative methods in research on teaching. In M. Wittrock (Ed.), *Handbook of research on teaching* (3rd ed., pp. 119–161). New York: Macmillan.

Fonzi, J., & Smith, C. (1992, August). *Communication in a secondary mathematics classroom: Some images.* Paper presented at the Seventh International Congress on Mathematics Education, Quebec City, Quebec, Canada.

Fonzi, J., & Smith, C. (1998). Communication in a secondary mathematics classroom: Some images. In H. Steinbring, M. Bartolini Busi, & A. Sierpinska (Eds.), *Language and communication in the mathematics classroom* (pp. 317–340). Reston, VA: National Council of Teachers of Mathematics.

Fosnot, C. (1996). *Constructivism: Theory, perspectives, and practice.* New York: Teachers College Press.

Gambrell, L., & Almesi, J. (Eds.). (1996). *Lively discussions!* Newark, DE: International Reading Association.

Gee, J. (1990). *Social linguistics and literacies: Ideology in discourses.* London: Falmer Press.

Ginsburg, H. (Ed.) (1983). *The development of mathematical thinking.* New York: Academic Press.

Ginsburg, H. (1989). *Children's mathematics* (2nd ed.). Austin, TX: Pro-Ed.

Gitlin, A., Siegel, M., & Boru, K. (1989). The politics of method: From leftist ethnography to educative research. *Qualitative Studies in Education, 2*(3), 237–253.

Gollasch, F. (Ed.). (1982). *Language and literacy: The selected writings of Kenneth S. Goodman* (Vols. 1 and 2). London: Routledge and Kegan Paul.

Goodlad, J. (1984). *A place called school.* New York: McGraw-Hill.

Goodman, K. S. (1967). Reading: A psycholinguistic guessing game. *The Journal of the Reading Specialist, 6*(4), 126–135.

Goodman, K. S. (1985). Unity in reading. In A. Purves & O. Niles (Eds.), *Becoming readers in a complex society* (pp. 79–114). Eighty-third Yearbook of the National Society for the Study of Education, Part 1. Chicago: University of Chicago Press.

Goodman, K. S. (1994). Reading, writing, and written texts: A transactional sociopsycholinguistic view. In R. Ruddell, M. Ruddell, & H. Singer (Eds.), *Theoretical models and processes of reading* (4th ed., pp. 1093–1130). Newark, DE: International Reading Association.

Green, J., & Meyer, L. (1991). The embeddedness of reading in classroom life: Reading as a situated process. In A. Luke & C. Baker (Eds.), *Towards a critical sociology of reading pedagogy* (pp. 141–160). Philadelphia: John Benjamins.

Griffiths, R., & Clyne, M. (1991). *Books you can count on.* Portsmouth, NH: Heinemann.

Grouws, D. (Ed.). (1992). *Handbook of research on mathematics teaching and learning.* New York: Macmillan.

Halliday, M. A. K. (1975). *Learning how to mean*. London: Edward Arnold.

Halliday, M. A. K. (1978). *Language as social semiotic*. Baltimore, MD: University Park Press.

Harste, J., & Short, K. (with Burke, C.). (1988). *Creating classrooms for authors*. Portsmouth, NH: Heinemann.

Harste, J., Woodward, V., & Burke, C. (1984). *Language stories and literacy lessons*. Portsmouth, NH: Heinemann.

Heath, S. B. (1983). *Ways with words*. Cambridge: Cambridge University Press.

Hoffman, P. (1988). *Archimedes' revenge: The joys and perils of mathematics*. New York: Norton.

Huff, D. (1954). *How to lie with statistics*. New York: Norton.

Janvier, C. (Ed.). (1987). *Problems of representation in the teaching and learning of mathematics*. Hillsdale, NJ: Erlbaum.

John-Steiner, V., Panofsky, C., & Smith, L. (Eds.). (1994). *Sociocultural approaches to language and literacy*. Cambridge: Cambridge University Press.

Juster, N. (1961). *The phantom tollbooth*. New York: Alfred A. Knopf.

Kantor, R., Miller, S., & Fernie, D. (1992). Diverse paths to literacy in a preschool classroom: A sociocultural perspective. *Reading Research Quarterly*, *27*(3), 185–201.

Kline, M. (1980). *Mathematics: The loss of certainty*. Oxford: Oxford University Press.

Knorr-Cetina, K. (1981). *The manufacture of knowledge*. Oxford: Pergamon Press.

Knorr-Cetina, K. (1983). The ethnographic study of scientific work: Towards a constructivist interpretation of science. In K. Knorr-Cetina & M. Mulkay (Eds.), *Science observed* (pp. 115–140). London: Sage.

Kort, E. (1989). *Taxicab geometry: An exploration of taxi-triangles*. Unpublished manuscript.

Krause, E. (1986). *Taxicab-geometry*. New York: Dover.

Kuhn, T. (1970). *The structure of scientific revolutions*. Chicago: University of Chicago Press.

Lakatos, I. (1976). *Proofs and refutations*. Cambridge: Cambridge University Press.

Lampert, M. (1990). When the problem is not the question and the solution is not the answer: Mathematics knowing and teaching. *American Educational Research Journal*, *27*(1), 29–63.

Lappan, G., Fey, J., Fitzgerald, W., Friel, S., & Phillips, E. (1998). *Connected mathematics*. Menlo Park, CA: Dale Seymour.

Latour, B. (1987). *Science in action*. Cambridge, MA: Harvard University Press.

Latour, B., & Woolgar, S. (1979). *Laboratory life*. Princeton, NJ: Princeton University Press.

Lave, J. (1988). *Cognition in practice*. Cambridge: Cambridge University Press.

Lave, J., & Wenger, E. (1991). *Situated learning: Legitimate peripheral participation*. New York: Cambridge University Press.

Lemke, J. (1990). *Talking science: Language, learning, and values*. Norwood, NJ: Ablex.

Luke, A. (1991). Literacy as a social practice. *English Education, 23*(3), 131–147.

McCabe, P. (1981). The effect upon comprehension of mathematics material repatterned on the basis of oral language. *Reading World, 21*, 146–154.

McMahon, S., & Raphael, T. (Eds.). (1997). *The book club connection: Literacy learning and classroom talk.* New York: Teachers College Press.

Moyer, J., Moyer, J., Sowder, L., & Threadgill-Sowder, J. (1984). Story problem formats: Verbal versus telegraphic. *Journal of Research in Mathematics Education, 15*, 64–68.

Myers, J. (1992). The social contexts of school and personal literacy. *Reading Research Quarterly, 27*(4), 297–333.

National Council of Teachers of Mathematics (NCTM). (1989). *Curriculum and evaluation standards for school mathematics.* Reston, VA: Author.

National Council of Teachers of Mathematics (NCTM). (1991). *Professional standards for teaching mathematics.* Reston, VA: Author.

National Research Council (NRC). (1989). *Everybody counts: A report to the nation on the future of mathematics education.* Washington, D.C.: National Academic Press.

Newman, J. (Ed.). (1961). *The world of mathematics.* New York: Simon & Schuster.

Pappas, T. (1987). *Mathematics appreciation.* San Carlos, CA: Math Aides/Math Products Plus.

Papy, F. (1974). *Frederique's stories.* St. Louis, MO: CEMREL, Central Midwestern Regional Laboratory.

Paulos, J. A. (1988). *Innumeracy: Mathematical illiteracy and its consequences.* New York: Hill and Wang.

Pearson, P. D., & Fielding, L. (1991). Comprehension instruction. In B. Barr, M. Kamil, P. Mosenthal, & P. D. Pearson (Eds.), *Handbook of reading research* (Vol. 2, pp. 815–860). White Plains, NY: Longman.

Peirce, C. S. (1877/1982). The fixation of belief. In H. S. Thayer (Ed.), *Pragmatism: The classic writings* (pp. 61–78). Indianapolis, IN: Hackett.

Peterson, R., & Eeds, M. (1992). *Grand conversations.* Richmond Hill, Ontario: Scholastic Canada.

Petit, J. (n.d.). *The adventures of Archibald Higgins: Here's looking at Euclid (and not looking at Euclid).* Los Altos, CA: William Kaufmann.

Phillips, D. C. (1995). The good, the bad, and the ugly: The many faces of constructivism. *Educational Researcher, 24*(7), 5–12.

Piaget, J. (1970). *Genetic epistemology.* New York: Columbia University Press.

Pimm, D. (1987). *Speaking mathematically.* London: Routledge & Kegan Paul.

Project Mathematics! (1989). *The theorem of Pythagoras* [Videotape]. Pasadena: California Institute of Technology.

Resnick, L. (1988). Treating mathematics as an ill-structured discipline. In R. Charles & E. Silver (Eds.), *The teaching and assessing of mathematical problem solving* (pp. 32–60). Reston, VA: National Council of Teachers of Mathematics.

Reynolds, J. (1985). Build a city. *Arithmetic Teacher, 33*(1), 12–15.

Richards, J. (1991). Mathematical discussions. In E. von Glasersfeld (Ed.), *Radical constructivism in mathematics education* (pp. 13–51). Dordrecht, The Netherlands: Kluwer Academic.

Richards, L. (1990). Measuring things in words: Language for learning mathematics. *Language Arts, 67*(1), 14–25.

Rogoff, B. (1990). *Apprenticeship in thinking: Cognitive development in social context.* New York: Oxford University Press.

Rosenblatt, L. (1938). *Literature as exploration.* New York: Appleton Century.

Rosenblatt, L. (1978). *The reader, the text, the poem.* Carbondale: Southern Illinois University Press.

Rosenblatt, L. (1980). What facts does this poem teach you? *Language Arts, 54*(4), 386–394.

Rosenblatt, L. (1994). The transactional theory of reading and writing. In R. Ruddell, M. Ruddell, & H. Singer (Eds.), *Theoretical models and processes of reading* (4th ed., pp. 1057–1092). Newark, DE: International Reading Association.

Rowe, D., & Harste, J. (1986). Reading and writing in a system of knowing. In M. Sampson (Ed.), *The pursuit of literacy* (pp. 126–144). Dubuque, IA: Kendall Hunt.

Rudduck, J., & Hopkins, D. (1985). *Research as a basis for teaching: Readings from the work of Lawrence Stenhouse.* Portsmouth, NH: Heinemann.

Rumelhart, D., (1977). Toward an interactive model of reading. In S. Dornic (Ed.), *Attention and performance VI.* Hillsdale, NJ: Erlbaum.

Schifter, D., & Fosnot, C. (1993). *Reconstructing mathematics education: Stories of teachers meeting the challenge of reform.* New York: Teachers College Press.

Schiro, M. (1997). *Integrating children's literature and mathematics in the classroom.* New York: Teachers College Press.

Schoenfeld, A. (1985). *Mathematical problem solving.* New York: Academic Press.

Schoenfeld, A. (Ed.). (1987). *Cognitive science and mathematics education.* Hillsdale, NJ: Erlbaum.

Schoenfeld, A. (1989). Exploration of students' mathematical beliefs and behaviors. *Journal of Research in Mathematics Education, 20*(4), 338–355.

Schoenfeld, A. (1992). Learning to think mathematically: Problem solving, metacognition, and sense making in mathematics. In D. Grouws (Ed.), *Handbook of research on mathematics teaching and learning* (pp. 334–370). New York: Macmillan.

Schwartz, D. (1985). *How much is a million?* New York: Lothrop, Lee, & Shepherd.

Scribner, S. (1984/1988). Literacy in three metaphors. In E. Kintgen, B. Kroll, & M. Rose (Eds.), *Perspectives on literacy* (pp. 71–81). Carbondale: Southern Illinois University Press.

Scribner, S., & Cole, M. (1981). *The psychology of literacy.* Cambridge, MA: Harvard University Press.

Sfard, A. (1998). On two metaphors for learning and the dangers of choosing just one. *Educational Researcher, 27*(2), 4–13.

Sheedy, J. (1996). Beyond straight lines. In R. Borasi, Ed., *Reconceiving mathematics instruction: A focus on errors*. Norwood, NJ: Ablex.

Short, K., & Pierce, K. (1990). *Talking about books: Creating literate communities*. Portsmouth, NH: Heinemann.

Shuard, H., & Rothery, A. (1984). *Children reading mathematics*. Portsmouth, NH: Heinemann.

Siegel, M. (1984). Reading as signification (Doctoral dissertation, Indiana University, 1984). *Dissertation Abstracts International, 45*, 2824A.

Siegel, M. (1995). More than words: The generative power of transmediation for learning. *Canadian Journal of Education, 20*(4), 455–475.

Siegel, M., & Borasi, R. (1994). Demystifying mathematics education through inquiry. In P. Ernest (Ed.), *Constructing mathematical knowledge: Epistemology and mathematics education* (pp. 201–214). London: Falmer Press.

Siegel, M., Borasi, R., & Fonzi, J. (1998). Supporting students' mathematical inquiries through reading. *Journal for Research in Mathematics Education, 29*(4), 378–413.

Siegel, M., Borasi, R., Fonzi, J., Sanvidge, L., & Smith, C. (1996). Using reading to construct mathematical meaning. In P. Elliott & M. Kenney (Eds.), *Communication in mathematics K–12 and beyond* (pp. 66–75). 1996 Yearbook of the National Council of Teachers of Mathematics. Reston, VA: National Council of Teachers of Mathematics.

Siegel, M., Borasi, R., Fonzi, J., & Smith, C. (1996). *Beyond word problems and textbooks: Using reading generatively in the mathematics classroom*. (ERIC Document Reproduction Service No. ED 403 144)

Siegel, M., Borasi, R., & Smith, C. (1989). A critical review of reading in mathematics instruction: The need for a new synthesis. In S. McCormick & J. Zutell (Eds.), *Cognitive and social perspectives for literacy research and instruction* (pp. 269–277). Thirty-eighth Yearbook of the National Reading Conference. Chicago, IL: National Reading Conference.

Siegel, M., & Carey, R. (1989). *Critical thinking: A semiotic perspective*. (Monographs on Teaching Critical Thinking, No.1). Bloomington, IN: ERIC Clearinghouse on Reading and Communication Skills and Urbana, IL: National Council of Teachers of English.

Siegel, M., & Fonzi, J. (1995). The practice of reading in an inquiry-oriented mathematics class. *Reading Research Quarterly, 30*(4), 632–673.

Skagestad, P. (1981). *The road of inquiry*. New York: Columbia University Press.

Skrykpa, A. (1979). *Effects of mathematical vocabulary training on problem solving abilities of third and fourth graders* (Unpublished Master's thesis). New Brunswick, NJ: Rutgers University. (ERIC Document Reproduction Service No. ED 172 169)

Smith, F. (1971). *Understanding reading*. New York: Holt, Rinehart.

Steen, L. A. (Ed.). (1990). *On the shoulders of giants: New approaches to numeracy*. Washington, D.C.: National Academy Press.

Steffe, L., & Gale, J. (Eds.). (1994). *Constructivism in education*. Hillsdale, NJ: Erlbaum.

Steffe, L., von Glasersfeld, E., Richards, J., & Cobb, P. (1983). *Children's counting types: Philosophy, theory, and applications*. New York: Praeger Scientific.

Street, B. (1984). *Literacy in theory and practice*. Cambridge: Cambridge University Press.

Szwed, J. (1981/1988). The ethnography of literacy. In E. Kintgen, B. Kroll, & M. Rose (Eds.), *Perspectives on literacy* (pp. 303–311). Carbondale: Southern Illinois University Press.

TERC. (Susan Jo Russell, PI). (1998). *Investigations in number, data, and space*. Menlo Park, CA: Dale Seymour.

Tierney, R., & Pearson, P. D. (1981/1994). Learning to learn from text: A framework for improving classroom practice. In R. Ruddell, M. Ruddell, & H. Singer (Eds.), *Theoretical models and processes of reading* (4th ed., pp. 496–513). Newark, DE: International Reading Association.

Tierney, R., & Pearson, P. D. (1992/1994). A revisionist perspective on "Learning to learn from text: A framework for improving classroom practice." In R. Ruddell, M. Ruddell, & H. Singer (Eds.), *Theoretical models and processes of reading* (4th ed., pp. 514–519). Newark, DE: International Reading Association.

Tyler, S. (1985). Ethnography, intertextuality, and the end of description. *American Journal of Semiotics, 3*(4), 83–98.

U.S. Department of Education. (1996). *Pursuing excellence* (NCES 97-198, by Lois Peak). Washington, D.C.: U.S. Government Printing Office.

van Maanen, M. (1988). *Tales of the field: On writing ethnography*. Chicago: University of Chicago Press.

Vygotsky, L. S. (1962). *Thought and language*. Cambridge, MA: MIT Press.

Vygotsky, L. S. (1978). *Mind in society: The development of higher psychological processes*. Cambridge, MA: Harvard University Press.

Walter, M., & Brown, S. I. (1969). What if not? *Mathematics Teaching, 46*, 38–45.

Wells, G., & Chang-Wells, G. (1992). *Constructing knowledge together: Classrooms as centers of inquiry and literacy*. Portsmouth, NH: Heinemann.

Wertsch, J. (1985). *Vygotsky and the social formation of mind*. Cambridge, MA: Harvard University Press.

Wertsch, J. (1991). *Voices of the mind*. Cambridge, MA: Harvard University Press.

White, A. (Ed.) (1993). *Essays in humanistic mathematics*. Washington, D.C.: Mathematics Association of America.

Whitin, D., Mills, H., & O'Keefe, T. (1991). *Living and learning mathematics*. Portsmouth, NH: Heinemann.

Whitin, D., & Wilde, S. (1992). *Read any good math lately?* Portsmouth, NH: Heinemann.

Whitin, D., & Wilde, S. (1995). *It's the story that counts*. Portsmouth, NH: Heinemann.

Willinsky, J. (1990). The lost reader of democracy. In J. Clifford (Ed.), *The experience of reading* (pp. 85–103). Portsmouth, NH: Boynton/Cook.

Index

About the Authors

Raffaella Borasi is Professor of Education in the Warner Graduate School of Education and Human Development at the University of Rochester. A native of Italy, she earned a *Laurea* in mathematics and education at the University of Torino before receiving an M.Ed. and Ph.D. in mathematics education from the State University of New York at Buffalo. Among her publications are *Learning Mathematics Through Inquiry* and *Reconceiving Mathematics Instruction: A Focus on Errors*. Her research interests include rethinking the uses of error in mathematics instruction, inquiry-oriented mathematics instruction, and the professional development of mathematics teachers.

Marjorie Siegel is Associate Professor of Education in the Department of Curriculum and Teaching at Teachers College, Columbia University, where she teaches courses on literacy education and research, and qualitative research methods. A former reading teacher, she received an M.S. and Ed.D. in reading education from Indiana University–Bloomington. Her scholarly interests include the contribution of transmediation (juxtaposing multiple symbol systems) to literacy learning, students' negotiations of multiple literacies, and critical approaches to literacy theory and research.